HUMANITARIANS
IN HOSTILE
TERRITORY

Kathleen,
Nice working with you
and good luck at 'school' :)

Glenn R Smith
July 2010

HUMANITARIANS IN HOSTILE TERRITORY

EXPEDITIONARY DIPLOMACY AND AID OUTSIDE THE GREEN ZONE

Peter W. Van Arsdale

Derrin R. Smith

Walnut Creek, CA

LEFT COAST PRESS, INC.
1630 North Main Street, #400
Walnut Creek, CA 94596
http://www.LCoastPress.com

ISBN 978-1-59874-443-9 hardcover
ISBN 978-1-59874-444-6 paperback

Library of Congress Cataloging-in-Publication Data
Van Arsdale, Peter W.
   Humanitarians in hostile territory : expeditionary diplomacy and aid outside the green zone / Peter W. Van Arsdale and Derrin R. Smith.
     p. cm.
   Includes bibliographical references and index.
     ISBN 978-1-59874-443-9 (hardcover : alk. paper) — ISBN 978-1-59874-444-6 (pbk. : alk. paper)
   1. Humanitarian assistance. 2. International relief. 3. War. 4. Humanitarianism. I. Smith, Derrin R. II. Title.
   HV639.V36 2010
   361.2'6—dc22
                            2010002574

Printed in the United States of America

♾™ The paper used in this publication meets the minimum requirements of American National Standard for Information Sciences—Permanence of Paper for Printed Library Materials, ANSI/NISO Z39.48—1992.

Unless otherwise indicated, all photographs were taken by Derrin R. Smith.

Cover design by Andrew Brozyna

Cover illustration: Amy Shaw and Evan Elliott secure a tent at the University of Denver-Romanian Land Forces joint training site in the Transylvanian mountains, 2004.

CONTENTS

List of Illustrations 9

List of Acronyms 11

Preface and Acknowledgments 17

PART I: SETTING THE STAGE 27

CHAPTER 1 HUMANITARIANISM, DEVELOPMENT, AND INTERVENTION .. 29
       A Moral Template 29
       The Humanitarian Enterprise 35
       The Development Enterprise 45
       Warriors, Builders, Chaplains, and Humanitarians 54
          Box: Engineering Aid in Afghanistan 57
       Types of Change and Intervention 58
       An Ethics of Cooperation and Intervention 65
       The Reciprocity of Humanitarianism and Development 67

CHAPTER 2 OUTSIDE THE GREEN ZONE: NONPERMISSIVE AREAS OF
       OPERATION 71
       The Green Zone 71

"Country Operations" and "Country Teams" 73

Humanitarianism and Warfare 76

The Accidental War: The 2006 Crisis between
Israel and Lebanon 82

Armed and Unarmed NSAs 93

The Privatization of War 97

CHAPTER 3 IN-SITU PRELIMINARY ASSESSMENTS, THREAT ANALYSES,
AND KOFI ANNAN'S LESSONS 103

The Necessity of Preliminary Assessments 105

Box: Tigrayan Water Systems 112

Provincial Reconstruction Teams (PRTs) 115

The Country Operations Plan 117

Preliminary Assessments and Humanitarian
Interventions 120

Threat, Risk, and Vulnerability Analyses 121

Box: Salvadoran Water Resources 127

Kofi Annan's Lessons 130

PART II: ON SITE, IN ACTION 133

CHAPTER 4 TRAINING AND EQUIPPING FOR DEPLOYMENT 135

Personal Preparedness 135

Equipment Needs and Checklists 145

Box: Operation Jaque 149

Training Protocols 151

Self-Doctoring Kits and Medical Training 157

Legal Checklists 160

CHAPTER 5 TRANSIT OPERATIONS, COMMUNICATIONS, AND SMART
TECHNOLOGIES 161

Transit Operations: Always Necessary, Often
Controversial 161

Planning for Threats: Obviously Needed,
Occasionally Ignored 171

Box: Ubiquitous Threats 175

Communications 177

Smart Technologies and Electronic Innovations 182

Message Dissemination and Public Relations 188

CHAPTER 6 BEST PRACTICES FOR HAZARDOUS AREAS OF OPERATION:

FIXED SITES AND FIELD SCHOOLS 191

Military Fortresses, Bases, and Camps 191

Romanian Military Camps and Operations 196

Fixing Perimeters, Establishing Sites, and

Securing Operations 212

Permanent Urban Facilities 215

Permanent Rural Facilities 220

Permanent Remote Facilities 225

Temporary Remote Operations 227

Disengagement 229

PART III: APPLICATIONS AND IMPLICATIONS 231

CHAPTER 7 FOREIGN SERVICE, TRIBAL OUTREACH, AND

SPECIAL OPERATIONS 233

The United States Foreign Service 234

Tribal Outreach and Transition 238

Three Case Studies 240

Box: Best Practices, Lessons Learned #1 248

Box: Best Practices, Lessons Learned #2 249

The Battle for Anbar Province 251

Box: Best Practices, Lessons Learned #3. 257

Special Operations 261

Box: The Roles and Methods of HTTs 271

Sustaining Operations through DEFTs 273

CHAPTER 8 CONCLUSION: BACK TO THE FUTURE 277

A Non-Ideological Stance 277

Civil Society and Pragmatic Humanitarianism 281

The Co-Evolution of Warfare and Humanitarianism 282

Anthropology and the Military 287

Scenarios and Simulations 297
Coming Full Circle 300

Appendix 303
References 321
Index 339
About the Authors 351

LIST OF ILLUSTRATIONS

FIGURES

Preface   Helicopter diplomacy 23

Acknowledgments   Romania: 2004 University of Denver
 training class 25

1.1   Ethical "rules of engagement" 33
3.1   Mai Misham village 107
3.2   VASK model 111
3.3   Salvadoran farm family 128
4.1   Camel trek 139
4.2   Martial arts training 144
4.3   Extraction by helicopter 147
4.4   First aid training 158
5.1   Crippled convoy Iraq 164
5.2   Convoy vigilance Iraq 168
5.3   Convoy parking Iraq 169
5.4   Mexico City protests 173
6.1   Staged ambush, Romania 202

7.1   Tarin Kowt interview 242
7.2   CMAX Afghanistan 245
7.3   Sunni Endowment cadre 253

Tables

2.1   Comparing "old" and "new" wars 81
6.1   Romanian field exercise: Best practices/
        Lessons learned #1 208
6.2   Romanian field exercise: Best practices/
        Lessons learned #2 209
6.3   Romanian field exercise: Best practices/
        Lessons learned #3 211

LIST OF ACRONYMS

AAA	American Anthropological Association
AFSA	American Foreign Service Association
AFRICOM	United States Africa Command
AFSOC	Air Force Special Operations Command
AHC	Anbar Higher Committee
ANZAC	Australia and New Zealand Army Corps
AO	area of operations
AQI	Al-Qaeda in Iraq
AU	African Union
C4S	command, control, communications, and computer systems
CAG	Civil Affairs Group
CALL	Center for Army Lessons Learned
CB	citizen band radio
CEAUSSIC	Commission on the Engagement of Anthropology with the U.S. Security and Intelligence Communities
CENTCOM	United States Central Command
CF	Coalition Forces
CHE	complex humanitarian emergency
CHU	containerized housing unit

CIA	Central Intelligence Agency
CMAX	civilian medical assistance exercise
CMOC	Civil-Military Operations Center
COCOM	United States Combatant Command (for example, AFRICOM, CENTCOM)
COIN	counterinsurgency operation
CPE	cultural preparation of the environment
DDR	disarmament, demobilization and reintegration
DEFT	Diplomatic Expeditionary Field Team
DEVGRU	Naval Special Warfare Development group
DIME/PMESII	Diplomatic, Information, Military, Economic/Political, Military, Economic, Social, Information, Infrastructure LinkedIn Group
DoC U.S.	Department of Commerce
DoD U.S.	Department of Defense
DoS U.S.	Department of State
DRC	Democratic Republic of Congo
EAP	emergency action plan
EMT	emergency medical training
EOD	explosive ordnance disposal
ePRT	embedded (or enhanced) Provincial Reconstruction Team
EU	European Union
FAO	Foreign Area Officer
FARC	Revolutionary Armed Forces of Colombia
FARDC	DRC government troops
FEMA	Federal Emergency Management Agency
FHA	foreign humanitarian assistance
FOB	forward operating base
FPIC	free, prior, and informed consent
FRT	field reconnaissance team
FSO	Foreign Service Officer
FSS	Foreign Service Specialist
G8	Group of Eight Forum (including United States, France, Germany, Italy, Japan, United Kingdom, Canada, Russia)
GDP	Gross Domestic Product

GNP	Gross National Product
GPS	global positioning system
HET	Human Exploitation Team
HLA	helicopter landing area
HOC	Humanitarian Operations Center
HQ	headquarters
HRAF	Human Relations Area Files
HSCB	Human, Social, Culture, Behavior Modeling Program
HTS	human terrain system
HTT	Human Terrain Team
HumInt	human intelligence
IBRD	International Bank for Reconstruction and Development ("World Bank")
I&CS	information processing and communications system
ICG	International Crisis Group
ICP	integrated communications plan
ICRC	International Committee of the Red Cross
IDP	internally displaced person
IED	improvised explosive device
IFOR	Implementation Force for Bosnia
IGO	inter-governmental organization
IHEC	Independent Higher Electoral Commission
IMF	International Monetary Fund
INES	International Network of Engineers and Scientists for Global Responsibility
IO	international organization
IRB	institutional review board
IRDG	International Recovery and Development Group
J2	intelligence and knowledge development
JFOR	Joint Special Operations Command
JTF	Joint Task Force
KFOR	Kosovo Stabilization Force
LCD	liquid crystal display
LES	Locally Engaged Staff
LN	local national

LOGCAP	Logistics Civil Augmentation Program
LRA	Lord's Resistance Army
LRP	long range patrol
MANDAP	man-portable air defense device
MMT	military movement team
MNC	multinational corporation
MONUC	United Nations Organization Mission in the DRC
MRAP	mine resistant ambush protected
MRE	meal ready to eat
MSF	Médicin Sans Frontières (Doctors Without Borders)
NATO	North Atlantic Treaty Organization
NFATC	(George P. Shultz) National Foreign Affairs Training Center
NGHO	non-governmental humanitarian organization
NGO	non-governmental organization
NSA	non-state actor (both unarmed and armed)
NTIA	National Telecommunications and Information Administration
OCHA	United Nations Office for the Coordination of Humanitarian Affairs
OMB	Office of Management and Budget
ONR	Office of Naval Research
OOTW	operations other than war
OP	observation post
Ops	operations
OPSEC	operational security
PAO	press/public affairs office
PD	public diplomacy
PET	Proactive Engagement Team
PFT	personal fitness test
PIC	Provincial Iraqi Control
PMC	private military company
PMF	privatized military firm
POW	prisoner of war
PRT	Provincial Reconstruction Team
PSD	personal security detail

PsyOps	psychological operations
PTSD	post-traumatic stress disorder
PVO	private voluntary organization
QRF	Quick Reaction Force
R&R	rest and recuperation
REA	rapid ethnographic assessment
RF	radio frequency
RPG	rocket-propelled grenade
RSO	Regional Security Officer
SAR	search-and-rescue
SAS	Special Air Service (British Special Forces)
SDR	software-defined radio
SFOR	Stabilization Force for Bosnia
SigInt	signals intelligence
SME	subject matter expert
SOG	Special Operations Group
SPF	sun protection factor
SSTR	security, stabilization, transition, and reconstruction
ST6/DEVGRU	Navy SEAL commando group
THT	tactical human intelligence team
TOC	tactical operations center
UN	United Nations
UNAMI	United Nations Assistance Mission for Iraq
UNAVEM III	United Nations Angola Verification Mission III
UNHCR	United Nations High Commission(er) for Refugees
UNICEF	United Nations Children's Fund
UNIFIL	United Nations Interim Force in Lebanon
UNIRIN	United Nations Integrated Regional Information Network
UNITA	National Union for the Total Independence of Angola
UNOSOM II	United Nations Operation in Somalia II
USAID	United States Agency for International Development
USSOC	U.S. Special Operations Command
UXO	unexploded ordnance
VASK	protocol/model for conducting REA
VBIED	vehicle-borne improvised explosive device

VHF	very high frequency
VRC	vehicle radio communications
VSAT	very small aperture terminal
WFP	World Food Programme
WHO	World Health Organization
YMCA	Young Men's Christian Association

Types of teams[1] covered in this text:

CAG	Civil Affairs Group
DEFT	Diplomatic Expeditionary Field Team
ePRT	embedded (or enhanced) Provincial Reconstruction Team
FRT	field reconnaissance team
HET	Human Exploitation Team
HTT	Human Terrain Team
IRDG	International Recovery and Development Group
Mission	ambassadorial/embassy team
MMT	military movement team
PET	Proactive Engagement Team
PRT	Provincial Reconstruction Team
PSD	personal security detail
QRF	Quick Reaction Force
ST6/DEVGRU	Navy SEAL commando group
THT	tactical human intelligence team

---

[1]Some of these teams also are considered to be country teams, depending on operational context and assignment.

PREFACE

EXPEDITIONARY INITIATIVES

From former U.S. Secretary of State Condoleezza Rice's proclamations regarding expeditionary diplomacy to the deployment of nongovernmental organizations and humanitarian projects in active war zones such as Afghanistan, Iraq, Sudan, and Somalia, the U.S. commitment to operations in hostile and remote territories is on the rise. Most recently, this has also included a concern with piracy. More than ever, the provision of humanitarian relief and aid, as well as diplomatic outreach, to vulnerable populations is occurring in areas that previously would have been considered closed or too hazardous for operations. Rather than "closed" areas, we now speak euphemistically of "nonpermissive or semipermissive areas of operation" in which a full range of humanitarian service, stabilization, and reconstruction services nonetheless can be provided. It is especially in these danger zones—outside the so-called Green Zones of safety—where the skill sets and knowledge presented in this text are most important. One must cross the line, step out of one's comfort zone and one's buffer zone, and often confront danger in order to provide needed services to target populations. One also must return safely to tell the tale.

A military presence, therefore, often frames the outreach context. Yet for us, as civilians, non-engagement is not an option. There are many ways to engage, some of which are both helpful and humane. One viable mode—with several variants—involves *country teams*. However, "country team operations" as an area of theory and practice is imperfect and in many ways embryonic. Much (but not all) of it occurs at the civilian-military interface. Personnel occasionally are lost as government authorities struggle to find the best transition timelines and security models to fit each field situation. Best-fit principles still are emerging. This text, geared particularly to U.S. civilians and social science practitioners (including graduate students and social scientists who serve as consultants to the military), provides additional guidelines. We hope that, through education, further casualties can be prevented among those working on site in conflictive and postconflictive environments. Country teams are our *modus operandi.*

We begin this book by defining what we mean by a *country team,* since the term invokes various understandings in different disciplines. For the U.S. Department of State, the country team is generally the select group of senior managers on an ambassador's staff; they also are known as the ambassador's "direct reports." Consequently, in the Department of State environment, country team meetings or country team staff notes involve only senior embassy or direct-report consulate personnel. This narrow definition is not ours. Rather, a country team, writ large in our lexicon, consists of all the government-affiliated deployed personnel—other than combat troops—in a foreign nation or territory. The overall team includes the executive and staff leadership and also the field personnel, international staff members, local hires, workers, and, in many cases, contractors. (A specific country team, in essence a subteam, consists of the eight or ten people tasked with a specific directive, such as agricultural/ irrigation assessment or military outreach support.) In short, an American country team in our context consists of *all the lives* for which an international government operation has a position/post and has a responsibility, on its overseas organizational chart. Locally employed staff and service workers (who may also be third-country nationals hired to work on a specific project or to provide services across-theater) are every bit a component of a country team as are the country director and international executive staff.

As members of U.S. country teams establish ever more complex presence posts, in ever more hostile and remote territories, the success of their missions—and preservation of their lives—depends on the thoroughness of their planning and logistics practices. It also depends on a genuine and humane interaction with indigenous populations. In the remainder of this preface, we highlight some of the hows and whys involved in what indeed is emerging as a set of "new humanitarianisms." Casualty case studies, mission planning, theater studies, and ethnographic observations, as well as a host of political issues, need to be understood in preparation for stepping outside the Green Zone.

WHY ARE WE CROSSING A THRESHOLD INTO HARM'S WAY?

In the past, relief and aid workers simply acknowledged that some areas were too hot to handle, and either would refuse to provide services or would quickly withdraw when threatened (or as casualties were taken on). For example, since the beginning of the new century, Doctors Without Borders withdrew from operations in Afghanistan after the deaths of several personnel in a remote province; Catholic Relief Services withdrew from Basra, Iraq, under similarly trying circumstances; Save the Children withdrew from western Sudan under duress; the United Nations abandoned Baghdad after the deadly bombing of its headquarters. The U.S. Department of State has evacuated dependents and personnel from dozens of overseas posts during the same period, while at times also providing significant aid for evacuation projects in countries ranging from Haiti to Lebanon. Several Christian groups left India after attacks on their humanitarian missionaries; international medical groups left Somalia, Sierra Leone, Sudan, and the Democratic Republic of Congo because of deteriorating security and personnel losses. This book examines similar cases in greater detail, as casualty case studies. Iraq is of particular interest, because we both have had strong ties to efforts there: Smith on the overseas front, through involvement in on-site country team operations, and Van Arsdale on the home front, through an Iraqi civil society initiative.

In recent years, there have been dramatic changes in the challenges and demands of the overseas environment for humanitarian relief, development, and SSTR (security, stabilization, transition, and reconstruction) personnel. Dangers are ubiquitous. Alyson Welch has summarized some of the casualty statistics. Citing various sources, she reports that attacks against aid workers rose significantly since 2000. One of her sources noted that 2008 was the most dangerous year on record, with 260 aid workers being seriously injured, killed, or kidnapped (2009: 3). Comparing the three-year period 2003–2005 with the three-year period 2006–2008, we see that there was an 89 percent increase in the number of attacks—and the kidnapping rate shot up even more (2009: 4, 5). Although most of those abducted have survived and eventually been released, the disruption of services and the traumatization of personnel have been tremendous. As Welch stresses, the unwritten rules of engagement for field workers have changed drastically.

According to casualty statistics for 2004–2009, a humanitarian aid worker supporting water/sanitation or food distribution projects for the UN overseas has a greater likelihood of being killed in the line of duty than does a New York City police officer. In a comparison of on-the-job death rates for humanitarian aid workers to the ten most hazardous U.S. civilian occupations, aid work received a number-five ranking (Welch 2009: 5). The international emblems of NGOs and aid organizations, which once were honored as shields, have now become targets. Yet, skilled men and women every day step across the thresholds of the Green Zones in their respective homelands, as well as lands far afield, to provide much needed services to local populations. In many cases, they live within these local communities, conducting their day-to-day lives "in the thick of the battle," both metaphorically and literally. Why do these humanitarians put themselves in harm's way?

Many people feel a moral imperative, a humanitarian obligation, to help those in need. Technology has brought us closer to the daily disasters of the world, and from cable news coverage to internet blogs, citizens of the world feel a "public pull" to help those in need. Perhaps this development is also a characteristic of the human condition—the dance between need and service—since acts of charitable outreach are engaged in notable frequency among poor as well as among wealthy people. We have observed members of some of the most impoverished populations in the world, from Indonesia to Afghanistan, reaching out in remarkable ways. A villager might have only one chicken and one bag of corn meal to feed the family for a long time, but it is not uncommon to see the meal shared with another villager who has less. Although such common acts of kindness generally go unannounced, one benefit of deployed communications technology by professionally trained personnel is that certain acts of kindness—as well as atrocities and disasters, even in the remotest of areas—can receive wide visibility with virtually instantaneous distribution and public response. Such visibility cannot easily be ignored by politicians; there is often a concomitant public cry to correct the injustice. A groundswell of concern emerges, moving a government to action; the United Nations (with its affiliate sections and partnered NGOs) steps forward with a possible solution. Speeches are made, pledges of funds and aid are announced, contracts for service initiated. The humanitarian enterprise, to borrow a phrase popularized by Larry Minear (2002), is being engaged. In the best of circumstances, some assistance actually reaches those in the direst need.

Nations, including those seen as superpowers, also have come to appreciate the need for overseas aid engagements as elements of national security imperatives. In the twenty-first century, no region seemingly is too remote, too weak, or too poor to be unimportant in the greater scheme of national security. From the perspective of the United States, if there is one primary lesson learned from the September 11, 2001, attacks on the World Trade Center and the Pentagon, it is this: "Ignore poor, remote regions at your own peril." The apparently blind eyes of the U.S. government and its national security apparatus toward the disenfranchised and impoverished "minimalist populations" of the Taliban and al-Qaeda sects—employing operatives and training camps in Sudan, Pakistan, and Afghanistan that were once perceived by outsiders as having little tactical or strategic value—resulted in unprecedented disaster. The attack of the weak against the powerful is resulting in new types of vulnerability, mirrored in the awkward juxtaposition of dusty rural terrorist training sites and rich urban financial centers.

We are witnessing an era of increased asymmetrical warfare, remote engagement, and civilian suffering. The United States is engaged along a number of fronts, both on site and remote. Although successes (as judged by non-American analysts) have been noteworthy, so, too, have been failures. Criticisms of U.S. aid projects and humanitarian interventions should be used to improve strategies and reinforce fundamental noncolonial intentions. The United States, according to senior analysts, still is ill prepared for major attacks and mega-disasters (Redlener 2006). Aid projects, reconstruction programs, transformational diplomatic outreach, and longer-term development schemes continue, but in altered forms, as the ancient footpaths of the martyred missionaries and humanitarians of previous centuries are now being trod by country team staff and their counterparts. Unlike *conquistadores*, who came to subdue and exploit indigenous populations and resources for the benefit of the crowned heads, country teams ideally—but still imperfectly—come to assist, to repair, to build. Unlike trade companies, which came to exploit the resources and the peoples of new lands—for example, the Netherlands' East India Company—country teams attempt to empower local inhabitants in resource development. Unlike some ambassadors of old—seventeenth-century England's George Downing being a stark and imperious example—senior mission personnel attempt to negotiate effective diplomatic relations. Some personnel still suffer the equivalent of the martyr's death; Fred Cuny is one famous example.

Much country team work transpires at the civilian-military interface, as noted above. The lines once thought to separate such providers as civilian humanitarians and military peacekeepers, or doctors without borders and battlefield corpsmen, no longer are distinct. A Joint Task Force is often used by the American military to deliver foreign humanitarian assistance, engaging various arrangements of civilian and military personnel. In turn, civilians are engaging and helping to empower various innovative configurations of United Nations, military, and NGO personnel, as exemplified by the recently formed Friends of Security group. As we note later in the book, the UN Office for the Coordination of Humanitarian Affairs plays a key coordinative role as responses are implemented for many disasters. Although the civilian presence and practices can help temper the more savage beast in the infantry, the military can improve mission focus and goal-based performance in partnering civilian organizations, some of which are very process oriented. Just as the most powerful nations cannot afford to ignore the least powerful, civilian humanitarians and other overseas workers—from chefs to engineers—cannot afford to ignore trained military personnel. They have much to offer. Like it or not, we're in the game together.

Although not referenced explicitly in this book, Derrin Smith has worked on the applications of math-based constructal theory to the understanding of country operations (2009). This book is about praxis, the intersection of

Helicopter Diplomacy and tribal outreach turned the tide in Iraq's Anbar Province, on this trip with Provincial Governor Sami Ma'moun, Chairman of the Provincial Council Dr. Abdul Salaam, and Marine Corps Colonel William Dwiggins.

theory, practice, and ethics in challenging and often conflictive environments. It is about both concept and method. It also is about both education and training. As we stress in Part Two, there is a difference between what is learned in the classroom and what is learned in the field. At one extreme, the prospective country team member must be able to understand the political processes associated with humanitarian intervention. At the other extreme, he or she must be able to understand the problems associated with foot infections resulting from poor hygiene. Many of our examples come from our own overseas deployments, as well as from our work with University of Denver-sponsored student training programs.

As the preceding photo indicates, civilian-military bridges can work.

ACKNOWLEDGMENTS

It seems that out of battle I escaped

Down some profound dull tunnel, long since scooped

Through granites which titanic wars had groined...

And no guns thumped, or down the flues made moan.

"Strange friend," I said, "here is no cause to mourn."

Tenor solo, from Benjamin Britten's War Requiem, Opus 66 (words by Wilfred Owen), as performed by Mark Van Arsdale on April 22, 2009, in concert at Indiana University

We would like to acknowledge the ideas, assistance, and support of the following individuals: Linda Roan, Mark Yager, Jack Schultz, Ed Knop, Beret Strong, Angela Bengtson, Jonathan Chu, Rebecca Goolsby, Tsegaye Hailu, Tsegay Wolde-Georgis, Lt. Col. Andrew Overfield, Lt. Col. Randy Odom, Col. William J. Bonner, Jr., Col. Ros Viorel, Col. M.S. "Skip" Raimer, Greg, Moser, Michael Baranick, Shayna Cram, Evan Elliott, Pam Puntenney, Bruce Finley, Joe Rice, Jim Chase, Alan Moorer, Jill Bausch, Rich Rodriquez, Gerald LeMelle, and Susan Weinstein. Peer reviews provided by two skilled individuals added a great deal. The technical editing of Stacey Sawyer and the detailed indexing of Erica Hill were essential. The overall editorial advice provided by Jennifer Collier of Left Coast Press proved to be invaluable.

On a personal note, Peter Van Arsdale would like to thank Kathy, Amy, Mark, Sarah, and John. Thanks in remembrance go to Prof. Robert Hackenberg. On a personal note, Derrin Smith would like to thank Shannon, Allison, Micayla, and Nicole. Mihaela Biliovschi Smith was a tremendous inspiration, providing constant encouragement. Thanks in remembrance go to Major John W. Macroglou, USMC.

The members of the 2004 University of Denver class (see photo) who worked with us in Romania are to be credited for their insights, hard work, and good humor; Jen Buzza served as the student commander. Romanian Land Forces and Air Force personnel were extremely helpful. This book is dedicated to all of them.

The opinions expressed herein are entirely those of the authors and in no way should be interpreted as official opinions or policies of any branch of the U.S. government. All information that pertains to U.S. Department of State and U.S. military operations is unclassified in its entirety.

PART I

SETTING THE STAGE

CHAPTER 1

HUMANITARIANISM, DEVELOPMENT, AND INTERVENTION

A Moral Template

Famed historian David McCullough stresses that humans need history "as much as we need bread or water or love" (2006: 1). He makes this point in the broader context of an analysis of the life and contributions of U.S. President John Adams. As is well known, early in his career Adams chose Thomas Jefferson to write the Declaration of Independence. As is less well known, during the late 1770s Adams authored the Constitution of the Commonwealth of Massachusetts, the oldest written constitution still in use in the world today. It came to serve as a template for the national constitution a decade later. In one section the Commonwealth's constitution states that it is necessary "to countenance and inculcate the principles of humanity and general benevolence, public and private charity, industry and frugality, honesty and punctuality in their dealings, sincerity, good humor, and all the social affections, and generous sentiments among the people" (McCullough 2006: 4). In short, Adams offered one of the first definitive statements of modern humanitarianism.

Whereas many others during the same era, such as Henry Home (aka Lord Kames), had written on principles of morality and justice, it had been more in the abstract philosophical sense (Moran 2005). It was thought that "naturally benevolent inclinations," through the principle of justice, could become lawlike and thus institutionalized, enabling help to be rendered. Some religious leaders of that era took complementary perspectives. For example, John Wesley (founder of the Methodist church), delivered sermons about God's "moral attributes" (Haynes 2006: 17a). Human troubles could be contravened through attention to Biblical doctrine, played out in the actions of humans helping humans. Relatively liberal for his time, Wesley saw human behavior as reflective of human circumstance and opportunity. Also contributing to this theme, and also relatively liberal for his time, Alexander Hamilton promoted antislavery principles in New York, through the Manumission Society (which he had cofounded in 1785). His primary mentor, George Washington, had set a good example: despite their earlier atrocities, the Hessians he battled at Trenton during the Revolutionary War were shown a good deal of humanitarian compassion (Fischer 2004: 62–65, 427). Washington also had written about helping the oppressed and needy within one's society.

The question of what constitutes "a moral template" also has confronted, and in some cases confounded, Western philosophers (and later, Western social scientists) since the eighteenth century. The nature/nurture debate has played a major role as issues of the relative contributions of genetic/heritable and cultural/behavioral factors have been analyzed. As Meredith Small (2006) notes, philosophers have vacillated between calling human beings "naturally kind" to calling them "naturally brutal." She discusses the work of primatologist Frans de Waal, who goes so far as to suggest that forms of justice and morality exist among higher, nonhuman primates. This controversial possibility aside, a related debate about altruism versus self-interest in humans continues unabated.

Debates about morality, in the context of Western culture writ large, were unfolding at about the same time as were debates about the notion of (what would become) the modern state, and the nature of war and peace. European scholars were at the epicenter. The medieval idea of the state as monarch-centric and under the umbrella of Christendom was collapsing; the concept of the state as an independent political entity, with the people having a say in governance, was emerging. Setting the parameters, as Shorto (2004: 99) would say, was the Dutch jurist Hugo de Groot, known more widely as Hugo Grotius. Considered by many today as the father of international law, from his base in Leiden he laid out principles on which war could be justified, about how it could be fought, and about how it affected the citizenries involved. "Natural law" was key. Human reason was essential. Grotius put it this way: an act could, and should, be judged "from its conformity or nonconformity with rational nature itself" (Shorto 2004: 100). One of Grotius's disciples, Piet van der Cun, known to history as Cunaeus, went so far as to proclaim that a republican form of government was morally superior to that of a monarchy. What was good for the people, how could every-day citizens become more involved, and how were those they were encountering in the lucrative international trade markets engendered by the likes of the Dutch East India Company and Dutch West India Company to be treated?

The concept of *benevolence* has come to play a central role in understandings of modern humanitarianism. As detailed by one of us elsewhere (Van Arsdale 2006: 182–185), in its simplest form it means "doing good in serving others" and can be understood fully only in juxtaposition to three sister terms. *Justice* emphasizes "doing what is right" for people at risk. *Autonomy* refers to respect for the sanctity of the individual as assistance is offered. *Nonmalevolence* refers to assistance that does not lead to secondary negative consequences (for example, violation of privacy). Taken together these terms represent what we call "deep justice." Taken together they also provide conceptual glue for understanding the reasons for reaching out to help others.

This chapter lays out our understandings of modern humanitarianism. We feature paradigms, theories, and practices derived not only from the field of humanitarianism but also from the field of development, because the interplay of the two has been essential during the post-World War II era as short-term relief and long-term aid have been offered those in need. Issues of humanitarian intervention are briefly addressed as we set the stage for understanding civil-military cooperation and country operations. Although contributions from several disciplines are noted, those from the disciplines of anthropology (primarily) and economics (secondarily) are emphasized for two reasons. They represent our primary foci and are key to understanding the bridge we build between humanitarianism and development.

Ethical "Rules of Engagement"

Although not a book of anthropology, this is a book informed by anthropology and by current debates involving the nature of war, of moral discourse, and of essential ethical encounters "on the ground," as humanitarian activities are undertaken in conflictive and postconflictive areas. We are ideologically neutral but not ethically neutral. Non-engagement at the military-civilian interface, in the toughest of conflictive and postconflictive situations outside the Green Zone, is not an option.

The phrase "rules of engagement" (Figure 1.1) usually is meant to pertain to a theater of war, specifying when and how soldiers can fire on the enemy. Firing only when fired on is one example. Here we are proposing a radically different use of the phrase. For us, "rules of engagement" means when and how humanitarians (in this context, members of country teams) can ethically engage a field operation, project, or program. Ours is a strategy of on-site humanitarian engagement. It is accompanied by a tactic of ethical engagement. Country teams—and new derivatives thereof—are our *modus operandi*.

The most penetrating and useful examination of what we would term the "ethics/accountability nexus" has been offered by George Lucas, Jr. (2009). Trained as a moral philosopher, he most recently has turned his attention to the ethics of military anthropology. Building on (and critiquing as necessary) the

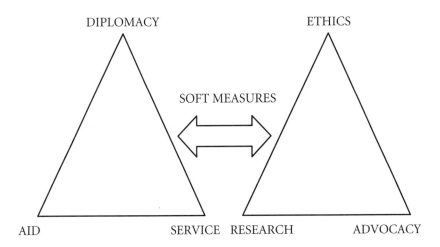

FIGURE 1.1   Ethical "rules of engagement" require consideration of so-called soft measures. In our interpretation, these consist of the intersection of the six factors shown here. Inevitably, there will be an imbalance "on the ground," but both humanitarian assistance and humanitarian intervention benefit from tactical analyses involving the first set of three and strategic analyses involving the second set of three. Free, prior, and informed consent (FPIC) must be pursued simultaneously.

essential work of David Price, Gerald Berreman, Terence Turner, and Carolyn Fluehr-Loban, among other anthropologists, he stresses that the principle of autonomy is central. Whether involving a potential project beneficiary, a colleague in the field, or an injured civilian at battle's end, the issue revolves on a respect for their agency and (especially) their wishes—unfiltered (at least initially) by well-intentioned outsiders. Following Lucas, we believe that certain nonrhetorical questions should be asked: Do those we encounter understand the complexities of what's happening? Do they want to be involved? Do they want their privacy preserved? Immanuel Kant's influence is significant here historically, as Lucas notes, and as we reiterate in Chapter 2. "The ability to act, choose, and decide on a course of life . . . is our most essential and (for each individual moral agent) most precious possession. [Following Kant] we cannot do things to ourselves or to one another that deprive ourselves or others of that capacity [for moral deliberation and consequent action]" (Lucas 2009: 173).

This is a crucial insight. The ethical fulcrum does not balance on the right or wrong of secrecy or clandestine operations per se, but more broadly on transparency and the ethical principle of autonomy—specifically one of its corollaries, informed consent. The "Kantian assessment procedure" suggests "that we have an overriding obligation *never* to act on strategies we formulate for dealing with one another, to which the subjects implicated in, or involved with those strategies could not *give their full and unqualified, voluntary consent when fully informed* about them" (Lucas 2009: 174, emphases in original). In developing this perspective Lucas takes careful account of the work of the Commission on the Engagement of Anthropology with the U.S. Security and Intelligence Communities (CEAUSSIC). We reference this commission in Chapter 7.

Running parallel to this argument are the viewpoints and questions raised by Katsuhiko Masaki (2009). Reminding us that in 2006 the UN Human Rights Council adopted the UN Declaration on the Rights of Indigenous Peoples, he stresses that a key feature is its recognition of the principle of free, prior, and informed consent (FPIC). This consent, to be given or withheld, applies to humanitarian and development enterprises, among other kinds of assistance and intervention. It is imperative that indigenous people—and by extension, any people—not be coerced or pressured as they make their choices. Consent involves tackling complex questions that may have different answers in different situations on the ground, including: Who recognizes, records, and responds to these people's felt needs? Who speaks for whom as consent is given? Who reciprocates and affirms the integral value of the projects undertaken? If needed, who offers postproject criticism?

To paraphrase an important insight of Carolyn Nordstrom (2009), who is an anthropologist specializing in the effects of war, violence, and anthropology's role therein, social scientists have the opportunity to provide an account—and must be held accountable. Those living (for example) in the Afghanistan of one hundred years future will be affected by actions taken today. Although she likely would not support much of what we suggest herein in terms of work with country teams, she likely would support much of what we suggest in terms of pursuing an ethical engagement.

THE HUMANITARIAN ENTERPRISE

New Humanitarianisms

Humanitarianism, as we define it, refers to the "crossing of boundaries" in the service of others. Although the boundaries literally can be geographic or geopolitical, they also can be ethnic, cultural, religious, and/or economic. Both conceptually and operationally, humanitarian actions clearly are intended to assist those in need, to help those whose lives are threatened. In most cases the needy are under duress, and those providing aid also are at risk (at least minimally) for their own safety and security. Those providing assistance must move out of their comfort zones. In most cases, too, those receiving aid find themselves in situations in which their own resources have been compromised owing to warfare or disaster.

In a more academic sense, humanitarianism represents a discourse about the underlying values and moral problematics of humanitarian relief operations, as Ian Smillie and Larry Minear (2004) indicate. Ethics are debated, obligations are assessed, advocacy is engaged (Redfield 2006). Although we address these here, of equal concern in this volume is the operational side of things, as activities play out in the field, on site in nonpermissive areas, outside the so-called Green Zones. Also of central concern is how teams of individuals are constituted and how they become involved.

To date, as Smillie and Minear affirm, no unified "humanitarian regime" has emerged (2004: 3). That is, there is no widely accepted set of standards, enforcement sanctions, and processes of accountability as humanitarian assistance is rendered to those in need. (By contrast, such regimes do exist in the refugee, trade, and nuclear nonproliferation arenas.) There is what Smillie and Minear term a "humanitarian imperative" that is played out through what they call a "humanitarian enterprise." Although taking various forms, some very nebulous, this enterprise can be said to be worldwide, enacted through a global network of agencies and organizations. It is shaped by rapidly emerging protocols, covenants, and conventions contained in international/humanitarian law. These include the UN Charter of 1946, the Universal Declaration of Human Rights of 1948, and the Geneva Conventions of 1949.

In their book *Sword & Salve* (2006) Peter Hoffman and Thomas Weiss
introduce the phrase "new humanitarianisms." Their premise is that new wars
(that is, those occurring in the post-Cold War world, some in not-before-seen
forms) are helping create both the need for, and the development of, new types
of humanitarian endeavor. The "Pollyannaish humanitarianism" of the Cold
War era is a thing of the past; the "good guy Westerner" invoking a singularly
positive humanitarian change has been dispelled as an image. Civil wars such
as those in Afghanistan, Sierra Leone, and Timor-Leste have come to engage
warring parties and humanitarian service providers in new ways. Civilians are
being swept up in unparalleled fashion; many also are carving out unusual
roles in the service of others. Some are attaining remarkably powerful positions in military situations, such as Paul Bremer, who served as proconsul for
the United States in Iraq (and thus Administrator for the Coalition Provisional
Authority) from 2003 to 2004. Some military personnel also are carving out
unusual roles, as Derrin Smith's work attests. Hoffman and Weiss suggest that,
since the early 1990s, realignments have appeared in the system of service,
between traditional principles and emergent operational protocols in war-
torn environments.

New humanitarianisms are taking many forms. Some are being activated
when natural disasters, such as the 2005 Pakistan earthquake, strike. Others are
being brought forth when purposeful human-caused disasters, such as the 9/11
attacks on the World Trade Center and Pentagon, occur. As indicated above,
many are emerging in response to war, such as that during the 1990s in Bosnia;
these activities can benefit combatants, detainees, civilians in situ, and refugees.
Humanitarian intervention is becoming a powerful and more frequently used
option. Following Weiss (2005: xxix), this process is defined as coercive measures employed by outside military forces to ensure access to at-risk civilians
and/or enforcement of a population's rights without the permission of that
state. The ways in which this process will play out as the recently defined and
UN-backed "responsibility to protect" plays out remain to be seen. For example,
while a high-intensity conflict like that in Darfur offers continued opportunities for intervention, a low-intensity conflict like that in Uganda might afford
new opportunities to protect and reintegrate former child soldiers.

New humanitarianisms can take place at the smallest scale, with one person assisting another. However, they usually take place on a larger scale; groups with defined risk characteristics are targeted for assistance. They can occur through the actions of nonprofit agencies (including NGOs) and civil society institutions, as members of vulnerable groups are aided by trained personnel. They can emerge through the mandated actions of intergovernmental and transnational organizations, such as the United Nations High Commission for Refugees (UNHCR). Red Cross and Red Crescent societies and chapters respond to disasters of various kinds. Other humanitarianisms occur under the auspices of nation-states, as the United States (through FEMA and its affiliates) exemplified with 2005's Hurricane Katrina. It is particularly important to stress that new humanitarianisms are being shaped, largely, by innovative responses to complex emergencies. Military personnel are adding key insights.

New humanitarianisms can take on noble proportions. The spotlight can shine appropriately on these activities, as it often does when Doctors Without Borders is operative on site and advocating for those at risk (Redfield 2005). Nobel Peace Prize winners, such as our colleague José Ramos-Horta (serving as president of one of the world's newest independent nations, Timor-Leste), can attract publicity and thus benefit those in need. Announcements can be broadcast rapidly via the internet and worldwide web, bringing attention to vulnerable populations. This tactic is used weekly by the International Crisis Group; the crisis in Darfur has been one situation ICG has featured repeatedly since 2003.

A Brief History of Humanitarianism

As long as people with the wherewithal have tried to assist those without, to aid those who are suffering, and to bring relief to those affected by disaster, there has been humanitarianism. Religious figures such as Buddha, Jesus, and Mohammed have been considered humanitarians by their followers, and their achievements have become legendary. Although such contemporary religious figures as Mother Teresa also have made significant contributions, most humanitarians are not associated with religious movements and do not receive public acclaim. Most have operated behind the spotlight.

From the 1862 publication by Henri Dunant of *A Memory of Solferino*, based on his analysis of the tragedies surrounding battlefield casualties and the need for humane care, to the founding of the Red Cross and the promulgation of the first Geneva Convention, humanitarianism as a field of endeavor in the West has gained considerable traction. Individuals, institutions, and events have shaped the Western humanitarian enterprise.

When viewed from an American perspective, many humanitarians have traced their own inspiration to such nineteenth-century activists as Florence Nightingale, Frederick Douglas, Elizabeth Cady Stanton, Susan B. Anthony, and Clara Barton. Improved health care, civil rights, and human rights—the latter encapsulated in the antislavery movement—were the U.S. focus. When viewed from a broader Western perspective, others trace their inspiration to those working in European war zones (such as Henri Dunant) and in Africa (for instance, Albert Schweitzer). Some become founders of organizations, foundations, or movements; others serve as organizational members; still others operate solo.

Barbara Metzler (2006) suggests that humanitarianism is best framed by studying the lives of individuals, both famous and not-famous, whose actions have benefited groups of vulnerable people. Her book features such people as the late actor Paul Newman (among the famous) and our colleague Dawn Bodo (among the not-famous). Some humanitarians remain anonymous, never choosing to have their contributions made public. Others emerge unexpectedly, as Daniel Goleman did in 2006; it turns out he has helped people in significant ways for years. Stars come forward, some with one name and some with two: Bono, Madonna, Angelina Jolie. Recently they especially have been drawn to Africa. They confront leading politicians, adopt children, speak out against the forces that impoverish others. In some instances it is not easy to distinguish among opportunism, assistance, and humanitarianism.

Exemplifying the individuals whose efforts have substantively shaped Western humanitarianism is Jane Addams. She has been described as "the secular saint of social work" (Douthat 2006: 74). Less theoretician than activist-humanitarian, her work with Hull House, founded in a multi-ethnic immigrant neighborhood in Chicago in 1889, was revolutionary. Early "settlement services" included daycare and kindergarten for the children of working mothers, as well as an employment office. Aided by her colleagues, most of whom were women, she went on to establish a social reform movement that came to include an immigrants' protection league, a juvenile protection association, and a mental health clinic for young people. Labor rights remained key throughout her career, as did concerns about social ethics. She later served as the first female president of the National Conference of Charities and Corrections (a.k.a. the National Conference of Social Work) and still later, through the duration of World War I, as a peace activist. In 1931 she was awarded the Nobel Peace Prize. Thirty years earlier, this prize had been awarded to Henri Dunant.

In contrast, Ian Smillie and Larry Minear (2004), as well as Thomas Weiss (2005), suggest that humanitarianism is best framed by studying institutions and events. Warfare and responses to its effects are central. Viewed through a Western historical lens, we would add that concerns with industrialization, poverty and welfare, immigrant rights, and "classism" were keys to the nineteenth- and twentieth-century evolution of humanitarianism. Religious conversion and colonial outreach provided justifications for some, antitheses for others.

The London Missionary Society, founded in 1795, was among the first organizations to "reach out to the heathen" in the South Pacific, North America, and Africa. Although its presumed (or presumptuous) humanitarian mandate can be critiqued in retrospect, at the time it was seen by Westerners as a helpful organization, one that inspired still others to undertake outreach and missionization in challenging environments. The Aborigines' Protection Society, founded in 1837, also worked in the South Pacific and took a more secular approach. It nonetheless was tied, albeit indirectly, to colonial initiatives that were administratively oppressive. Founded by well-heeled people with little overseas experience, this society formulated a plan to assist Australia's aboriginal population. Although lacking substantial input from the intended beneficiaries, the effort nonetheless had other hallmarks of humanitarianism—for example, the preservation of culture and indigenous language.

The Young Men's Christian Association (YMCA) was founded in London in 1844. The first branch in the United States was formed in Boston in 1851. Building on Christian values and ethical precepts, the intent was to work in recreational and social spheres to tackle social issues and transform communities. Some 150 years later the movement had grown within the United States to encompass 19 million members participating through more than 2,500 branches and camps. Worldwide, activities and outreach engaged those in 120 countries (Metzler 2006: 105). Humanitarianism, as exemplified by efforts in Lebanon in 2006 (see Chapter 2), now is widely touted by the YMCA.

It was during this same period of time, circa 1850, that written references to humanitarian intervention first began to appear. As Weiss (2005: 8) notes, contributors to the international legal literature began dissecting events in Greece, where England, Russia, and France had interceded in 1827 to stop Turkish massacres. Several interventions undertaken by European states against incursions by the Ottoman Empire gained attention from 1840 through 1908. "By the 1920s, the rationale had broadened to include the protection of nationals abroad. Intervention was invoked against a state's abuse of its sovereignty by brutal and cruel treatment of those within its power. . ." (Weiss 2005: 8).

Within the United States the Civil War served as a benchmark. Whereas the "underground railroad" demonstrated the risks that humanitarians were willing to take as they assisted escaping slaves, prisoner of war camps such as that at Andersonville, Georgia, demonstrated the gaps in humane care that still persisted. Health care for injured soldiers was adequate in some cases, inadequate in others. While over 600,000 died in the fighting on both sides, some 56,000 men ultimately died in captivity, nearly the same number as died a century later during the Vietnam War. The issue of civilian casualties caused ripples but did not receive significant attention until the Red Cross movement took hold years later. Yet the war spurred improvements in public health, in scientific and investigative technologies, and eventually in civil-rights-related legislation (Van Arsdale 2006: 169).

Through the first half of the twentieth century a humanitarianism evolved that was shaped by the events of the two world wars. Ominous battles, such as the protracted and extremely deadly conflict at Verdun in World War I, and the pre-Hiroshima firestorm bombings of Japanese cities during World War II created uproars among humanitarians. So did such combat-related events as the 1942 Bataan death march in the Philippines, which was later labeled a war crime. Just one of the many thrusts to assist vulnerable populations, bridging both world wars, involved refugees. Forcible displacement issues stemming from World War I led Norwegian Fridtjof Nansen to establish an office that was the first in world history to systematically address the needs of refugees *en masse.* Armenians who had been targeted by Turks were among the first to receive aid. Working in concert with the League of Nations, this office proved a precursor to the UNHCR, formed three decades later.

The subdiscipline of political anthropology has made surprisingly fewer contributions to the understanding of contemporary warfare and humanitarian outreach than might have been predicted. It has played only a modest role, for example, in our understandings of war and human rights abuse in Iraq (Rothenberg 2009).

The role taken by the United Nations, in concert with NGOs and the International Committee of the Red Cross (ICRC), in shaping contemporary humanitarian outreach is well known. It has been outlined and critiqued by Smillie and Minear (2004), among others. Within half a century tremendous visibility (and associated publicity) has been garnered for this multipronged and somewhat disparate effort. Major relief operations in such places as Kosovo and Timor-Leste recently have demonstrated that partnerships among UN, IGO, NGO, and military units can be helpful. Viewed from a unit service perspective, the UN can be seen to have achieved some of its greatest gains as its UNHCR unit tackles refugee issues, its WFP unit addresses food issues, and its UNICEF unit handles issues involving women and children. It can be seen to have encountered some of its greatest problems as issues of burden sharing, cross-agency outreach, and long-range strategic planning have arisen. What Smillie and Minear term "mega-NGOs," such as Oxfam International and World Vision, have come to dominate nearly 50 percent of the global humanitarian "pie" (Smillie and Minear 2004: 195). The problems of inter-NGO competition over resources were first detailed with particularly powerful effect by John Prendergast (1996).

In 1991 the UN General Assembly established the Department of Humanitarian Affairs, under the auspices of the Emergency Relief Coordinator. From negotiating access for humanitarian workers to mine action programs, this represented the United Nations' most pragmatic attempt to date to coordinate among—and act on—the diverse range of logistical issues its units were confronting. It even ran the much-maligned Oil-for-Food Program in Iraq. The department was consolidated in 1997, at the behest of Kofi Annan, into the Office for the Coordination of Humanitarian Affairs. Some of its earlier functions were spun off, but advocacy of humanitarian principles remained paramount (Eliasson 1999: 189–190).

Still another way to look at the evolution of humanitarianism is to consider the notion of *teams*. Teams have a common purpose, a unifying set of training principles, and a mandate to work together, on site, to tackle the task at hand. Although in one sense members of the London Missionary Society can be considered to have represented an institution, in another sense those members assigned (for example) to East Africa can be considered to have represented a team. The seventeenth-century Dutch colonists who, through a simple council, spoke out against abuses of Native Americans in New Netherland, also can be considered to have been a team. John Adams and the small retinue of colleagues assisting him in France in the late eighteenth century on his diplomatic mission also can be conceived as being a team. Apart from its obvious usage in the field of sports, the term became crystallized in the nineteenth century as groups of professionals—medical teams—assisted the wounded in makeshift tent camps and mobile hospitals during the American Civil War. The term became popularized in World War II, as American military patrols— such as that involved in "saving Private Ryan"—worked in sync to secure the European countryside.

Country teams, in their various manifestations and in their pursuit of a wide variety of objectives, can trace their origins to these types of "team outreach." It is a Western tradition of service and intervention. It is not without controversy.

A Contemporary Paradigm

Humanitarianism has become a big business. By one account it involves expenditures of over $10 billion annually. "New actors now mingle with the traditional players and include private corporations such as Bechtel. . . and military contingents such as the Marine Expeditionary Force" (Smillie and Minear 2004: 8). NSAs (non-state actors) are increasingly central in shaping what occurs.

Just as there is no single set of players, there is no single "theory of humanitarianism." Social scientists based in academe, as well as those who serve as consultants both to the military (from outside) and for the military (from inside), are contributing; so are military analysts, Department of State personnel, and NGO/IGO representatives. However, we would suggest that a single paradigm encompassing relevant theories and actions can be identified. That is, there is a useful "umbrella" that can aid the organization of, establish guidelines for, and provide integrity to several complementary initiatives. In putting a point to this paradigm we have relied on the writings of Farmer (2003, 2009), Hoffman and Weiss (2006), Prendergast (1996), Smillie and Minear (2004), and Williams (2001). The synthesis authored by Nguyen and Peschard (2003) also has proved helpful. Several of the key points previously have been laid out by Van Arsdale (2006).

From a paradigmatic and theoretical perspective our book builds on postpositivism and "a pinch of critical theory." In the first sense, this approach is not to be understood in the narrow perspective of quasi-experimental research, and, in the second sense, it is not to be understood in the narrow perspective of ideological inquiry. Rather, reality is seen to exist imperfectly but nonetheless to be rooted in the observable and measurable actions of men and women "on the ground," in definable cultural contexts. When field research is undertaken empiricism is essential; field data must be collected that feature a balanced array of demographic, behavioral, and attitudinal variables. As work is being triangulated, the cross-checking of sources and the protection of sources are key.

Whether conducting field research or field operations, one must make analyses of decision-making processes, of options confronting a diverse array of actors—in this case ranging from military personnel to NGO workers to government officials to insurgents—and of definable outcomes. Ethical considerations are paramount. Yet a critical realism also is seen to be useful, since the fact-value distinction can be blurred, especially as the voices of diverse actors in war zones are taken into account. The views of every-day soldiers (not just field commanders) and every-day villagers (not just tribal leaders) are appreciated. In short, we believe in the valued intersection of theory, practice, and ethics—*praxis*—and in the admonition of Susan Sontag: it is not the position but the disposition.

This perspective draws from such schools as cultural materialism, feminism, and political ecology. It is attuned to the voices of those who are victimized and suffer, focusing on ways to incorporate these persons in nontoken fashion into discussion and debate, but it is not a discursive approach per se. It is dialogic and reflexive as the researcher/practitioner engages the subject/beneficiary; each is recognized as substantively shaping the views of the other. A perspective bridging postpositivism and critical theory also incorporates an analytic approach wherein key events, including those associated with warfare, are reinterpreted as necessary in light of new voices and new empirical findings. The field of human rights informs these reinterpretations; the evaluation of abuses against persons (including injuries on and off the battlefield) and the analysis of interventions undertaken on their behalf (including medical care) must both be considered.

If there is a single theory on which the paradigm relies more heavily, it is that of structural violence. In our application it is able to accommodate both the obvious (and at times spectacular) violence found on the battlefield and, especially, the less obvious (but more insidious) violence associated with hierarchical power relationships that differentially affect the poor. This theory focuses on inequality as manifest in institutional arrangements sponsored by states and inequity as manifest in problematic access to essential resources. To paraphrase Nguyen and Peschard (2003: 456), whose synthesis covers health but is more widely applicable to humanitarianism, this allows us to address "political spaces" along three axes: (1) the ways in which inequalities are embodied institutionally; (2) the ways in which therapeutic power is legitimated; and

(3) the ways in which the management of misfortune is handled. In other words, working in three domains we must investigate and address (1) unequal relationships, paying particular attention to those who are most vulnerable and are being victimized; (2) the manner in which agencies charged with helping the vulnerable and the victims are legitimizing and institutionalizing their power; and (3) the ways in which these agencies are utilizing their power as relief, aid, and associated human services are rendered.

Misfortune and affliction are reflected in psychological, socioeconomic, and political circumstances. The negative physical factors affecting a civilian victim of a low-intensity conflict such as that in Myanmar and the negative factors affecting a military victim of a high-intensity conflict such as that in Iraq are similar. Viewed from this perspective the suffering of a wounded soldier is not substantively different from that of a wounded civilian, but when viewed in the context of structural violence—where great differences in resource access, encompassing institutional structures, and political power are considered—the calculus shifts. Both inequality and inequity emerge. Physical pain may be manifest in similar ways, but affliction is not.

The nexus of health, poverty, and sustainable development had become a paradigmatic focus by the late 1990s. The issue of structural inequalities became the touchstone. Since then humanitarian initiatives in nonwar zones and low-intensity conflict areas increasingly have come to embrace this, as the writings of Cahill and associates (2003), Thomas-Slayter (2003), Van Arsdale (2006), and many others illustrate.

Our paradigm is event-driven. That is, it intends to be responsive to what is being learned from the latest humanitarian crises and complex humanitarian emergencies. These crises fall within five broad areas: impoverishment, disease, natural disaster, terrorism, and warfare—the last a special focus of this book.

THE DEVELOPMENT ENTERPRISE

A Brief History of Development

The humanitarian paradigm outlined above is reliant on what has been learned from the field of international development. Our own activities in the field have relied heavily on "learnings" from the development enterprise. We have engaged in what might be called "classic development projects" in such diverse settings as Iraq, Guyana, and Indonesia. We also have engaged in what might be termed "nontraditional development projects" in such settings as Romania, Afghanistan, Timor-Leste, and the United States.

Proponents of traditional overseas development programs built on the notion that citizens of less-developed nations desire—and can benefit from—the expertise afforded by the citizens of developed nations. Plans, processes, and programs that have improved the quality of life of those living in such places as the United States, Britain, and Norway are to be studied and emulated. One premise has been that "underdevelopment" is the obverse of "development" and that the former is inferior to the latter. A second premise has been that there is an imbalance that is to be "righted" by appropriate action and by the infusion of adequate resources. A third premise has been that an integration of useful elements from social and economic spheres must be accomplished, with attention certainly paid to political exigencies.

Since World War II four prominent approaches, at times labeled as theories, have dominated the development discourse (Archer 2009; Little 2005; Thomas-Slayter 2003; Van Arsdale 1993). The neoclassical (also termed "modernization theory") is most closely associated with capitalism. The nation-state is the focus. The concept of the rational actor, acting primarily on self-interest, is featured. Resources are deemed to be scarce, a situation that promotes competition and—as a frequent result—rosier economic outcomes. The marketplace is the driver. Processes of change are evolutionary and, indeed, ultimately will benefit all classes.

In sharp contrast is an approach emphasizing the political economy. Focusing on systems and institutional structures rather than on individuals and nation-states, this approach suggests that change does not proceed in smooth fashion. Capitalism is viewed more as an irritant than an effective driver. Inequalities and inequities emerge in the distribution of power and wealth. The so-called Dependency School aggressively promulgated this approach, based particularly on work being done in Latin America, during the 1960s and 1970s. Whereas those associated with the neoclassical approach would refer to "developing nations," those associated with the political economy approach would refer to "underdeveloped nations."

The third prominent approach is broadly postmodernist. Its adherents represent a variety of perspectives, but all hold in common the need to dispel grand, one-dimensional discourses on development and the need to rebut those offering uniform praise and support for strategies devised by outsiders. Illustrating but one vein, feminist scholars suggest focusing on the roles women can play in community settings, covering health care, literacy enhancement, and micro-entrepreneurial industry. An atmosphere must be created wherein "facilitative development" can take place. The interplay between "culture" and "development," informed by anthropologists, also has played out here; each term has to some extent become reified and then been deconstructed. For us, this aspect remains unsatisfactory.

The fourth approach is tied to emergent understandings of human rights. "Rights-based development" seeks an integration of trends that have evolved along different (yet potentially complementary) paths since World War II. Macro-level, socioeconomic development efforts have paralleled micro-level, sociopolitical human rights efforts. The former, very pragmatic and community development/infrastructure-oriented, has paralleled the latter, very systemic and individual protection/advocacy-oriented. An informed dialogue, aided by anthropologists and economists, is now bridging the two. Oxfam International is among the major NGOs actively promoting this. The goal/product orientation of development practitioners is now better being merged with the ethical/process orientation of human rights practitioners. It is this synthesized approach that most closely complements the on-site tactics and field strategies suggested in this text.

Development is not a discipline. However, it has been "appropriated" by various academic disciplines during the post–World War II era. "Development anthropology" and "development economics" (to name two of the most prominent) began providing considerable traction in the early 1970s (Cochrane 1971). Scholars in both disciplines have increasingly been able to bridge the theoretic and the pragmatic and to apply what is being learned to field settings (Little 2005). Country team members increasingly have the opportunity to do the same.

Cooperation and Change

Of particular importance to the development enterprise has been the post-World War II emergence of cross-cultural cooperative efforts, especially those that have promoted more bottom-up and fewer top-down strategies. The forging of what variously have been termed partnerships, collaborations, or cooperative change programs has become a clear—and obvious—necessity. Ward Goodenough was among the first social scientists to state this in the context of community development: the need to achieve cooperation among individuals and groups, each likely with different values, purposes, and traditions, as they attempt to implement programs of change. Simply put: "to accomplish purposive change in another usually requires the other's cooperation" (Goodenough 1963: 17).

Goodenough went on to lay out what some of us saw as an early manifesto for progressive development. At the same time he stressed essential criteria for a new profession of development professionals. These change agents were to study anthropology, sociology, economics, and political science. (Human rights and humanitarianism were not yet seen as central thrusts.) They were to be empiricists, data-collectors, and synthesizers of the first order. They were to be sensitive to the wants and needs of potential beneficiaries, as well as to the development of communication skills that would enable "cultural boundary crossing" as beneficiaries' felt needs were considered. Although not needing to become policy analysts or policy makers, they had to possess sensitivity to the policy implications of "induced change." The proper diffusion of knowledge gained to other professionals in other settings also was emphasized. Otherwise, "lessons learned" quickly could become "lessons lost." What were viewed by some as "exceptional" experiences with development projects, once contextualized, were usually found to be "normal" (Goodenough 1981).

Particularly during the 1960s, 1970s, and 1980s development (even of the most progressive sort) was viewed as "coming from the outside" and being project- and program-oriented. A field assessment designed by change agents—advisors, consultants, professors—would lead to the identification of felt needs. A project would be designed to address these needs. Resources would be marshaled. If successful, the short-term project would be turned into a long-term program and ideally be replicated elsewhere. Beneficiaries' standards of living and social well-being would be measurably increased.

Foreign Aid

Modern U.S. foreign assistance programs began to take definitive shape during the early years of the Cold War. The Foreign Assistance Act was passed in 1961. These programs followed on the success of the Marshall Plan, largely crafted by economist Charles Kindleberger and implemented in Europe soon after the conclusion of World War II. However, they were conceived and structured differently than the Marshall Plan was. As Hoben noted, these programs were as much conceived as policy responses to the spread of communism as to the needs of low-income people in underdeveloped countries. It was thought that "this primary objective of stopping communism was consistent with the mutually beneficial expansion of trade between rich and poor nations, the pursuit of humanitarian goals, and the fostering of democratic political institutions" (Hoben 1982: 352).

Support for foreign aid, much of it channeled through the U.S. Agency for International Development (USAID) and its network of overseas offices, came from a very loosely affiliated and unstable group of conservative, liberal, military, business, and humanitarian interests. Congressional support was present, but it was partisan and at times divisive. This atmosphere, in turn, led to a fragmented set of development goals, objectives, and mission priorities. Assistance was most assuredly delivered in such places as El Salvador, Pakistan, and Egypt, but it was not part and parcel of a unified development or humanitarian program. A benchmark was reached in the mid-1970s, when amendments to the Foreign Assistance Act were passed. They required that, as budget allocations were being considered, greater emphasis be given to promoting more equitable income distribution and employment options for the "poor majority," in concert with rural development, food crop enhancement, and labor-intensive appropriate technologies. Such programs were to include the

"poor majority" as coparticipants and, as a correlate, opened up more opportunities for anthropologists to work with USAID (Hoben 1982: 357–358).
Peter Van Arsdale became Chief-of-Party (and thus head of a specific country
team) for a 1984 Salvadoran irrigation assessment project through just such
an opening. The importance of employing anthropologists to work alongside economists as evaluators of foreign aid programs had been stressed two
decades earlier by Charles Erasmus (1961).

Models of foreign aid typically have been heavily influenced by the work
of development economists, an expertise of Derrin Smith. These models

> began by focusing mainly on the provision of physical infrastructures
> to developing countries in the 1960s and 1970s, through the [World
> Bank] and the IMF's structural adjustment programs. During the
> 1980s and 1990s, donor government-led approaches were progres-
> sively replaced by ideas of local partnership based on empowerment
> and capacity building. (Corrêa d'Almeida 2009: 12)

U.S. foreign aid initiatives are, by definition, government sponsored and
taxpayer funded. During the past fifty years they have variously been more
"country oriented," as (for example) when billions were pouring into El
Salvador on a multisectoral basis during the early 1980s, and more "program
oriented," as (for example) when millions were being spent on reproductive/
family planning programs during the late 1980s in Africa. In one of the most
incisive recent critiques on foreign aid, Nicholas Kristof (2006) analyzes prominent approaches being touted today. On the one hand, there are those such as
economist Jeffrey Sachs, who focuses on Africa and argues that rapid increases
in foreign aid will enable developing nations to extricate themselves from a
"poverty trap." He believes that a renewed and improved strategy combining
internal and external resources, both human and fiscal, is essential. A number
of developed nations supported the so-called Monterrey Consensus, wherein
a government pledges 0.7 percent of GNP to official development assistance.
The United States, despite supporting the consensus and increasing its commitment, still has not reached this level.

On the other hand, there are those such as William Easterly, who argue that Sachs's approach—and indeed the entire humanitarian approach of the United Nations—is misdirected. He cites statistics for twenty-two African nations that indicate public investment, in concert with foreign aid, yielded no increase whatsoever in productivity over the 1970–1994 period. As opposed to approaches emphasizing quantitative enhancements (for example, number of dams built, number of products exported), these in turn tied to dollar amounts given, Easterly advocates a more qualitative, "best practices" approach wherein improvements in well-being are emphasized. A bottom-up, incremental policy design is preferred.

In another of the most incisive recent critiques, Dennis Shin and associates (2008) argue that American foreign aid planning needs to be turned on its head. A reauthorization of the Foreign Assistance Act will require rethinking, such that relationships are redefined among the executive and legislative branches and others involved in U.S. foreign assistance, including host-country governments and representatives of civil society. The dichotomous big-power relations formed during the Cold War, which drove the types of assistance offered, no longer exist. Top-down strategies no longer work. Nonconsultative, non-empowering strategies are to be dismissed. A type of development that is linked to poverty reduction, as well as to health promotion and basic education, must be the central goal of foreign assistance. It must be framed holistically, with careful consideration given to factors affecting trade, the role of the private sector, and the capacity "for country ownership through anticorruption aid and democracy promotion" (Shin et al. 2008: 51–52).

A contemporary approach being touted by a number of experts resident in Foggy Bottom builds on the findings of economists Craig Burnside and David Dollar (2004). Their study found that aid did boost growth in countries where better forms of governance were practiced. Institutional stability makes a difference. Yet other studies—including one by Easterly, Levine, and Roodman (2003)—dispute these findings. Government officials nonetheless have been touting Millennium Challenge Accounts, which channel aid to countries where the governments are judged to be more competent and less corrupt. We believe that this approach makes sense but that it must be done in concert with indigenous programs targeting local felt needs and incorporating culturally attuned socioeconomic strategies. "Aid isn't the preferred path to development" (Kristof 2006: 43), but it can be an essential building block.

A Contemporary Paradigm

Barbara Thomas-Slayter (2003: 15) suggests that any useful development paradigm will consider the following: the interplay of development and underdevelopment; value assumptions about human nature and about what the "good life" should be; operational criteria for achieving that kind of life; and a strategy for getting there. She goes on to suggest that, as development for nations of "the Global South" is considered, structural characteristics such as health care, literacy, and household-based standard of living (viewed socioeconomically rather than economically) must be emphasized. Innovative qualitative indicators include dependency burden (as this relates to a family's responsibility for young children) and political vulnerability (as this relates to political parties' abilities to substantively assist citizens). Innovative quantitative indicators include the rate of underemployment and the export dependency ratio.

Since the 1970s a development paradigm has been emerging that recognizes the following criteria: (1) that low-income residents of developing nations base their economic decisions as much on pragmatic choice as on tradition; (2) that local institutions and local technologies usually are adaptive, offer sound foundations for development, and must not be brushed aside; (3) that equitable income and asset distribution are desirable ends that can help a society attain sustained growth; and (4) that programs promoting equitable growth will be more likely to succeed if they are fine-tuned to address local situations and interests (Hoben 1982: 350). Anthropologists and economists alike have paid increasing attention to behavioral analyses, that is, to those patterned activities that members of developing nations engage in to adapt to changing socioeconomic and political circumstances. They also have paid increasing attention to the activities that agents of change engage in as they attempt to assist others. Empirical grassroots analyses, targeted locally and regionally, have proven more useful than macro-analyses targeted nationally and internationally (Thomas-Slayter 2003).

This paradigm arises in response to calls for localized projects that benefit micro-entrepreneurs and rural smallholders and that create minimal changes in the landscape. It arises as a counterpoint to mega-projects like dams and reservoirs, which have dominated the discourse of development for 50 years. Despite notable successes, such as the Way Seputih/Way Sekampung dam, irrigation, and hydroelectric project in south Sumatra (for which Peter Van Arsdale and his Indonesian colleagues conducted feasibility studies), cost-benefit analyses have yielded "net negative" results for a number. Most recently, controversy has arisen over the proposed series of dams on the Salween River. Running from China through Myanmar (Burma) and bordering Thailand for a stretch, it is the world's longest undammed river. Opponents claim that certain features of the dam cascade were secretly negotiated and that its development would further damage members of the dozen or more ethnic groups who live in the region. The Salween Watch Coalition states that the dams "are part of a military strategy by the [Myanmar] dictatorship to increase control over the ethnic peoples of Burma, their lands, and their rich natural resources" (2006: 6).

Dissecting the work of NGOs allows an analytic bridge between the development and humanitarian enterprises. Most NGO activity has concentrated on development programs, but some (for instance, in refugee camps) has come to target emergency humanitarian relief (Williams 2001: 2). An emergent perspective, which perhaps will achieve consensus status during the twenty-first century, is that development efforts should be aimed at local and regional (rather than national) levels; that health and education/literacy are the sectors where the greatest measurable gains can be achieved; that women's socioeconomic roles, especially in highly gender-diversified and gender-stratified societies, should be targeted; and that further innovations in civil-military cooperation—complemented by the work of NGOs—should be explored. The UN's eight Millennium Development Goals provide a broad but useful umbrella that complements much of this. Goal Number Eight, to develop a global partnership for development, is germane. The deadline set to achieve these goals is 2015.

Our contemporary development paradigm is responsive to the "second triangle" of factors presented in Figure 1.1. Ethics, research, and advocacy provide a focal point for applied anthropologists and economists. Even those opposed to engaging the military in any way whatsoever are afforded a window of opportunity here. Complementary perspectives on this issue are presented later in this chapter, in the subsection on types of change and intervention (specifically, in the discussions on economics and anthropology).

WARRIORS, BUILDERS, CHAPLAINS, AND HUMANITARIANS

Warfare clearly has shaped the course of history. It is "event-specific." As modern warfare has evolved, strategies for intervention also have evolved. Of particular importance here are the interventions associated with Western warfare, over the past millennium. In addition to the political sphere, interventions occur in three arenas: (1) on the battlefield, as warriors engage in combat; (2) in the immediate battlefield environment, as engineers and builders deal with logistics, matériel, and infrastructure; (3) in the broader battlefield environment, as humanitarians—including chaplains—assist warriors and civilians in need.

Emergent Civil-Military Cooperation

Normative and pragmatic concerns intersect dramatically in the field of humanitarianism, as Hoffman and Weiss (2006) stress. Utilitarianism, reflecting a kind of situational ethics, emerges. As warriors, builders, and humanitarians confront displaced populations, injured civilians and soldiers, and damaged infrastructure, hard choices have to be made. The ideal stance of neutrality and impartiality in service to others may have to be replaced by a pragmatic, nonneutral stance of intervention to save others. There is an emergent "responsibility to protect" norm, derived from the actions of human rights, security, and military specialists, which is working in roughly complementary fashion to a long-existing but amorphous "responsibility to serve the needy" norm.

Although not as systematic as in the present era, various examples of civil-military cooperation in assisting the ill and wounded have been noted for centuries. The Knights of the Hospital of St. John—the Hospitallers—were a military order dedicated to providing medical aid to pilgrims traveling to the Holy Land during the era of the Crusades. The Hospitallers' Crac des Chevaliers (Castle of the Knights), suggested by Adrian Boas (2006) as possibly the greatest surviving example of medieval military architecture, sits in the area of Qal'at al-Hisn, Syria, near the border with Lebanon. It symbolizes both might, with its balconies and chutes for dropping rocks and pouring liquids on enemy combatants, and compassion, with its dispensaries to aid the wounded.

Civil-military cooperation was enhanced early on—and often at the expense of indigenous peoples—by religious specialists. Aspects of the hospice movement, in part, can be traced to members of such religious orders as the Crosiers, who assisted wayfarers (including soldiers) in need. The roles played by priests and chaplains serving the military became central. According to Dale Herspring, in England the lord of a manor was responsible not only for procuring supplies and arming men who would fight on his behalf but also for providing a chaplain who would offer spiritual guidance, comfort on the eve of battle, and solace once the fighting had ceased (2001: 18–20). Across the Atlantic, chaplains or the equivalent were recorded as having served colonists battling Native Americans as early as 1637 (while also having served to crush indigenous religious practices). By the early eighteenth century continental commanders had come to expect the assistance of chaplains. During the French and Indian War, most were Congregationalists, Presbyterians, or Episcopalians. During the Revolutionary War, a similar pattern held. George Washington was among the early American military leaders who stressed the importance of civilian chaplains in military service. In a few instances chaplains even took leadership positions on the battlefield.

This emergent type of chaplaincy was one-sided. Little regard was shown for other beliefs, particularly those of Native Americans or recent immigrants. It was seldom informed by what now would be called "cross-cultural insights." Issues of belief and practice usually were presented as black and white, when in fact a blurry gray would have been more appropriate.

By the Civil War the Union had a better-organized chaplaincy system than did the Confederacy. Nonetheless, the importance of clergymen continued to be emphasized by those on both sides. Orders also were issued by Union and Confederate commanders that chaplains should not be held as prisoners. It also was during this period that the first Jewish chaplain was appointed; the first rabbi appointed to regular chaplaincy service took his post half a century later. By the end of World War I there were over 2,200 chaplains in the U.S. Army and by the end of World War II more than 9,000 (Herspring 2001: 27–39 *passim*).

Ray Giunta has written about his service as a Christian chaplain at "ground zero," that is, in New York City immediately after the 9/11 attacks (2002). He was one of those who assisted with the services for "Victim #1," a firefighter who lost his life in the north World Trade Center tower. Working alongside relief workers, search and rescue experts, and police officers for two months, Giunta found that being a good humanitarian means being a good listener, especially for those who are grieving. He also found that being a good humanitarian means offering assistance to other humanitarians.

Military Engineering and Innovations

As modern warfare emerged, so, too, did modern military strategies associated with preservation of life and conservation of resources. Terrorist and counterinsurgency activities of the latter twentieth and early twenty-first centuries have skewed this ideal, but it fortunately persists. Off-battlefield strategy involving civilian interests, personnel support and logistics, the assessment of matériel (including unexploded ordnance), and the care of prisoners are four of the areas where humanitarian innovations are increasingly being explored.

Engineering Aid in Afghanistan

"Imagine 130-degree temperatures and intense humidity. Meat-eating lizards 3 feet long ambling past. Spiders bigger than a dinner plate. Earthquakes, regularly. Enough mice, rats, scorpions, and mosquitoes to last a lifetime. Welcome to Afghanistan—Forward Operating Base Fenty." Employing a touch of hyperbole, this is how Julie Hutchinson (2009: 2) introduces the area where three members of the 204th Civil Engineering Flight of the Colorado Air National Guard worked recently. The construction management and engineering support jobs of Col. Mike Crader, Maj. Anthony Fontanetta, and Chief Master Sgt. Jim Martin took them to a river valley in the Tora Bora area of Afghanistan. They worked on building an air-traffic control tower, a dining facility for American troops, military operations buildings, and barracks for Afghan troops. Crader reported that their experience was not unlike "coming into a subdivision that was built without any infrastructure" and then trying to add electricity, sewers, and running water. He reports that the engineers tried to carefully respect Afghan construction techniques. These involve the use of extensive amounts of mortar, brick, and plaster, but no drywall. While eating MREs (meals ready to eat), the three men and their colleagues also were not short of goodies sent by family and friends—Girl Scout cookies, M&Ms, and beef jerky. Cargo planes arrived at FOB Fenty twice daily. American and allied teams in the area were supported by over 1,000 Afghans from the nearby city of Jalalabad. The three reported gaining "a deep respect for the Afghan people" given their overall experience in-country.

The cross-fertilization between civil and military operations has benefited from innovations in engineering. Construction engineers regularly have accompanied soldiers in the field since the Roman era; however, professional engineering in the West developed at the same time—in the late nineteenth century—as did humanitarianism as a social philosophy. "From its beginnings, humanitarianism was allied with an ethical vision for the use of science and technology [including medicine] irrespective of nationality, race, or other restrictive description" (Lucena et al. 2006: 1). In part spurred by what had taken place on the battlefield, an "idealistic activism" took hold among increasing numbers of engineers in the twentieth century, with some joining the International Network of Engineers and Scientists for Global Responsibility

(INES). Founded in 1991, INES inspired (and, in turn, continues to be inspired by) several groups, such as Engineers Without Borders. Many of their services are offered without compensation to those in need overseas. The late Fred Cuny, whose work spanned Bosnia to Chechnya, was among the leading inspirations as a humanitarian-engineer (Lucena et al. 2006: 2).

At the height of the war in Iraq, journalist Frank Viviano visited the Kurdish-controlled areas in the northeast. He interviewed members of the *peshmerga*, engaged in both defensive and offensive military operations, as well as representatives of civilian agencies, engaged in various kinds of urban development projects. He believes that although an obvious distinction can be made between "warriors" and "builders," both are essential in understanding how a war-ravaged society functions (Lucena et al. 2006). We would add that both types of person usually believe in justice, in complementary fashion. Both usually believe, in complementary fashion, that a civil society can be created. While battling the enemy, warriors can contribute via policy clarification, infrastructure support, and security enhancement. Although builders literally design and build structures, more importantly some contribute to policy development, educational support, and economic development.

Types of Change and Intervention

Although there is no single "theory of humanitarianism," the paradigm we have outlined suggests which types of change and intervention match our criteria. When viewed historically, a number of patterns and disciplinary trends can be identified. Some are linked to complementary theoretical stances taken by practitioners and advocates of humanitarian activities; these stances usually derive from their particular disciplines (ranging from anthropology to law). Other patterns and trends are linked solely to actions and interventions that have played out (with varying degrees of success) on site, in the field. In the post-World War II era these often have been associated with NGO and IGO operations.

We identify eight disciplinary trends during the twentieth and twenty-first centuries that have helped shape "modern humanitarianism." Although space limitations prevent in-depth analysis, it is imperative to provide high-lights from the two that have been most relevant to our own work: economics and anthropology. The others are military science, sociology and social work, medicine and public health, engineering, law and political science, and theology and religious missionization. (The field of human rights, although obviously key, is not a "discipline." It is touched on in our coverage of law and political science.) In several instances we identify key individuals within these disciplines whose work has inspired us.

Economics

Derrin Smith draws much of his expertise from the field of economics and its related subfield, development economics. Tremendous strides have been made in this discipline as it relates to both the humanitarian enterprise and the development enterprise. Albeit in fits and starts, innovations have been reflected in certain World Bank and International Monetary Fund initiatives, especially in agricultural development. Structural adjustment programs have been touted and, when appropriate, criticized. Debt forgiveness also has been touted and, when appropriate, criticized. Large-scale development projects, such as dams and reservoirs, have been promoted in such diverse locations as Brazil and India; small-scale development projects, such as textile mills, have been promoted in such diverse locations as Indonesia and El Salvador. Economists such as Jeffrey Sachs have become leading advocates of creative financing, the improved use of foreign aid, and an "evangelism for aid" associated with poverty reduction (Kristof 2006: 41). The writings of Amartya Sen and 2006 Nobel Laureate Mohammad Yunus have focused on economic capabilities and freedoms, within the broader context of human rationality, things economist *cum* systems thinker Kenneth Boulding hinted at a half-century earlier (cf. Ryan 2003). Socioeconomist Kajni Kothari writes persuasively of poverty not as an economic problem "but a function of exclusion, abandonment, and disenfranchisement" (Thomas-Slayter 2003: 21). Socioeconomic factors, such as those associated with sustainable livelihoods addressed at the household level, have become a focus.

The economic modernization schemes of the mid- to late-twentieth-century largely have been abandoned. "Growth" still is the watchword, as well as a primary goal, but it is being tackled from a number of innovative angles. Some of these focus on modest infusions of outside capital linked to substantive infusions of inside work. Others focus on supporting microenterprises (Thomas-Slater 2003). Still others focus on grassroots partnerships, where capacity building through ecologically responsible development has become key (Van Arsdale and Witten 2006). Indeed, the effects of conservation practices on market economies (and vice versa), as these involve indigenous peoples, are being analyzed in a number of South American locales (Godoy et al. 2005).

This was not always the case. As Glynn Cochrane (1971) stressed, economists of the Cold War era had been attuned to the ways in which infusions of capital could be made to generate useful change. These were primarily unidirectional and unidimensional, aimed at market growth. Despite the efforts of George Dalton ([1961] to cite one exemplar working in Africa) and Charles Erasmus ([1961] to cite another exemplar working in Latin America), a gap in economic rationality was perceived to exist among those involved in "primitive and peasant economic systems" and those involved in "Western capitalist economic systems." The promotion of advantageous allocations, linking economic means to economic ends, was seen as important and, indeed, in the writings of some (for example, Kindleberger 1965) as the needed engine of growth as "economic lifecycles" unfolded. Fiscal measures were advocated that, although at times appearing punitive, were deemed essential to achieve market integration and transformation. Western market economies could be infused into non-Western societies and, once entrenched, could serve as models for new patterns of preference.

Economic insights are continuing to be reframed and reiterated. For example, during the 60th Session of the UN General Assembly, spanning 2005/2006, a draft resolution was introduced by its president. Among elements of interest here were the emphasis on crisp national development strategies by member states, the value of partnered approaches to development, the significance of macro-economic interpretations to the development enterprise, and—again—the importance of meeting the Millennium Development Goals by 2015.

Anthropology

Peter Van Arsdale draws much of his expertise from the field of anthropology. In the most general sense this field traces its roots to an array of philosophical, linguistic, biological, archaeological, and cultural studies. These have both enriched the field, leading some to call it "the broadest of the social sciences," and entangled the field, leading others to call it "the most maddening of the social sciences." The term *anthropology* was not used on a consistent basis until the mid-nineteenth century. During the 1800s it was *ethnography*, emerging from cultural studies (as broadly defined), that not only began to provide rich information on the diverse array of societies worldwide but that also began to point to cross-cultural problems that might need to be addressed.

The ethnographic studies that came to identify problems in need of rectification, in retrospect, can be described as studies identifying "problems of 'the Other'" in need of "assistance by Western outsiders." By the 1880s relatively comprehensive information was emerging from "the field" in Australia and Oceania, Southeast Asia, South Asia, East Africa, Latin America, and North America, in particular, suggesting "indigenous problems" in need of "humane solutions." Among the first organizations to attempt to tackle the problems of indigenes was the Aborigines' Protection Society of London, cited earlier. Some of their activities came to be informed by ethnographers and anthropologists. Such explorer-anthropologists as John Wesley Powell had an effect as well, in his case further exposing indigenous populations of the American Southwest to scrutiny and disparate attempts at intervention.

Racism, "cultural disappearance," and disease—especially within the context of colonialism—were paramount among those concerns that shaped emergent humanitarianism within anthropology (Moore et al. 1980: 82–89). Before the post-World War II development of what variously has been defined as *applied anthropology, practicing anthropology,* or *public anthropology,* academically based cultural anthropologists took the lead in identifying populations at risk and the problems most likely to adversely affect them. Most recently, cultural anthropologists have taken the lead in analyzing "military culture" and have contributed to studies of troop well-being and psychosocial adjustment.

A sensitivity to the need to facilitate change, based on felt needs, rather than induce it from outside, based on presumed needs, was powerfully advocated by Charles Erasmus (1961), whose work was noted earlier. He was one of the first anthropologists of the post-World War II period to systematically examine overseas development and technical assistance programs. He focused on Latin America, especially its land reform initiatives. His catch-phrase "man takes control" referred to what now is termed *agency*, that is, the role of the individual as a viable and proactive agent of change. His approach complemented that of Sol Tax, one of the earliest advocates of "action anthropology."

Erasmus went on to stress the roles that social scientists should play. He believed they could be of greatest value in "areas ripe for development" at a strategic level, "by helping to guide technical assistance. . . where the projects under consideration would have the least cause to depend upon their services thereafter" (1961: 324). Social cost accounting was deemed essential. Agriculture was seen as the sector of prime importance; military opportunities were yet to achieve high levels of visibility. Although his vision of conceptualizing and promulgating a "general theory of cultural development" was not fully realized, his insights were of great heuristic value. Contemporary anthropology, as it now engages arenas as diverse as agriculture and military affairs, builds directly on these ideas (Kedia and van Willigen 2005).

The intersection of anthropology and development, mirrored by concerns with humanitarianism, has become increasingly strong during the past 30 years. This is seen both in theory (for instance, Little 2005) and practice (for example, Van Arsdale and Witten 2006). Building on the work of Satish Kedia (2008), who looks at career opportunities for applied anthropologists, a panoply of external and internal forces is creating new demands for transdisciplinary, issue-oriented knowledge. Such stark disasters as Hurricane Katrina remind one of the need for anthropological interpretations of governmental and NGO functionality. Ongoing social problems associated with HIV/AIDS, particularly in Africa, have necessitated fresh insights into customs that enhance and customs that hinder responsiveness. More nuanced understandings of social and "grassroots" (including labor) movements are emerging. Agricultural development is now better understood in terms of intended and unintended ecological transformations. Migration, including issues involving forcibly displaced populations, is seen to be multidimensional rather than linear. Investigations into ways to improve partnered community development work (especially in rural settings), while seemingly more "traditional," remain essential. Critical reflection, coupled with on-site research, into what best promotes "sustainability and viability of environments" (Kedia 2008: 18) is vital. Many of these efforts require solid cross-cultural communication and diplomatic skills, as Kedia suggests. At broad conceptual levels, they also require an appreciation of the UN's Millennium Development Goals.

To summarize, development is no longer about "doing things for others, relying on field data" but rather about "doing things with others, engaging critical reflection and ethical sensitivity." Regarding issues covered in this text, these opportunities can be realized through relief operations, human rights, human security, food security, and peace-building activities. Better anthropologically attuned understandings derived from each of these domains, in turn, will have direct bearings on interpretations of civilian-military relations and postconflictive development/reconstruction scenarios.

Other Contributions

Humanitarianisms, old and new, have drawn from a number of other fields as well. Military science is key, but—since it underpins much of the remainder of this volume—it will not be dealt with here.

Regarding sociology and social work, the contributions of Jane Addams to the latter already have been mentioned. Whereas the work of Mimi Silbert exemplifies sociology's contributions (via criminology) to modern humanitarianism, the work of Robert Merton exemplifies sociology's theoretic (albeit more indirect) contributions. With his most prominent work spanning the 1940s, 1950s, and 1960s, as Cuzzort and King (1989: 150–157) stress, his ability to analyze function and dysfunction enabled him to identify societal fracture lines. Dysfunctional events create disequilibrium; disequilibrium is manifested in societal problems. Interventions must be conceived accordingly, as later analysts of military affairs have reaffirmed. Yet of even greater importance here is the stance he took on ethics. Merton was among the earliest social scientists to stress that a functional approach to social action has ethical and moral consequences. Naive moral judgments must be supplanted by rigorous scientific analyses.

Regarding medicine and public health, key contributions to the humanitarian enterprise are legion. It can be argued persuasively that the greatest humanitarian strides of the past half-century have been made in the health care field. Smallpox has been eliminated, polio almost so, and the rates of endemic diseases such as onchocerciasis (African river blindness) reduced significantly. This is one reason that Bill and Melinda Gates have targeted most of their philanthropic outreach toward health. As Nicholas Kristof (2006: 42) astutely observes, the public health arena also is the one where measurable outcomes can be most effectively and efficiently charted. The number of children who have been assisted by oral rehydration therapy can readily be recorded, village by village, district by district, region by region. These data then can be systematically compared with data obtained from other areas worldwide. The Centers for Disease Control have demonstrated analytic, curative, and policy-oriented leadership in this regard.

Regarding engineering, key contributions already have been noted. Here it is important simply to remind that, once plans for a humanitarian and/or development project involving infrastructural enhancements have been laid out, engineers are brought in. Their roles are crucial as large projects such as refugee camps, impoundments, and access roads are being designed and built. Although less visible, their roles also are crucial as small projects such as sanitation systems, village irrigation schemes, and rural health clinics are being implemented. As Juan Lucena and associates (2006) write, few engineers have had formal training in principles of humanitarian assistance. Even fewer have had training in the ethical precepts associated with intervention, relief, and aid delivery. The Colorado School of Mines, a premier engineering institution with hundreds of graduates working overseas, is among the first to initiate an educational training program in "humanitarian engineering."

Regarding law and political science, the contributions, of course, have been substantial. These best can be framed from the perspective of human rights. From the founding of the United Nations and the promulgation of the Universal Declaration on Human Rights, to the early work of the Nuremberg Tribunal and the recent work of the International Criminal Court, lawyers and political scientists have played lead roles. Conventions, protocols, and declarations spanning such diverse issues as torture, child labor, and refugee security have gradually gained traction (Van Arsdale 2006). The modern Geneva Conventions have been seminal as (for example) the treatment of prisoners of war is considered. So-called truth and reconciliation commissions have been convened successfully in a number of countries, such as El Salvador. Analyses of political power and its abuses, in times of war as well as peace, have engendered substantial insights into the issue of ethnocide and genocide. The political ramifications of humanitarian intervention continue to be explored.

Regarding theology and religious missionization, some analysts would assert that this is the most controversial arena as the disciplinary history of humanitarianism is considered. In contrast, we see it as simply one more important set of initiatives. Proselytizing and conversion have had demonstrable adverse effects on indigenous peoples; less well known are the positive effects as missionaries have brokered relations among oppressive government officials and indigenous peoples. In some cases (for example, Papua Province, Indonesia, as witnessed by Peter Van Arsdale), human rights abuses have been directly averted by missionary intervention. Within the United States, the humanitarian contributions of a pastor, Martin Luther King, Jr., have attained legendary status.

An ETHICS OF COOPERATION AND INTERVENTION

The information and ideas presented in this chapter provide the backdrop for the remainder of the book. As cooperative work within nonpermissive military environments is considered, we clearly favor progressive strategies that engage "outsiders" and "insiders," interactively and reflexively, in programs effecting change. We appreciate the foundational insights that the fathers and mothers of our social sciences, as well as those who pioneered on-site projects, have provided. From Charles Kindleberger to Kajni Kothari, from Jane Addams to Ward Goodenough, theory and practice have intersected and unfolded, albeit often in rough and imperfect form. We believe that civil-military cooperation is essential as the world moves into "post-Pollyannaish humanitarianism." Emphasis on the singularly transformative impact of the well-intentioned Western civilian *cum* aid worker is no longer adequate. In many instances, nonneutrality—linked to political humanitarianism—is not only more practical for outsiders but also more beneficial for insiders. It also is clear that we are not armchair theorists. We have cut our teeth on fieldwork and country operations.

The principles of differentiation (the selection of military targets with a precision allowing civilian populations and property to avoid unnecessary damage) and proportionality (that there be a reasonable correlation between any damage inflicted on civilian populations and property and the strategic value of the military operation) have become central to the military/humanitarian specialist. Principles of just war must be followed. The Geneva Conventions must be fully upheld. Recent innovations in transnational criminal court and tribunal procedures must be supported. The proscriptions of international humanitarian law, such as that involving the emplacement of military or guerrilla combatants among civilians (so that they can be concealed), have gained traction.

The ethical implications of this integrated array of perspectives are significant. Following Weiss (2005), a more utilitarian approach, which shies away from moral absolutes, is appropriate. An understanding of the political, social, and economic context in which humanitarian assistance is offered is essential. A utilitarian approach is complemented by a functional approach; outcomes are reflected in measurable changes in the lives of vulnerable people—civilians and soldiers alike. Actions have consequences. Personal responsibility and institutional accountability must be the hallmarks of the humanitarian, whether that person works for the military, a government agency, a university, or an NGO.

Ethics is the science of morals. Members of the military can take on seemingly high moral mantles. For example, in an informal survey of potential U.S. voters, Joshua Green (2006: 42) found a majority perceiving "service in Iraq or Afghanistan as not just a desirable credential but one that confers unchallengeable moral standing" in veterans running for national office. As potential interventions balancing life and death are weighed by soldiers-turned-politicians, from the late John Murtha to John McCain, ethical practices and transparent decision making must transcend partisan disagreements. The notion of a "high moral mantle" also must not be overblown or overshadow the important contributions of nonmilitary personnel.

THE RECIPROCITY OF HUMANITARIANISM AND DEVELOPMENT

Humanitarianism and development are interactive, reciprocal fields. Each informs the other. Each benefits from the achievements of the other. We believe that practitioners in one regularly should engage practitioners in the other, sharing what works and does not work. Themes stressed by development specialists should emphasize poverty reduction, human development as reflected in literacy and health, and economic growth attuned to local conditions (Thomas-Slayter 2003). These themes mirror those that should be stressed by specialists in humanitarian assistance, including the alleviation of human suffering, the buttressing of local infrastructure and supply networks in times of crisis, and the implementation of locally sustainable relief-and-assistance programs. Taken together, these form a nexus that is central to the notion of rights-based development.

Whereas a simple definition of humanitarianism might be "systematic efforts to correct deficits in the human condition, with an emphasis on the sociopolitical," a simple definition of development might be "systematic efforts to augment deficits in the human condition, with an emphasis on the

socioeconomic." We have worked in both areas and believe them to be complementary and interactive. Learnings from one (for instance, on programmatic
capacity building and sustainability) can and should influence learnings in the
other. Country operations and military operations can and should contribute
learnings in turn.

Poverty is the foundational issue for development. Suffering is the foundational issue for humanitarianism. A number of scholars and activists now
are addressing the intersection of these two, in ways that bode well for the
future. Drawing on the field of human rights, Amartya Sen (1999) stresses the
need to actualize a moral imperative; poverty eradication becomes an obligation, not just an option. Drawing on the field of medicine, Kevin Cahill and
his colleagues (2003) stress the need to be compassionate while also "doing
humanitarianism." Compassion, in and of itself, is only self-indulgent. To borrow a phrase from Thomas-Slayter (2003: 309), "synergetic improvements"
are needed, as intersections between the fields of development and humanitarianism are identified and built on. Just as development ideally is reflected
in people ("the beneficiaries") being empowered to access resources and leverage decisions that are favorable for themselves, humanitarianism ideally is
reflected in people ("the service providers") being able to assist in ways that
respect dignity, increase prospects for autonomy, and facilitate opportunities
for empowerment.

Modern humanitarianism can, and must, transcend the "Pollyannaish
humanitarianism" of the recent past. What we call "pragmatic humanitarianism" (as expanded in the concluding chapter) is needed. This in no way
sidesteps a moral imperative but in fact (as emphasized by Nockerts and
Van Arsdale 2008) builds directly upon it. Service, outreach, and intervention are offered where the "morally possible" and "materially possible"
intersect. Those injured, impaired, and otherwise at risk must be assisted
by those with the resources, capabilities, and opportunities to help them.
Such humanitarian activity usually takes place in response to crisis. That
first responders, second responders, logistical experts, and support personnel (from chaplains to engineers) are drawn from both civilian and military
sources is a plus.

Humanitarianism must be built on understandings of deep justice and moral obligation. It must confront structural violence. As noted earlier, humanitarianism is not an unassailable moral good but a kind of ideology, shaped by the ideas and actions of a wide range of activists, philosophers, on-site field staff, and others. Although drawing on the ideas of non-Westerners, it is largely a product of Western approaches to dealing with vulnerable populations. Interventions must target the alleviation of suffering in the short run, the reduction of risk in the long run, and the overall improvement of human security. Country teams can make significant contributions.

CHAPTER 2

OUTSIDE THE GREEN ZONE: NONPERMISSIVE AREAS OF OPERATION

THE GREEN ZONE

A news report emanating from Iraq on July 30, 2007, was not very different from the many that had been issued earlier or those that have followed. Suicide bombers had been active, renegade militias continued to be problematic, the Iraqi government continued to struggle. But there was a distinctive note. A new type of Green Zone had been established: a legal zone consisting of a heavily fortified compound to shelter judges and their families, as well as aid attorneys trying some of the country's most dangerous suspects. It officially is called the "Rule of Law Complex" and is located in the Baghdad neighborhood of Rusafa (Gordon 2007).

The Rule of Law Complex is located across the Tigris River, to the east of the more well-known and much larger Green Zone. Also known as the Emerald City or Versailles on the Tigris (Chandrasekaran 2006), this 4-square-mile area of Baghdad originally consisted of Iraqi government buildings, palaces, and villas. After the American invasion, it was taken over by the Coalition Provisional Authority. Soldiers, diplomats, private contractors, mercenaries, and others increasingly congregated here. Coalition representatives—Poles, Brits, Aussies, Spaniards, Italians—have all lived here. Some displaced Iraqis, as well as original residents, also have lived within its boundaries.

Early on most of those living in the Green Zone were (seemingly) brought together by what was referred to as "'the mission'—the Bush administration's campaign to transform Iraq into a peaceful, modern, secular democracy where everyone, regardless of sect or ethnicity, would get along" (Chandrasekaran 2006: 11). The zone—now also referred to as "the International Zone"—has come to take on almost legendary status, pro and con. Tilting pro, for example, when the January 1, 2009, security pact took effect, the U.S. military turned over zone security to Iraqi forces (although several foreign organizations continued to maintain separate guarded compounds therein). Tilting con, for instance, on August 9, 2009, Iraqi authorities arrested a British contractor over the shooting deaths of two coworkers therein (Gamel 2009: A2). Fenced, barricaded, and closely guarded, today it remains the focal point of international authority and action within Baghdad. The U.S. and British embassies are located there, as are Iraqi government headquarters. Most foreign journalists file their reports from inside; some rarely venture outside (a critique leveled in 2008 against BBC representatives). Certain country team operations also are planned from inside.

Our concern is with activities and organizational operability outside such Green Zones, in semi- or nonpermissive areas of operation. Sometimes these are referred to as "Red Zones," but more often they have no particular denotation. In extreme cases, their connotation is "zones of danger."

"COUNTRY OPERATIONS" AND "COUNTRY TEAMS"

Comprehensive, externally designed programs intended to assess, implement, and monitor a set of interventions in a particular country usually are referred to as "country operations." Such operations target specific objectives, such as refugee relief, the rebuilding of infrastructure in postconflict environments, and food aid. Sometimes they are primarily military in objective. They usually are built on "country assessments," which have long been employed by government agencies (such as the U.S. armed forces and USAID), by nongovernmental organizations (such as Save the Children and Oxfam), by advisory institutions (such as Human Rights Watch and the International Crisis Group), and by the United Nations (such as through UNAMI, the United Nations Assistance Mission for Iraq).

A country operation usually is organized, vetted, and operated by a country team. A country team, in U.S. Department of State parlance, is much different from those conceived and implemented by the military, corporations, NGOs, and IGOs. At the Department of State the country team for a nation such as Iraq consists only of the ambassador's most senior staff, whereas in the other instances—those of direct relevance in this book—the team comprises all personnel stationed at that post and its satellites, from the country director to the locally employed, indigenous support staff. Sometimes what is described as a "country team" will, in fact, be a subteam, such as a Provincial Reconstruction Team (PRT) operating in a place like Anbar Province, Iraq.

Country teams, conducting country operations, can be found within four primary sectors or arenas, as suggested above: the military (through a particular branch, such as the U.S. Marines), corporate (including "development banking"), nonprofit/nongovernmental, and intergovernmental. Banking provides a useful example. The operations of the Islamic Development Bank are typical. Its country operations department is headed by its vice president of operations. Operating in seventeen nations, from Afghanistan to Uzbekistan, the bank has seven "national shareholders" (ranging from Saudi Arabia to the United Arab Emirates). Its central department of country operations is based in Jeddah, with subdepartments based in each of the nations it is assisting through its loans and sectoral initiatives: human development, agricultural development and food security, infrastructural development, and private sector development. By comparison the African Development Bank conducts its country operations in similar fashion but has divided its operations into regions. Key communications, project by project, are handled by project officers also known as "country team secretaries."

Major corporations that engage in overseas development projects and programs cosponsored by the governments in question also are considered to be conducting "country operations." An example is Chevron. In Australasia, Chevron Australia is a major actor in the exploration, development, and production of oil and gas resources. It is central to the development of reserves that are intended to benefit Timor-Leste, currently ranked as Southeast Asia's poorest nation. The $3.7 billion Sunrise Project, intended to exploit reserves that have been located in the Timor Sea between Timor-Leste and Australia, has been delayed owing to political instability in the region and disputes as to how to divide the large royalty amounts anticipated. President José Ramos-Horta recently told us that he anticipates at least $1.2 billion annually in royalties. Chevron Australia employs over 1,000 people in its Perth office alone; all are considered members of its country team.

The United Nations, the world's largest and most influential IGO, fields country teams and mounts country operations through its various agencies. UNAMI (noted above) coordinates the sixteen-agency/program UN country team for Iraq. Included (for example) are representatives of the World Food Programme, the World Health Organisation, and the Food and Agriculture Organisation. Although it can be said that the overall country team is mounting country operations, it also can be said that a specific agency/program under its umbrella is doing so. An example is the United Nations High Commission for Refugees (UNHCR), working recently in Timor-Leste.

For each country where a need has been identified and operations are intended, an annual country operations plan is developed by the organization in question. Since such plans often stem from in-situ preliminary assessments, they are covered in Chapter 3.

As implied in this book, country operations involving the military are known superficially to a wide public but not well known in terms of their training, applied methodological/research, and cooperative/partnering attributes. Most of the more progressive operations, which are peaceful and conducted in conjunction with civilian partners, are poorly understood in the "outside world." This, in part, is due to the fact that military activities labeled as "country operations" can appear to be ominous and oppressive. For example, as Colombian Third Division Army troops continued their long-standing battle with the FARC (Revolutionary Armed Forces of Colombia), in January of 2007 commanders reported "country operations" that led to the capture of nine individuals. This capture was part of a regional sweep, itself part of a national initiative, the "National Exercise of Columbia." Guerrillas who have gained the sympathy of a wide public, and who have been viewed by some as liberators, were being rounded up. Derrin Smith has witnessed similar exercises in Anbar Province, Iraq; Peter Van Arsdale similar exercises in Papua Province, Indonesia.

Just as country operations are all-encompassing, the responsibilities of a country operations coordinator are comprehensive and complex. In addition to serving as director of the agency's activities throughout a particular nation, this person's general duties can include the development and maintenance of collegial relations with indigenous leaders; monitoring and maintaining compliance with administrative procedures; managing and reviewing management systems; and coordinating activities among field sites. Specific duties can include leading or assisting in drawing up proposals, plans, and budgets for new field projects; ensuring that communications are maintained efficiently; ensuring that field reports are completed on time and transmitted to key recipients; ensuring that security guidelines are followed; and managing senior line staff. In most cases the coordinator is expected to try to enhance the agency's position relative to similar agencies working within the same sector. Sometimes the coordinator will be asked to change course unexpectedly, as happened in Iraq in 2003 when the looting of the Baghdad Museum caused a special subteam of military and civilian personnel to be formed. The team found that the museum had been used as a military fighting position and weapons cache. The team's diligence led to the recovery of a number of valuable artifacts (Bogdanos 2005).

Country operations are to be differentiated from "field operations," such as those conducted by U.S. Customs and Border Protection personnel or those conducted by the CIA. Some such overseas operations can be controversial. Human Terrain Teams operating in Iraq and Afghanistan are seen to complement country operations, and in a sense, to be subsets of certain country teams. Their pros and cons are discussed in Chapter 7.

HUMANITARIANISM AND WARFARE

From a Euro-American perspective a convincing argument can be made that the evolution of humanitarianism and warfare is an interlinked process. The writings of scholars as diverse as Max Hastings (2005) and Max Boot (2006) suggest that the latter drives the former. Freeman Dyson (2005), renowned for his work in what came to be called operational research during World War II, believes the two are interactive. We also believe that the two are reciprocal and interactive, which, far more than warfare, contributes to innovations in humanitarian action. It is imperative to understand the historical patterns between warfare and humanitarianism.

Some analysts would go farther than Hastings and Boot, claiming that a war—or specific battles—serve as a kind of glue, binding together otherwise disparate political entities, as occurred during World War I at the Battle of Vimy Ridge, in France, the first time that all four divisions of the Canadian Corps went into battle at the same time. Each April 9th the battle is commemorated in Canada in nationalistic fashion, as are the lives of the approximately 3,500 who died that day in 1917. Also in World War I, during the latter months of 1915, over 2,700 New Zealand troops were killed in fighting at Gallipoli, Turkey. ANZAC (Australia and New Zealand Army Corps) Day is celebrated dramatically each year in commemoration of what was the latter nation's first major series of battle engagements, and first major defeat. As the late Slobodan Milošević frequently and perversely reminded his Serbian compatriots, referring in 1989 to the Battle of Kosovo Polje fought 600 years earlier against the Ottoman Turks, even a defeat can serve as a nationalistic, unifying event.

Boot has outlined what he sees as four major revolutions in Euro-American warfare since 1500, linking each to innovations in technology. These are the Gunpowder Revolution of the sixteenth century (as exemplified by the British Navy's defeat of the Spanish Armada in 1588), the First Industrial Revolution in military technology of the mid-nineteenth century (as exemplified by metallurgical advances, many of these in turn reflected in field artillery and rifles), the Second Industrial Revolution in military technology of the mid-twentieth century (as exemplified by tanks, aircraft carriers, and heavy bombers), and the Information Revolution of the 1990s (as exemplified by cruise missiles, sophisticated electronic navigation systems, and stealth aircraft). Boot is particularly interested in the interface of command-and-control systems with military technology, believing that the former often lag behind the latter.

Clausewitz and "Other Means"

Theories of warfare abound. It is not our intent to summarize them here. However, it is our intent to briefly outline one of those theories and several related concepts that directly pertain to understanding the work of those "at the civilian-military interface." Therefore, it is fascinating and perhaps surprising to note that a "classic" theory of the early nineteenth century, that of Carl von Clausewitz, is still in vogue—and still being avidly debated. From our perspective the most cogent overview and re-evaluation has been provided by Nikolas Gardner (2009). He reiterates the importance that Clausewitz's work continues to have on contemporary scholars and military theorists. Gardner adamantly disagrees with those who have suggested that Clausewitz was almost exclusively focused on "the primacy of slaughter" and "the destruction of the enemy in a bloody, decisive battle" (2009: 120) and that somehow, Clausewitz's position has been translated into violent, close-combat prescriptions being enacted in Iraq today. Rather, Gardner stresses Clausewitz's broader interpretation of the very nature of war. Although in a pure (and abstract) logic, war between belligerents should continue to escalate to extremes as each side attempts to win, there are (in the non-abstract) a number of countervailing forces. Various political objectives, the value of defensive postures, and the imperfection of intelligence all come into play. Escalation is thwarted, and other off-site and on-site factors come into play, leading to Clausewitz's most well-known aphorism: war is a continuation of political activity by "other means."

Political considerations reach into the "military means," to borrow a phrase from Posen (1999: 27). Advocating an analytical approach similar to that of Gardner, but doing so a decade earlier, he stresses that Clausewitz firmly believed that statesmen should ensure that policy infuses military operations. Those in charge of policy, although not needing to be soldiers themselves, require a firm grasp of military affairs. However, Posen adds: "Functional specialization between soldiers and statesmen, and the tendency of soldiers to seek as much independence from civilian interference as possible, combine to make political-military integration an uncertain prospect" (1999: 27). The setting of priorities by well-versed civilians enhances the likelihood of integration; we would add that effective on-site operations by country teams can dramatically improve these prospects. Many, after all, will have been working with soldiers daily.

Certain of these seemingly irreconcilable factors are brought together by Clausewitz in a conceptual model, his so-called "paradoxical trinity"—emotion, chance, and reason (Gardner 2009: 121–123). Using both the aphorism and the model as springboards, we assert that country operations in conflictive environments—particularly when adverse military circumstances are being encountered—are helping to continue political activity by "other means" while also being affected by emotion, chance, and reason. That Clausewitz also addressed the issues of insurgency and guerrilla warfare is germane, because what are now termed NSAs (non-state actors) inject "nontraditional" elements of emotion, chance, and reason into the mix as well. Actors' objectives vary widely in conflictive environments, and the scale, intensity, and duration of warfare also vary widely.

The Responsibility to Protect

Within the past decade the long-running debate about "the right to intervene" has been turned on its head. As the International Crisis Group's Gareth Evans summarized (2006), a new international norm has emerged: the responsibility to protect. Following the presentation in 2001 to the UN Secretary General of a major Canadian government-sponsored report (entitled using the same phrase), possibilities for international policy change began to reverberate. Language reflecting this norm was adopted at the UN's 60th Anniversary Summit in 2005 and was later reaffirmed by the Security Council:

> Each individual State has the responsibility to protect its populations from genocide, war crimes, ethnic cleansing and crimes against humanity. . . . The international community, through the United Nations, also has the responsibility. . . . In this context, we are prepared to take collective action, in a timely and decisive manner, through the Security Council . . . on a case-by-case basis and in cooperation with relevant regional organizations as appropriate, should peaceful means be inadequate and national authorities are manifestly failing to protect their populations.

Evans described the codification of this norm as a major breakthrough and as a fascinating piece of intellectual history. From our perspective, the norm complements a current notion of "human security." A useful UN working definition of this phrase is "the protection of the vital core of all human lives in ways that enhance human freedoms and human fulfillment," further entailing "protecting people from critical and pervasive threats and situations" while enabling the creation of systems "that together give people the building blocks of survival, livelihood and dignity." From our perspective these interpretations also complement the intellectual history found in the creative writings of Hans Binnendijk and Richard Kruger. In *Seeing the Elephant* (2006), they contrast what they term neo-Hobbesian and neo-Kantian approaches. Early on Hobbes had sought solutions to conflict and issues of governance through appropriate applications of state power, Kant through appropriate applications of moral conduct and law. "Neo-Hobbesians" such as Zbigniew Brzezinski (*Out of Control*, 1995) seek solutions to "a world of turmoil," advocating (for example) the assertive trilateral leadership of the United States, Western Europe, and

Japan. Chaos might reign, global order must be maintained. "Neo-Kantians" such as Francis Fukuyama *(The End of History and the Last Man,* 2006 [1992]) see "a world of progress" and seek solutions through the application/evolution of liberal democracies. It is interesting to note that both Brzezinski and Fukuyama stress that political ideas, along with their associated values and belief systems, play critical roles in determining the future (Binnendijk and Kruger 2006: 60). Also, these co-authors believe Samuel Huntington (*The Clash of Civilizations and the Remaking of World Order,* 1996) to have been a neo-Kantian early on, but a neo-Hobbesian more recently. We lean toward the neo-Kantian approach, while recognizing that liberal democracies most assuredly do not work—and should not be imposed—for all. This is part and parcel of our stance on ethical engagement, as discussed in Chapter 1.

Old Wars and New Wars

The seminal war-related crises spanning 1991 through 2004 are laid out masterfully by Thomas Weiss (2005) in *Military-Civilian Interactions: Humanitarian Crises and the Responsibility to Protect.* These interactions include Northern Iraq, Somalia, Bosnia, Rwanda, Haiti, East Timor (aka Timor-Leste), Kosovo, Afghanistan, and Iran. Their integrated analysis leads to insights as to what is happening at the civilian-military interface in the "post-Pollyannaish" era of humanitarianism. Understandings of cooperation and conflict in the context of humanitarian intervention are featured. Our text builds on these, as well as (in part) Ryan's notion of the post-imperial state (2008). Complementing this text is that of Hoffman and Weiss (2006), *Sword & Salve: Confronting New Wars and Humanitarian Crises,* mentioned in Chapter 1, which includes a creative table (3.1: p. 58). Our text also builds, in part, on this. We have modified it slightly, as shown in Table 2.1.

Hoffman and Weiss, although not duplicating Boot, also refer to major revolutions or transformations in warfare and military technology and the "reciprocal social changes" (2006: 76) that have accompanied them. Of particular importance to them, and us, are the changes in political authority, the movement over the past several centuries generally being toward greater

Table 2.1   Comparing "Old" and "New" Wars.

Old Wars	New Wars
Locus—coincides with state boundaries	*Locus*—areas of fragmented political authority
Agents—states and their militaries; traditional alliances	*Agents*—increased role of non-state actors, such as militias and contractors
Economies—tax revenues underwrite government war effort	*Economies*—includes illegal activities, aid, plunder
Targets and victims—mainly combatants	*Targets and victims*—prevalence of civilian casualties
Technologies—large-scale conventional weaponry	*Technologies*—new technologies and non-traditional applications
Media coverage—nonexistent to minimal propaganda	*Media coverage*—greater coverage; shapes inclination toward force

centralization. Although modern guerrilla warfare and certain of the unorthodox approaches used by Al Qaeda do not conform to this trend, most major military operations do: more centralized command-and-control, more sophisticated use of feedback loops as field data are received and processed, more attention to the sociopolitical consequences of battlefield operations. In fact, as of 2009, certain more liberal military strategists were beginning to refer to processes of "command-and-collaboration."

Although inextricably linked, the evolution of warfare and the evolution of humanitarian activity have not proceeded in lock-step fashion, as the polymath historian William McNeill (2006) implies. He builds his analysis on a critique of the four phases of warfare laid out by Boot. McNeill also is interested in the interface of military strategies, administrative bureaucracies and entanglements, and the intricacies of face-to-face combat with insurgents in current operations in such places as Iraq and Afghanistan. McNeill believes that "the larger human setting—moral and intellectual as well as social and economic—within which wars are fought [must be better emphasized]" (2006: 20).

An understanding of warfare and the roles played by soldiers is essential to this book. Fighting grabs the headlines, but the varied activities surrounding danger zones and the maintenance of defensive, peacekeeping forces is of primary concern to us. "Country operations" include modes of preparation, logistical support, training programs, and administrative processes. We believe that, when viewed through a humanitarian lens, the interface between civilian and military personnel can become more well-defined. A new synergy is apparent, one integral to the humanitarian enterprise. It is represented in the activities of those defined and redefined as "peacekeepers," "citizen soldiers," and "national guardsmen." Civil-military cooperation to the benefit of at-risk populations likely will become a byword of the twenty-first century.

THE ACCIDENTAL WAR: THE 2006 CRISIS BETWEEN ISRAEL AND LEBANON

At the broadest level World War II has been called "the war that never ended" (Dallas 2006). Yet, in the Middle East there is a set of loosely intertwined conflicts that also have never ended. A look at one series of events serves to illustrate key points emphasized throughout this book. Our example refers to what editors of *The Economist* (2006) called "the accidental war."

We believe the crisis that unfolded so dramatically between Israel and Lebanon during 2006 can serve as a contemporary benchmark in understanding civil-military cooperation in the context of battle. Issues surrounding our ethical "rules of engagement" also emerge. "The Lebanon war must serve as a wake-up call," said Robert Malley, director of the International Crisis Group's Middle East Program (ICG 2006: 1). It was most assuredly a kind of new war. Its analysis also affords insights into country operations. As the crisis became full-blown during July, 2006, UN Secretary-General Kofi Annan referred to it as "humanitarian" (Keath 2006: 1A). He called for the opening of "humanitarian corridors" to assist those trying to escape and to assist those trying to render assistance. The Deputy Secretary-General referred to the disproportionately heavy toll being taken on civilians. Indeed, within the first week, over 200 civilians were killed (King 2006: 1A). Similar numbers were killed during each of the next several weeks. (By comparison, even more tragic statistics were reported from Iraq during July, 2006. During the preceding two months nearly 6,000 civilians were slain across the country. The first six months of the year saw over 14,000 persons, most of them civilians, being killed [Lenz 2006]). More than 1 million people ultimately were displaced owing to the fighting in Lebanon (El Sayed et al. 2007: 20).

Military Campaigns and Humanitarian Concerns

The crisis first broke on July 12th. Hezbollah, the Shi'ite faction largely in control of southern Lebanon since 1982, captured two Israeli soldiers, killed several others, and began firing short-range rockets across the border. An initial hope was that the two soldiers could be exchanged for a long-imprisoned Lebanese named Samir Kuntar. Among the largest towns hit were Haifa (on the coast), Nazareth, and Tiberias (on the Sea of Galilee). Israel quickly responded with military bombardment of its own; this was followed by air raids on a range of cities and towns in south Lebanon thought to harbor Hezbollah fighters. Sections of Beirut were hit, as were runways at Beirut International Airport. Ten days after the fighting began, and after having killed a number of combatants, Israel announced its first capture of two Hezbollah fighters.

Hezbollah's strategy, utilizing a total of about 3,000 militia, was to scatter among various cities, towns, and villages. As has been the case throughout its existence, there was no large, identifiable structure called "central command." There were no tarmacs where large numbers of aircraft and trucks were parked; indeed, there were no aircraft. Artillery, and rocket launchers were scattered across the countryside, hidden among buildings and moved along side streets. Israeli attacks thus targeted such areas, with the inevitable loss of many innocent civilians.

By the second week the United States had sent ships and military personnel to aid in the evacuation of civilians on both sides of the border. Representatives of the International Committee of the Red Cross had been able to enter areas on both sides of the border, although its logistical supply chain was deemed relatively weak. Sheik Hassan Nasrallah, the leader of Hezbollah, continued to defend his organization's initial attack (although after the war had ended, he stated that he had not anticipated the ferocious counterattacks by Israel).

He initially demanded prisoner exchanges. Lebanese Prime Minister Fouad Siniora called for an immediate ceasefire, emphasizing that Israeli attacks had turned the southern portion of his country into a disaster area in need of humanitarian assistance. He claimed that Israeli forces had deliberately targeted ambulances and medical convoys (Keath 2006: 6A). Israeli premier Ehud Olmert defended his country's counterattacks, while also noting concern for civilian casualties. By the second week it was estimated that over 600,000 people in south Lebanon and north Israel had fled or been forcibly evacuated. By this time the United States was backing a plan to destroy the militia and its rocket arsenal, resisting a French cease-fire counterinitiative (Hoge 2006). Medicine, food, blankets, and generators were among the first relief supplies reaching those displaced. The UN's top humanitarian official, Jan Egeland, estimated an immediate need for over $100 million in aid and a longer-term need for over $1 billion. The second figure later proved to be much too small, but by December 2006 more funds nonetheless had been received through United Nations appeals than were needed (*UNIRIN News* 2006).

Among the first organizations to offer substantive assistance was the World Health Organisation. A number of others, with representatives and volunteers already on site, also were quick to respond. These were exemplified by Refugees International.

A convoy of refugees was inadvertently hit on July 23rd. Some seventy Lebanese were fleeing the border village of Tairi with Lebanese Red Cross ambulances when missiles struck nearby. Three people were killed and sixteen wounded. A Lebanese photojournalist also was killed, the first such civilian casualty of the war. While some Lebanese were trapped in villages near the border, others were able to flee to the largest cities: Beirut, Tyre, and Sidon. The movements of IDPs (internally displaced persons) were paralleled by movements of refugees into Syria. Over 100,000 were estimated to have reached that country within the first twelve days of fighting. Americans (some aided by U.S. Marines sent by President George Bush) were evacuated on ships that steamed west through the Mediterranean Sea to Cyprus.

Proclamations of broader humanitarian concern began being voiced within three days of the first attack. First-tier concerns were expressed by leaders in Lebanon and Israel. Second-tier concerns were expressed by leaders of the United States, some European nations, Egypt, and Saudi Arabia. The last two nations urged Syria to end its support for the Hezbollah guerrillas directly involved in the fighting. Saudi Foreign Minister Prince Saud al-Faisal spoke openly about the need to "stop the bleeding" (Gannon 2006: 8A). U.S. Secretary of State Condoleezza Rice arrived on site on July 24th, and, although she was able to meet with representatives of both sides, she accomplished relatively little. As Israel moved to establish a "security zone" in south Lebanon, while killing several Hezbollah leaders in intense fighting, Rice did win pledges from Olmert to open up Beirut International Airport for humanitarian relief flights.

"Humanitarian corridors" on the ground also were being established. These efforts were complicated by the fighting that, at the same time, was expanding in Gaza between Israelis and Palestinians. Substantial relief supplies from the European Union, primarily in the form of food staples, began arriving by the end of the second week. With the United Nations facilitating its movement, ships and aircraft downloaded these supplies to waiting trucks. Not surprisingly, as they reached Lebanon's border, some drivers expressed concern for their own safety. Much of the food had to be transferred to often less-reliable Lebanese trucks, driven by sometimes less-reliable Lebanese drivers. Not all supplies reached their intended destinations. Beirut initially was better able to receive such shipments; smaller towns were less able.

Calls for an immediate ceasefire began within the first two weeks, as previously noted. Yet, by the third week bold attacks were continuing from both sides. Hezbollah claimed first-time usage of a mid-range missile, likely an Iranian Fajr-5, which was able to reach into north-central Israel. On July 30th an airborne Israeli attack on the Lebanese village of Qana killed fifty-six people, most of whom were civilians. Under broad-based international pressure, Israel agreed to a two-day ceasefire. During this period, large numbers of Lebanese civilians fled north. As Sabrina Tavernise reported on July 31st:

[Civilians] piled onto tractors, packed into cars, crowded children into open trucks, and even walked, lugging belongings on their back. . . . Those who could were getting out of town, though many who were elderly, infirm or lacking the means remained stuck. . . . The dead were brought out, too. The Red Cross [retrieved numerous bodies]. . . . Large buildings had folded in on themselves [owing to the shelling]. Roofs were on the ground. Chunks of concrete and power lines were piled waist-high. Cars were on their backs like turtles. (2006a)

Some aid was reaching those most at risk, but delivery lines remained inconsistent. By the third week supplies delivered by air were reaching larger Lebanese cities from France, Jordan, and Saudi Arabia, among other nations. Relief suppliers based in Syria were having difficulty getting consistent access by road. Humanitarian convoys crossing the border from Israel to Lebanon required permission from Hezbollah and/or Lebanese sources, as well as Israeli, with the consequence of bureaucratic entanglements being that some were denied access entirely. In several villages where ambulances met resistance (primarily because of damaged infrastructure), wounded civilians were carried by relatives moving solely on foot. In one case they were carried by reporters.

By the third week six brigades of Israeli troops had pushed their way into southern Lebanon. Their objective was to clear the area of remaining Hezbollah fighters. Bint Jbail, a town in the central portion of south Lebanon, witnessed some of the toughest fighting. A hospital was hit by Israeli fire in the Bekaa Valley early in August, although most of the personnel and patients already had been evacuated. By the end of the third week of fighting it was estimated that approximately 800,000 Lebanese had become internally displaced, with another 200,000 having left the country as refugees. In short, about one-quarter of the entire population was "in motion."

One Lebanese woman stated that she stayed in a shelter in her building for two days but then came to a shopping mall's parking garage in Beirut. It afforded more protection. She also needed items to assist her husband, who was in a wheelchair after suffering a stroke. Transport in and out of the capital city was made difficult by the Israeli destruction of virtually all bridges and portions of major roads (Refugees International 2006).

Estimates made at the end of the third week of fighting indicated that approximately ten civilians were being killed for every militiaman or soldier

(Wadhams 2006: 1A). At about this same time it was announced that Hezbollah would be handing out grants—ranging from $10,000 to $12,000—to as many as 15,000 families displaced by the conflict. Lebanese officials estimated that Iran sent approximately $150 million in cash to underwrite the effort. Said one official: "There's no doubt [Hezbollah] is endearing itself further with its supporters" (Blanford and MacLeod 2006: 25).

By the fourth week international parties had brokered several relatively successful lines of communications with the combatants. Later recounting the negotiations, U.S. officials said they involved "one of the most dramatic bouts of diplomacy that the United Nations Security Council has witnessed in years" (Hoge 2006: 1). UN Secretary-General Kofi Annan was actively engaged in the effort. (After the war ended he traveled to the region to meet first-hand with representatives of various factions and with displaced persons.) Pledges of interest in a ceasefire were made by combatants even as the fighting continued. The fighting finally came to an end thirty-four days after it had begun. In addition to those killed, in excess of 1,000, some 130,000 homes had been severely damaged or destroyed.

The Immediate Postwar Period

The United States was among the nations pledging substantive amounts of reconstruction aid to Lebanon; the initial amount (as presented by President Bush in a speech) was $230 million (Cooper 2006). However, more than the issue of monetary aid was the issue of assembling a viable international peacekeeping force. While, on the one hand, leading the debate, European nations, on the other hand, were relatively slow to commit specific troops. An early Italian pledge of 400 later was boosted to over 2,000. France similarly boosted what many saw as a too-small original pledge, especially given its longstanding (albeit originally colonialistic) relationship with Lebanon. Estimates of the total number of peacekeepers needed ranged from 6,000 to 15,000; the latter figure was derived from a UN resolution. They were to be deployed and to work alongside Lebanese troops. Security Council Resolution 1701, unanimously approved on August 11th, was holding.

Within days of the ceasefire hundreds of thousands of the Lebanese who had been displaced began streaming back to their home towns and villages. Far fewer Israelis had been displaced, but many of those who had been also began returning. Many who had resided in southern Lebanon reported finding little or nothing of their former homes. Re-entry and resupply were hampered by the Israeli air and sea blockade of key Lebanese ports and transport routes; this lasted for weeks.

The disarming of Hezbollah became a key sticking point. Its backers in Syria and Iran were loath to cut off supplies (including armaments), particularly at a time when the latter nation was exerting its muscle as a "nuclear wanna-be." Hezbollah's leader, Hassan Nasrallah, had noted that Iran saw his party (along with its rocket arsenal) as a necessary deterrent against potential Israeli or American aggression aimed possibly at disabling Iran's nuclear program (Rodenbeck 2006). By October, 2006, when a broad amalgam of 135 prominent individuals (many of them former prime ministers) called for a comprehensive five-point plan to improve conditions, the broader political situation had become clearer. Iran and Syria long had had an interest in prodding Hezbollah to challenge Israel, and clearly were not interested in promoting its postconflict disarmament. As Max Rodenbeck (2006: 6) implies, a systems perspective is useful as the diverse and entangled array of causal factors and corollaries throughout the Middle East are considered. If America could be seen to "burn its fingers on Iraq," attention could be diverted from the Iranian nuclear dilemma, and Syria could be praised for its recent attempts to restart negotiations with Israel over the Golan Heights. Long-simmering tensions among Lebanon's Sunni, Shi'a, Christian, and Druze communities also could be downplayed. Expressing a contrasting view before the battle had begun, Thomas Friedman (2005: 7b) had called Syria's occupation of Lebanon "naked imperialism."

The situation was again thrown into disarray when Pierre Gemayal, a Lebanese cabinet minister and opponent of Syrian influence in Lebanon, was assassinated on November 21st. A member of a prominent Maronite Christian family, his killing raised tensions between the anti-Syrian coalition, which was struggling to hold the government together, and the Syrian-allied opposition, led by Hezbollah. Prime Minister Siniora's colleagues blamed Syria for the killing (Slackman 2006). Several months later a prominent Sunni Muslim lawmaker was killed in a car bombing. He also had been a severe critic of Syria.

Hezbollah's political role within Lebanon was both reinforced and threatened by what transpired after the fighting ended. As a political party it had come to command respect in the eyes of some, a situation aided by the sectarian-balancing coalition that had been formed by the prime minister the previous year. Seen by many Shi'a as a protector and political patron, Hezbollah was (and is) seen by many Sunni, Christian, and Druze as "both a tool of Syrian and Iranian meddling and an obstacle to the assertion of full control by the Lebanese state" (Rodenbeck 2006: 6).

By December 2006, five months after the fighting had ended, the United Nations Interim Force in Lebanon (UNIFIL) had approximately 11,000 troops in place in the country. During January 2007, several major international donors reconvened to assess what still could be done. A more accurate assessment of overall structural damage and property loss had been received from Lebanese officials; the total was placed at about $3.5 billion. Additional losses in the service sector, among others, were estimated as reaching several billion more. With the Lebanese treasury nearly drained, over thirty countries and agencies (including the United States and Saudi Arabia) pledged assistance totaling $7.6 billion. Nearly fifty days of Syrian- and Iranian-backed protests had preceded this round of discussions, resulting in what had been termed a "stalemate in Beirut." It was estimated that these two nations were providing as much as $40 million a month to Hezbollah and other related interests in Lebanon (Cooper 2007).

The Later Postwar Period

By mid-2007 it had become clear that Hezbollah would continue as a major actor within Lebanon. Syria's position had shifted slightly. Other Arab neighbors showed occasional bluster but little substantive action. Israel's position seemingly remained unaltered, although a substantial minority of its citizens again were advocating for peaceful alternatives. The shuttle diplomacy of U.S.

officials continued, at irregular intervals. The European Union retained its cautious, nonprovocative stance.

It also had become clear that refugees and internally displaced persons would remain central to the situation, with their camps often serving as flashpoints. For example, the Nahr el-Bared refugee camp in northern Lebanon, populated by Palestinians, became a focal point in mid-2007 as Lebanese troops stormed the hideout of an Islamic group said to represent Fatah. Artillery, tanks, and rocket-propelled grenades were used to bombard the settlement; several persons were killed. During the thirty-four-day war itself, the notion of "camp relief" had become less useful and less realistic. As El Sayed and associates state, the new UN "cluster approach," which emphasizes protection and temporary shelter of refugees and IDPs, had been judged to be more useful (2007: 21).

Ramifications associated with the assassination of Rafik Hariri in 2005 continued to press. Syrian operatives had been blamed, yet culpability had not been clearly established. An extraordinarily wealthy man, Hariri had risen from humble origins and had —while serving two terms as Prime Minister— demonstrated a remarkable resiliency as his country was buffeted by a variety of economic, military, and political pressures. Although never harshly admonishing Hezbollah, he also frequently had spoken out for multilateral dialogue. He was widely regarded as a positive figure by analysts, fellow politicians, and every-day citizens of the region.

Ramifications associated with the initial abductions of Israelis by Hezbollah personnel also continued to press. Ehud Goldwasser and Eldad Regev were the soldiers captured on July 12th, sparking the war. Two years later, on July 15, 2008, their remains were returned, as part of a prisoner exchange. Goldwasser's widow, Karnit, continued a public speaking schedule through 2009 that took her to the United States and other locales. She discussed the issues of abductions and human rights abuse.

As of early 2010 the Hezbollah-dominated alliance and the pro-Western coalition still dominated the landscape in Lebanon. The U.S. Ambassador to Lebanon, Michele Sison, continued her efforts to broker interparty relations. UNIFIL still maintained its presence. A different kind of item also dominated the landscape: unexploded ordnance (UXO), consisting of unexploded cluster bombs, shells, rockets, and other devices still scattered throughout the southern and central regions of the country. Derrin Smith's on-site analysis in 2009 of Iraqi refugee Shi'a communities in Lebanon and their level of involvement with Hezbollah—at once a designated terrorist organization as well as a social welfare, aid, and political organization—indicates the difficulties in analyzing the situation holistically. Certain of the data appear in multiple shades of gray when one wears a civilian hat, then in stark black and white when one wears a military hat.

A Complex Humanitarian Emergency

This represents a classic example of a complex humanitarian emergency (CHE), couched within a broader sociopolitical and transnational context. "The country's infernally complex ingredients seem chemically incapable of melding into a digestible dish. . . . [With martyrs also regularly made and elevated, it is difficult] to untangle the network of shifting allegiances that make up the spider's-web-in-a-kaleidoscope of Lebanese politics" (Rodenbeck 2007: 10). That Lebanon had been the scene of one of the region's most protracted wars, the civil war of 1975–1990, only exacerbated this latest emergency.

By the second week of the battle speculations about the degree to which this was a proxy war between Iran and the United States already had become apparent. Related acrimonious debates continued months into the future. Hezbollah is funded largely by Syria and Iran; Israel receives substantial amounts of funding from the United States. Of concern to humanitarians was the extent to which a proxy war might be accompanied by "proxy humanitarianism." Despite claims that Hezbollah operates largely independently of Iran policy-wise, analysts had become increasingly concerned that Iran was pulling the strings. The complexity of the humanitarian emergency was further compounded at the local level by the fact that Hezbollah began assisting displaced persons even before the fighting had ended, at the regional level by the diverse and at times conflicting aid schemes being instituted, and at the international level by the broad statements about humanitarian concerns (and the role of the United States) being made by Iranian President Mahmoud Ahmadinejad.

The emergency could not be categorized as simply polarized between two parties. It represented tensions "between the U.S. and the Arab street, between fundamentalists and the West, between Sunni and Shi'ite Muslims" (Blanford and MacLeod 2006: 25–26). Referring to Chapter 1 and the three axes associated with structural violence, we clearly see that unequal relationships exist among each of these dualities; that the help afforded Lebanese victims by Hezbollah cannot be denigrated in comparison to that afforded by Western agencies; and that the "power of relief" further shapes the civilian-military environment. In one sense, the institutions in Lebanon are fluid, but, in another, their entrenched ethnoreligious statuses contributed to this complex humanitarian emergency.

During the months that followed, external analysts had a field day attempting to assess the motives behind the fighting and thereby attempting to determine correlates of the emergency as it played out in the lives of every-day people. One person who was particularly harsh in her analysis of Israeli activities was Lara Deeb (2006). Following the writings of Seymour Hersh she suggested that the United States and Israel had colluded in advance to attack Hezbollah. More important to the present analysis, her long-term fieldwork in Lebanon supports the notion that Hezbollah should not be considered as con-stituting "strongholds" (implying scattered sites that exist as enclaves within a greater Lebanese society) but rather as constituting "civilian communities" (implying a membership that is well-integrated into southern Lebanese soci-ety). That this organization runs what she terms "one of the most efficient and professional social welfare networks in Lebanon" (2006: 10), featuring hospitals and schools, bolsters the contentions of those who see Hezbollah as both a victim of Israeli aggression and a humanitarian organization. Deeb sees its popularity as a political party resting "on a combination of successful resistance to Israeli occupation and attacks, political platforms and practice in Lebanon, Islamic ideology and an approach to political-economic develop-ment that includes [the welfare network noted above]" (2006: 11). It should be stressed that her views have been sharply countered by other analysts.

A subtext to the fighting, and thus to the complex humanitarian emer-gency, was the issue of Palestinian prisoners held by Israel. As of August 2006 the prisoners numbered about 9,700, with about 100 of these being women and about 300 being children under the age of 18 (Smith 2006: 1). Most continued to be held well into 2007. That Israel already was engaged in an offensive operation in Gaza, begun after one of its soldiers was captured on June 25, 2006, further complicated the humanitarian emergency. Only later were significant numbers of prisoners released and repatriated. Information we obtained on site in 2009, as discussions with Shi'a, Sunni, and Christians continued to unfold, indicate the adamant position that Palestinians living in Lebanon—even those born there—should never be granted Lebanese citizenship. It would interfere with their stated "right to return to the homeland." Other political issues remain more fluid.

The array of actors involved in addressing this crisis was vast and differentiated. Those employing small- to mid-scale assistance strategies were among the most effective, in part because they "didn't bite off more than they could chew." At least implicitly, several NGOs interactively used what we since have identified as our "tactical triangle" of diplomacy, aid, and service (see Figure 1.1).

ARMED AND UNARMED NSAS

Some NSAs wage war and engage in militant actions; they also are referred to as "armed NSAs." Others conduct humanitarian operations and provide relief. Although occasionally labeled as "unarmed NSAs," they more commonly are referred to as NGOs, PVOs, IOs, and IGOs (cf. Hoffman and Weiss 2006: 57–58). The roles of unarmed NSAs in conflictive and postconflictive environments have been described especially well by scholars associated with the Humanitarianism and War Project (initiated in 1991 at Brown University, now based at Tufts University and supported by a broad array of UN agencies, donor governments, NGOs, and foundations). They are not covered in depth in this book.

In conflictive and even postconflictive environments, country teams likely will encounter armed NSAs. This was the case in Lebanon, as reported earlier. Such groups may have exacerbated a conflict, as is being seen in the Democratic Republic of Congo; may have contributed to its resolution, as was seen in the late 1990s in Timor-Leste; or may have played irregular and ill-defined roles, as was seen in the early 1990s with several factional groups in Sierra Leone. "Now that belligerents have proliferated and often control substantial areas of national territory, NGOs and UN agencies are required to relate directly to [armed] NSAs as well as central governments" (Hoffman and Weiss 2006: 94). Country teams usually are not charged with resolving or mediating tensions with such NSAs but rather with moving forward on a particular project in ways that minimize frictions with them. In a few instances, country teams may attempt to incorporate members of armed NSAs into an emerging collaborative socioeconomic action plan, as recently occurred in Afghanistan's northern provinces.

Armed NSAs, by definition, operate as organized, armed groups usually beyond state control. Expanding on the *Human Security Brief 2006*, which taps the work of Caroline Holmqvist and other scholars on "new wars," we include:

- Rebel opposition groups (with a stated incompatibility with the central government)
- Local militias (often ethnically or clan based)
- Vigilantes (seeking justice for perceived local grievances)
- Warlords (controlling certain resources and territories, usually within a loosely structured or failing state)
- Civil defense forces and paramilitary groups (when they are clearly beyond state control)
- Quasicivil defense forces (when they are in loose affiliation with a central state command)
- Private companies (when they are providing security and military services)

Frequent splintering, factionalization, and re-alignment, as has occurred among anti-al-Maliki groups within Iraq (for example, Shi'a leader Muqtada al-Sadr's army), makes it difficult for any prospective country team representatives who might be interacting with them for humanitarian purposes to systematize their approach. Some of the factions at one point judged "friendly" may at another by judged "hostile," as experiences in Iraq have borne out.

U.S. country teams, in virtually every contemporary circumstance, are working formally at the behest of both the American and a foreign government. Any regular contact with armed NSAs must be vetted by local representatives of both governments. In states where corrupt or ineffective governments hold sway, and where divide and conquer tactics rule, senior politicians may be supporting certain of the ominous NSAs subrosa while eschewing them formally and diplomatically. This practice has taken place within the past decade, for example, in Colombia and the Democratic Republic of Congo.

Armed NSAs can be both abusive and protective. Uganda's LRA (Lord's Resistance Army) exemplifies this. Its forcible recruitment of child soldiers, many of whom are abused at the hands of other LRA members, is seen in stark counterpoint to the protection it offers local constituents and allies in north Uganda and south Sudan. In a different context, the private contractor Blackwater Worldwide (now renamed Xe) has proven both abusive and protective in Iraq as well, as noted later in this chapter.

Armed NSAs are playing major roles in reshaping the face of twenty-first-century humanitarian efforts. The "humanitarian enterprise" is emerging as a fluid yet amorphous set of outreach operations engaging civil, quasicivil, military, and quasimilitary actors and contractors—in some cases simultaneously. Country teams engaged in stabilization, reconstruction, development, and/or diplomatic activities are increasingly being immersed in such situations, as Derrin Smith's recent work in Iraq and Afghanistan confirms. Like country teams, armed NSAs variously effect and are influenced by the confluence of political, economic, and cultural factors. These factors can play out, for example, as MNCs such as Newmont Mining are encountering in Indonesia. Like country teams, armed NSAs also variously affect and are influenced by the confluence of factors associated with the work of IOs, IGOs, NGOs, and such human rights advocacy/monitoring groups as Human Rights Watch and Amnesty International. These factors can play out amid tensions, as complex humanitarian emergencies unfold. The December 2004 tsunami that struck Sumatra's Aceh Province exemplifies this. Quasigovernmental civil defense forces, operating in loose affiliation with the Indonesian military, came to the assistance of villagers whose homes had been washed away in the flooding.

U.S. country team representatives, specializing in short-term relief and emergency reconstruction, were rebuffed, bullied, and at last reluctantly welcomed as the two-week mark passed, after the tsunami. The Indonesian military assumed an increasingly prominent coordinating role. The U.S. military (as well as those of several European and Asian nations) assumed a secondary advise-and-assist role. A number of country teams themselves succeeded in helping several thousand displaced persons. Medical aid, temporary shelters, and emergency food rations were distributed. Despite a desire on the part of some NGO affiliates to provide trauma counseling to survivors, this was eschewed. Quasigovernmental civil defense forces again stepped in.

Three points stressed by Hoffman and Weiss (2006: 96) as they consider local agencies' interactions with armed NSAs apply equally well to country teams' interactions. First, identify and promote those groups that already are facilitating humanitarian operations. Some will be representative of civil society interests. Second, limit relations and curtail the involvement of rogue actors that are attempting to profit politically or economically from war or the distress of others. (These are sometimes referred to as "spoilers.") Third, identify and distinguish those armed NSAs that have the potential to contribute to humanitarian action. They must be nurtured and, perhaps, structurally transformed. This approach had been suggested as a strategy to better engage Muqtada al-Sadr's Mahdi Army. Again, any pretext of neutrality will disappear in the process.

Soft Measures

Both armed and unarmed NSAs are subject to the influence of so-called soft measures (see Figure 1.1). These include efforts to raise awareness of sensitive human rights issues and influence attitudes (Human Security Report Project 2006). IOs, IGOs, NGOs, and country teams often are positioned to influence armed NSAs. The International Committee of the Red Cross (ICRC) occupies a unique position of influence in this regard. While following a more traditional concept of neutrality, it still wields significant influence on armed NSAs in such places as Colombia, the Philippines, and Palestine. Its reports also are influential; many offer practical advice on how to assist those who are most vulnerable. Of great importance—and highly unusual—is its scathing analysis regarding the torture of fourteen "high value detainees" held by the U.S. government at the Guantanamo Bay Internment Facility (ICRC 2009).The approach to rights-based development that was laid out in Chapter 1 is intended to complement the informed application of "soft measures." The development practitioners' emphasis on pragmatic socioeconomic goals must not supersede the human rights practitioners' emphasis on systemic sociopolitical goals. The former's emphasis on the macro/community level must not supersede the latter's emphasis on the micro/individual level. When the approach is balanced in this fashion, there is a chance than structural violence gradually can be reduced.

The Privatization of War

The wars in Iraq and Afghanistan have, in part, been outsourced. Most of the outsourced operations take place outside the Green Zone. Large private corporations, such as Blackwater/Xe, DynCorp International, Halliburton (and its Kellog, Brown & Root subsidiary), MPRI, and others, have secured large government contracts to provide an array of security, construction, and even supervisory services. Some of them are known as private military companies (PMCs) or privatized military firms (PMFs); some of them, in turn, are handling a majority of the logistics for certain of the field operations. By a set of twisted roots, PMCs' origins can be traced to the outfitters working to assist revolutionary-war-era troops. Subsequent wars saw a variety of private contractors, but they "worked the sidelines." Within the United States the outfitting of warriors officially remained in the public, tax-supported domain through much of the twentieth century. However, during recent decades, changes can be traced to the private security firms formed by such famed former military personnel as "Chargin' Charlie" Beckwith (noted in Chapter 7). His Austin consulting firm was called Security Assistance Services. According to Jonathan Alter (2007: xi), by one estimate nearly half of the American personnel involved in the war in Iraq are neither active duty military nor reservists, but contractors. According to Jeremy Scahill (2007: xviii), by another estimate there were about 100,000 private individuals *cum* contractors on the ground in Iraq by 2006. By still another estimate, aired on National Public Radio, there were nearly 300,000 noncombat personnel engaged in all types of support, security, and logistical/transport activities in the Iraq and Afghanistan theaters as of December, 2009. Although we believe these estimates to be imprecise they nonetheless provide a sense of the magnitude in the outsourcing of services. When operating in the field, a team representing one of these contracting firms is—in an oblique sense—a kind of country team.

PMCs "are business organizations that trade in professional services intricately linked to warfare" (Singer 2008: 8). According to Ivan Watson, reporting for National Public Radio and cross-referencing data from the Private Security Company Association of Iraq, from 2003 through 2007 well over $6 billion had been earned by private security personnel representing several of these corporations (2008). At any one time 3,000 or more individuals (mostly Americans) were being employed in security roles in the country, with thousands more foreign citizens and Iraqis in support positions (for instance, as drivers). More broadly, during this same period it is estimated that DoS, DoD, and USAID paid contractors more than $100 billion for goods and services to support war operations and rebuilding in Iraq and Afghanistan (Lardner 2009: 6A). Since the early 1990s such contractors have supplied a substantial array of services in Africa, Asia, the Balkans, and Latin America as well.

Increased privatization could occur, in part, because of programs such as LOGCAP. The Logistics Civil Augmentation Program was created in 1985. It is a U.S. Army initiative that uses civilian contractors to provide certain services such as post supplies, base construction, and feeding for deployed troops, with an emphasis on augmenting unplanned, short-notice contingency operations. It relies not on standard line-item but on supplemental, military funding (Rasor and Bauman 2007: 246). Overall cost savings and streamlined bureaucracy are seen as likely outcomes.

Increased privatization also could occur because of the resource reprioritization emphases of former Secretary of Defense under George W. Bush, Donald Rumsfeld. Former Vice President Dick Cheney also was an advocate. Yet before, during the Clinton administration, Virginia-based Military Professional

Resources, Inc.—staffed largely by senior retired military officers—had been authorized to train the Croatian military in its war of secession against Serb-dominated Yugoslavia, "a contract that ultimately tipped the balance" (Scahill 2007: xvi). By 2006 the DoD's "total force" had come to be officially redefined as consisting of active and reserve military, civil servants, and contractors.

The relative lack of government oversight that some teams representing PMCs have while in the field makes their status as legitimate country teams questionable. Peter Singer, formerly at the Brookings Institution and author of *Corporate Warriors* (2008), as early as 2003 stated: "Across the board, in pretty much every single area, there is a divide between how broadly and explosively this industry has become important . . . and how slow the government has been to deal with it, not only in terms of regulation but also how it contracts its operations" (Bourge 2003: 1).

PMCs have been both complemented and criticized for their work. If linked into a broader U.S. government policy mandate, with congressional oversight, favorable outcomes can result. MPRI was complemented by special forces commanders for its work in Bosnia while training soldiers and providing logistical support at the brigade and battalion levels. It was criticized for its efforts to train Kosovar forces during civil wars in the former Yugoslavia. The Kosovo Liberation Army was not turned into an effective fighting force in its battle against Serbian opponents (Bourge 2003: 2).

Blackwater

The company with the infamous name Blackwater Worldwide (now renamed Xe) is emblematic, part and parcel, of issues associated with the privatization of warfare. Many of its personnel have been involved in security work. Although most individual contractors espouse patriotic and/or humanitarian motives, some are moved primarily by financial considerations. Some of them, in turn, misunderstand or abuse the opportunity. And some of these mercenaries, in turn, were caught in the flashy, mismanaged web of Blackwater.

The original Blackwater name, ironically, proved to be darkly appropriate: founded by Erik Prince, a former Navy SEAL, a large tract near North

Carolina's Great Dismal Swamp was chosen as its base. Much of the 7,000-acre tract is used for training its contracted employees. It is described by Scahill as the world's largest private military facility (2007: xix). In recent years the company expanded to include the Blackwater Training Center, Blackwater Security Consulting, Blackwater Canine, Blackwater Armor & Targets, Blackwater Logistics, Blackwater Airships, and Raven Development Group (Rasor and Bauman 2007: 101). In short, it built on trends developing in the pre-9/11 era and cleverly expanded in the post-9/11 era to take advantage of niches needed by the U.S. military as its operations evolved and morphed, as some areas were being downsized yet overall operations were being amped up. Exemplifying the range of possibilities, food services were even explored by the company. That the White House in 2003 began outsourcing its protection services for senior officials in Iraq to Blackwater gave the company a real boost.

Blackwater quickly became a leading recruiter and purveyor of security personnel and services. The U.S. ambassadors to Iraq, since proconsul L. Paul Bremer, all initially were protected by Blackwater personnel, many earning six-figure annual salaries (Scahill 2007: xix). Peter Van Arsdale interviewed one former guard, who noted the nondescript (and boring) nature of most of his work in Iraq. Yet others found the activity energizing. Through one subdivision, Greystone Limited, "proactive engagement teams" (PETs) were formed. Recruiting personnel from as far afield as Nepal and the Philippines, these teams could be hired to meet emergency or security requirements for clients overseas—the United States government and its agents being but one among several bidders.

Most of the world first learned of the reach of private companies shortly after the March 31, 2004, ambush of four Blackwater personnel in Fallujah, Iraq, as Scahill (2007) recounts it. After their jeeps were attacked and burned, their charred bodies were dismembered, dragged through the streets, and hung from a bridge over the Euphrates River. Katy Helvenston sued the company for her son's death in this incident. "They have established themselves as the bad guys," she said (Baker 2009: 27). Others accused Blackwater's guards of taking an "aggressive, trigger-happy approach to their work" (Broder 2007: 1). Then in late 2008 five Blackwater convoy security guards indicted in the September

17, 2007, unprovoked deaths of seventeen unarmed civilians in Baghdad were found to have been operating in the area in direct defiance of U.S. government orders. After shooting erupted at a blockade, the Raven 23 convoy gunners also had fired their machine guns at civilian vehicles that posed no threat to the convoy (Meyer 2008: 2A). Indeed, the damage to Blackwater's reputation became severe as the earlier suit and later act of defiance played out. In December of 2009 it was revealed that Blackwater security guards earlier had participated in some of the CIA's most sensitive activities. Between 2004 and 2006 they had assisted agency officers in clandestine raids against suspected insurgents in Iraq and Afghanistan, as well as in the transportation of detainees. Even before the latest allegations were revealed, in February of 2009, the company had decided to rebrand itself as Xe.

That L. Paul Bremer had issued an order on June 28, 2004, immunizing such contractors from prosecution had further enflamed feelings on both sides. (This issue was addressed by Iraqi parliamentarians in 2008, and in early 2009 security guards were stripped of their immunity.) Neither quite military nor quite civilian, Blackwater had claimed that it operated by a trade association contract, through the International Peace Operations Association. Accountability became amorphous. "Private contractors largely operate in a legal gray zone that leaves the door for abuses wide open" (Scahill 2007: xxi). Early in 2009 the DoS decided not to rehire Blackwater/Xe to protect its diplomats in Iraq. The company in turn reported that it would retool to better focus on lines of business other than private security contracting. Later in 2009 the DoS also cut its ties with Armor-Group North America, the security contractor that had been hired to protect the U.S. Embassy in Afghanistan. The unacceptable behavior of some personnel was cited as the reason.

CHAPTER 3

IN-SITU PRELIMINARY ASSESSMENTS, THREAT ANALYSES, AND KOFI ANNAN'S LESSONS

On December 22, 2006, an Oxfam outpost in Darfur, Sudan, was attacked. No one was killed; the targets were vehicles. A staff member interviewed on National Public Radio said that a dozen vehicles were stolen or destroyed, and that—with no end to the violence in sight—chances for improvement in the humanitarian situation were bleak. Shortly before this, one of our colleagues on assignment in Darfur had reported to us on her discouragement regarding issues of gender violence at the hands of *janjaweed* militia.

Just five days earlier two dozen employees and visitors of the Iraqi Red Crescent Society were kidnapped in downtown Baghdad. The perpetrators were dressed in Iraqi army uniforms. They drove up to a main office building at mid-day in pickup trucks, which also were used in the getaway. Men were singled out, women left behind (Torchia 2006). Although some of the hostages were soon released, others were kept captive for an extended period. The kidnappers' apparent goal, as with other mass abductions targeting factory workers, sports conference delegates, and bystanders at bus stations, apparently was disruption of the aid network and the instilling of fear into an already chaotic environment. The Red Crescent kidnapping occurred at a time when internecine and sectarian attacks had reached record-high levels.

One of our colleagues, an American working for Catholic Relief Services, explained how she was forced to curtail her humanitarian efforts in Basra, Iraq, owing to similar problems. Still another of our colleagues, an indigenous Iraqi working for Women for Women International, explained how he travels the road from Baghdad's airport to his office, along a route infamous for its attacks via IEDs (improvised explosive devices). He always chooses a rickety car without logos or insignia, so as not to attract undue attention. Still other of our colleagues, Ukrainians working on de-mining and explosive ordnance disposal (EOD), in addition to military reconnaissance and matériel operations in eastern Iraq, were killed outright.

Humanitarian work is becoming increasingly dangerous, increasingly complicated, and—of necessity—increasingly innovative. Sudan and Iraq are but two (admittedly highly problematic) settings. On every continent except Antarctica, professionals are working with volunteers, academics with practitioners, civilians with military personnel. Projects are being engaged that benefit refugees, internally displaced persons, former child soldiers, victims of trafficking, rural herders, and urban barrio dwellers. Our students are finding internships and applied research opportunities in places as accessible as Louisiana and as remote as Timor-Leste, with organizations as well known as World Vision and as obscure as Wings of Hope.

In instances like all of these, the dangers can be diminished by conducting appropriate in-situ preliminary assessments.

THE NECESSITY OF PRELIMINARY ASSESSMENTS

Many of us, professionals and students alike, are charged with responding to complex humanitarian emergencies. These are defined as severe (often chaotic) situations in which excessive mortality is likely, damage is extensive, multiple systems are disrupted, and the management of resources is taxed. In many such situations, large civilian populations are exposed to warfare, food shortages, and population displacement. In all such cases, to quote Holly Ann Williams, the emergencies are "profoundly political processes" (2001: 2). Conflict, crisis and catastrophe are the terms often used. As Williams notes, the discourse on complex humanitarian emergencies emerged full-blown only during the 1990s. The discourse on assessing CHEs—and other situations that would engage country teams—is still emerging.

Initial first-hand assessments are a priority for country team operations in challenging environments and situations such as those in Sudan and Iraq. It is essential to get "the lay of the land" before starting an operation of any type. Demographic, cultural, socioeconomic, political, and ecological data usually must be collected and always must be analyzed. Our individual experiences working in a combined total of more than twenty countries, five of which were highly conflictive at the time, indicate that most villagers and other citizens (including administrators) remain enthusiastic when asked to share information of both a personal and general nature. In most instances it relates to development projects or humanitarian enhancements. In some instances it relates to sensitive political or military situations. In all instances the highest ethical standards and greatest degree of caution must be maintained by the team members/assessors; inappropriate methodological work and casual data dissemination can endanger the local citizenry.

The "anthropological touch" is especially beneficial as such assessments are being planned and conducted. This approach assures that diverse voices are represented and that the felt needs of the populace, shared emically, are obtained. Once *felt needs* become demands or petitions for action, they are referred to as *expressed needs* (Ervin 2005: 77). By contrast, what are termed *normative needs* are those determined by outside investigators or service professionals—in other words, they have been filtered through a scientific screen. There may be a high degree of congruence between felt and normative needs in a single setting; there may be little congruence, especially when a CHE is being assessed. Generally speaking, and to the detriment of local populations, the exposition of normative needs often has overridden the exposition of felt needs as field data are interpreted and projects are planned.

Types of Assessment

There are three general types of preliminary field assessment that can engage social scientists, as well as any military personnel and indigenous counterparts they might be working with on country teams: (1) needs assessments, particularly those that target locals' service needs within the health, education, and social service sectors; (2) reconnaissance surveys, where the "lay of the land" is addressed as a particular problem or a potential project is being contemplated; (3) systems assessments, whereby a preliminary macro-analysis is made of an entire existing system, such as that associated with a community's water resources. All three types seek "ground truth," something that cannot fully be appreciated until one is there, "walking on the ground among the people involved in the events in question" (Van Arsdale 2005a: 183). As Alexander Ervin reminds us, other types of assessment—not conducted during the preliminary phase—such as the social impact assessment, also are important (2005: 111–112).

With an eye toward anthropology, contributors to *Applied Field Methods: A Manual of Practice* (Van Arsdale 2005b) have laid out general principles for conducting such assessments. The kinds of questions that should be asked, from "grand tour" through "climate survey" to "culture change," are covered. Three sets of data are required: demographic/archival, behavioral, and attitudinal. The field protocol should be organized so that these sets are gathered in sequence, since demographic data tend to be the easiest to obtain, attitudinal the most difficult. A substantial level of rapport is needed before political opinions, in particular, can be plumbed in depth. The principle of triangulation is essential—that is, that the selection and use of three or more complementary methods allow the central issue to be tackled more effectively, with the likelihood of accuracy in findings enhanced accordingly. Participant observation, key informant interviewing, and semistructured surveying (conducted orally or by using a questionnaire filled out by respondents) usually constitute the basic "triangulated kit." Other methods are added as needed.

An Ethiopian Test Case

In Tigray Province, Ethiopia, a needs assessment of water resources was conducted in 1994 by Peter Van Arsdale and his colleagues (Figure 3.1); this was shortly after the civil war had ended and the postconflictive environment still was highly charged. Although the assessment was not done under the auspices of a country team, but under the joint aegis of the nonprofit Water and Sanitation Consultancy Group of Denver, Colorado, and the Tigray Development Association (Van Arsdale and Witten 2006), it set the stage for a much later systems assessment whereby methodological innovations of direct use to country

FIGURE 3.1   Women in the Tigrayan village of Mai Misham participate in a focus group session covering water resources. The two men on the left serve as facilitators (photo by Peter Van Arsdale).

teams were tested. The first—an in-situ needs assessment—therefore provided information of relevance for the second, which investigated/tested rapid ethnographic assessment (REA) methods as part of an in-situ systems assessment.

The second project in Tigray was conducted in 2008 under the auspices of eCrossCulture Corporation, a for-profit firm based in Boulder, Colorado, for which Van Arsdale serves part-time as a senior researcher. The corporation had received an award from the Office of Naval Research (ONR) to provide U.S. military planners and their interagency partners with an improved array of methods to quickly discover critical aspects of a society with respect to humanitarian, security, reconstruction, and/or stability missions. Computational modeling/simulation development was a complementary goal. DoD Directive 3000.05 requires that the military collect social and cultural data in support of SSTR missions, so that more comprehensive and grounded understandings of the contexts within which military missions operate can be obtained. Recent developments in Iraq and Afghanistan (as well as other theaters) contributed to this initiative, as did the pluses and minuses associated with the recent work of Human Terrain Teams.

An eCrossCulture premise, following ONR, is that new social science-based models and methodologies—when applied appropriately—allow military analysts not only to collect such data but also to know which data matter most. Fieldwork time frames in conflictive and postconflictive environments usually are brief. The settings tend to be dangerous. Prioritization is essential as analysts determine "how to use meaningful data to make sense of tribal, ethnic, and socioeconomic relationships, understand socioenvironmental factors (for example, who controls water use in arid climates), land rights, disputes, the role of religion in everyday life, and community power structures" (Schultz et al. 2009: 1).

The understanding of "culture," in the simplistic sense, is not the objective of this kind of applied research. Rather, the objective is the understanding of incentives, constraints, motivations, subtleties, and decision-making processes, in the broader context of functional networks, which themselves reflect "the culture" of the society in question. However, in other field contexts, as Brian Selmeski (2007) has stressed, asking broad questions about culture can affect and inform peacekeeping operations and in that sense can be valuable.

Specifically, the intent of eCrossCulture Corporation was to provide ONR, and eventually military-affiliated field-based teams, a framework built on ethnographic/qualitative insights and computational/quantitative modeling scenarios. "If . . . then" conditional scenarios also would be devised, to be used both as strategic tools and heuristic learning devices. The REA methods chosen would be field-tested in Ethiopia to ascertain which work best in challenging conflictive and postconflictive environments, when implemented by novice researchers. (Most of the military personnel likely to engage these methods would be novices.) A key element therefore was the testing of an array of methods, used in concert with a detailed field guide developed by eCrossCulture Corporation, which would constitute a "toolkit." A detailed literature review would be conducted in advance, covering the background to social science and military involvement in such activity, with specifics as to which rapid assessments methods work best in which settings. Interviews with practitioners, including those involved with country operations, would be conducted as well; adjustments then could be made in protocol and process as necessary.

Operational premises/assumptions therefore were these:

- Field personnel need reliable, ready-to-use methodological toolkits that are relatively simple yet adequately robust as they assess "terrain" and "landscape." Training in the use of such toolkits should be straightforward and uncomplicated. Community counterparts also should be incorporated into the process, without compromising their standing or stature.

- Water systems, within the water/sanitation sector and excluding irrigation, can serve as exemplars in this type of research. Their structures, access/use, and management are adequately complex, therefore illustrative of a community's—and perhaps a society's—sociopolitical and socioeconomic functioning. Details surrounding indigenous decision-making processes likely will emerge. Water systems per se are not the issue.

- The investigation of water systems in rural Ethiopia could demonstrate the application and use of rapid assessment methods in a challenging environment that is similar to those encountered in other operational theaters. More generally, field ethnographic research engaging REA can contribute to the development of models and methods of use to civil-military teams such as PRTs (Provincial Reconstruction Teams), Civil Affairs Groups (CAGs), embassy-based country teams, and humanitarian relief teams.

Having studied categories devised by anthropologists who developed the comprehensive HRAF (Human Relations Area Files) database over the past half-century, the researchers decided that data related to the following indicators could be targeted on site: degree of community cohesion, degree of privilege, power differentials within and among communities, and degree of factionalization. The researchers decided that decision process-wise, data could be obtained on variables linked to formal and informal leadership hierarchies, surface and subrosa communication patterns, and direct and indirect strategies that indigenous persons use to implement internal changes. All would provide insights into the structure and functioning of social networks, themselves of prime importance.

The University of Denver served as a subcontractor to eCrossCulture Corporation. Two graduate students in international relations, both with previous experience in Africa, were selected from among twelve applicants and trained over a period of three weeks—twenty-one hours of class time in total. With appropriate letters of introduction and Ethiopian embassy certifications in hand, they then were sent to Tigray to investigate water systems using the REA toolkit (including field guide) designed by eCrossCulture's senior researchers. The toolkit was built on the so-called VASK Model (Figure 3.2), developed by the team and contained "how-to" information on the following field methods, all amenable to REA, as reported by Schultz et al. (2009).

TRANSECTING (GROUP WALKS)   These activities enable the village "landscape" to be sketched physiographically and geographically. This technique was piloted successfully in another Tigrayan village in 1994 by

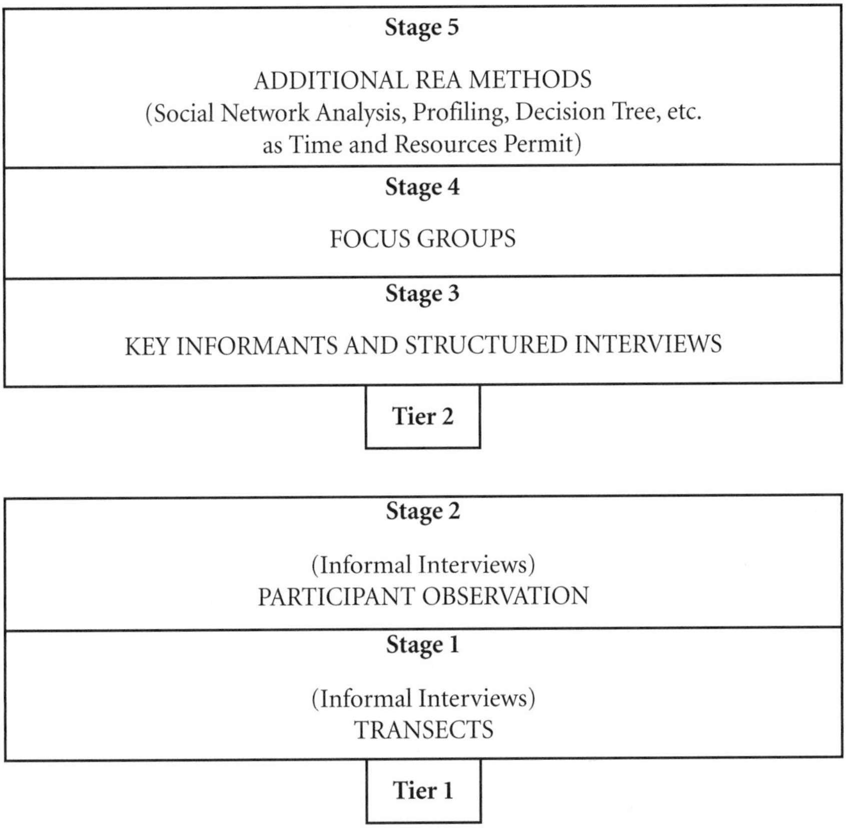

Stage 5
ADDITIONAL REA METHODS (Social Network Analysis, Profiling, Decision Tree, etc. as Time and Resources Permit)
Stage 4
FOCUS GROUPS
Stage 3
KEY INFORMANTS AND STRUCTURED INTERVIEWS

Tier 2

Stage 2
(Informal Interviews) PARTICIPANT OBSERVATION
Stage 1
(Informal Interviews) TRANSECTS

Tier 1

FIGURE 3.2   The VASK Model for Rapid Ethnographic Assessment suggests ways that field researchers can effectively employ rapid ethnographic assessment (REA) methods. Tier 1 techniques are basic and help to establish a qualitatively sound grounding. Tier 2 techniques add depth and breadth to the emergent analysis and are employed as resources warrant. "VASK" is an acronym reflecting the last names of the model's developers: Van Arsdale, Schultz, Knop.

Van Arsdale. At that time two intersecting transects were devised, each involving three team members. Each team literally walked through the village in as straight a line as possible, one from NE to SW and the other from NW to SE. Conversations were held with villagers encountered. Notes were compared when the two transect teams met in the middle, as well as afterward.

Tigrayan Water Systems

The assessment conducted in Tigray Province, Ethiopia, in late 2008 yielded a comprehensive understanding of water systems in the context of both "terrain" and "landscape." It demonstrated that the array of rapid assessment methods that had been chosen *a priori*, with the exception of the focus group technique, worked well—and also would work well in other challenging postconflictive settings. University of Denver graduate students Angela Bengtson and Jonathan Chu, aided by two Tigrayan translator/counterparts, followed the protocol that the eCrossCulture team had established as data were collected over a period of three weeks.

In two neighboring villages matched along sociocultural, sociopolitical, and socioeconomic dimensions, it was found that virtually all adult villagers, men and women alike, are familiar with the locations of water sources, water flow patterns, recharge times, seasonal variations, and norms associated with sharing and use. Women do more of the work. Neighboring villages function in reciprocal and linked fashion as access to water—always perceived as "scarce," even when there is plenty—is negotiated. Single sources are not tied inextricably to single user networks. Socioeconomic linkages are stronger than sociopolitical linkages. Strategies of shifting and reallocation among sources, which range from wells to artesian springs, are readily employed, especially during the dry season. Local water administrators help in coordinating but do not micro-manage the process. Records are kept but do not prove constraining as technicalities are considered. Village-level meetings aimed at mediation, coordinated by an indigenous *baito* (village council), are held as needed. Full-blown disputes are rare.

It was found that water can be conceived as a construct, not simply as a resource. Taken in their entirety, water resources—from the perspectives of access/use, management, monitoring, administering, and searching (for new sources)—can truly be conceived as constituting an integrated water system (Schultz et al. 2009: B1–B2). Hoped-for understandings of degree of cohesion, degree of privilege, power differentials within and among communities, and degree of factionalization all can be investigated with the toolkit that was chosen; these can be of broad use as "investigative templates" as country-teams and civilian—military research teams investigate relations in conflictive and postconflictive environments.

PARTICIPANT OBSERVATION   This entails low-level, low-intensity observation, recognizing that in-depth rapport (while desirable) rarely can be developed in such a short period. In Ethiopia it focused on work activities involving water use, on community meetings, and on informal "networked activities," some of these involving both adults and children. Complementary discussions over tea or coffee, held in villagers' homes, served to augment the observations.

KEY INFORMANT INTERVIEWS   Target persons include informants thought to be very knowledgeable on a particular topic and judged to be appropriate for "reputational ethnography" (that is, the informants valued reputation adds merit and enhances the likelihood that the data being collected are on target). In Ethiopia these interviews initially focused on district- and village-level administrators but gradually expanded to include church deacons, educators, former military personnel, and water specialists. They were nonstructured. Each informant read and signed an informed consent form, which had been translated into Tigrinya; these forms were retained by the researchers.

SEMISTRUCTURED AND STRUCTURED INTERVIEWS   These interviews must be designed to capture data from an array of individuals, thought to be representative of the overall adult population or—depending on the research objective—representative of a particular subset, such as female water gatherers or former guerrilla combatants. Nonprobabilistic (judgmental) sampling, rather than probabilistic (random) sampling, must be employed, although some degree of cross-cohort stratification can be used. In Ethiopia respondents included members of the *baito*, as well as farmers, laborers, transport workers, and community activists. Both adult males and females were included. The semistructured protocol consisted of ten primary questions related to water systems, accompanied by several "probes." The structured protocol consisted of questions obtained from the sixty-two-page eCrossCulture field guide, many of which relied on "confidence scales" (for example, "How confident are you [the researcher] that the community is egalitarian/situational and democratic/participatory?" [very confident, so-so, pure guess]). Questions about values were featured (for instance, "On security/safety/health, would you [the researcher] rate this as a community key value [high, medium, low] or a perceived challenge [high, medium, low]?"). Again, informed consent forms were obtained from each respondent.

EVENT CALENDARS   These items reflect the common notion that the life of each person is reflective of the most important events that have occurred in it. Such events may be more personal (such as marriage) but also may be more community-centric (such as the time a hand-dug well was dedicated). Some, of course, are reflective of tragedy. Data on these events are gathered using an unstructured, one-on-one interview format. In Ethiopia this method was not used extensively but (for example) did capture the otherwise-missed data on a water source whose primacy was revealed to be tied to the visit once paid there by outside religious specialists.

FOCUS GROUPS   These groups involve persons invited to participate because of their presumed expertise on a particular topic of research importance. Each group (ideally consisting of six to ten individuals) must be structured to be relatively homogeneous. That is, participants must be selected to represent a common set of demographic characteristics (age range, gender, education) and an a priori presumed common set of understandings about the topic in question. Participants ideally represent a cohort defined along both emic and etic lines. A focus group must be run by one researcher who focuses on keeping the discussion moving and who encourages interaction and even disagreement among participants, and another who assists with note-taking and (in the case of Ethiopia) on-the-spot translations. Complications (logistical and sociopolitical) in getting cohorts together dramatically reduced the effectiveness of this method in Ethiopia; it eventually was abandoned in favor of other of the methods previously noted.

Ethical Concerns

Assessments such as the two conducted in Tigray must be "innovative around the edges." Ways must be found to gather the necessary data without compromising the safety of the country/research team and without compromising the ethical basics of benevolence, nonmalevolence, justice, and truth. Neutrality is one such "innovative area." Although one vision of the founders of the International Committee of the Red Cross was that aid should be delivered in a fashion that favors neutrality, impartiality, and consent, as Thomas Weiss (2005: 211) stresses, a political humanitarianism tied to notions of nonneutrality and interventionism has taken hold in many sectors. The "military-civilian humanitarianism" that is emerging suggests that a utilitarian, situational ethics, based partially on on-site field exigencies, may be required. Moral absolutes are not useful, as is illustrated in Chapter 7, where we discuss "turning the tide through Fatwa" in the Battle for Anbar Province, Iraq.

The REA/Ethiopia project—from the Office of Naval Research through eCrossCulture Corporation to the University of Denver—did not budge nor fudge when it came to use of the Institutional Review Board (IRB) procedure. All involved adhered closely to the formal review requirements, as this procedure was carried out at the university. Processes protecting villagers' privacy, confidentiality, and informed consent were both documented and actualized on site. (These review requirements suggest a second reason why the focus group technique proved difficult to implement. Some respondents were skeptical that confidences could be maintained with what they perceived as the focus group's open discussion format.) "Innovation around the edges" therefore might address this constraint in future work. Kerry Fosher, a security anthropologist and specialist on this general topic, has emphasized the importance of working with the military to develop a code of ethics that incorporates anthropological insights (Nuti 2007). Ultimately, the researcher shares responsibility for how the data he or she has collected is used.

Provincial Reconstruction Teams (PRTs)

Some of the most important in-situ assessments—as well as programmatic inroads—are made by Provincial Reconstruction Teams (PRTs). According to the official "PRT Playbook" No. 07-34, a PRT is a joint DoS/DoD entity, operating under joint policy guidance from a civilian Chief of Mission and a battlefield commander. Whereas DoS personnel lead the PRT, team leaders being Foreign Service Officers (FSOs), the PRT deputy is a military officer. The

Chief of Mission may be providing guidance to several PRTs at once, setting political and economic goals as well as policy. Associated military personnel, under the direction of the senior military leadership in the theater, exercise authority over movement and security of the PRT personnel. They take the lead regarding logistics as activities play out at the brigade level. The FSOs and their team leaders determine who their interlocutors are to be and decide which members of the local community are to be engaged. Stated differently, U.S. PRTs have been organized to expressly limit the power of the military to control or dictate political-economic-governance contacts or the undertakings of civilian officers.

Certain PRTs become embedded. An ePRT, as a general rule, coordinates its activities with a paired provincial PRT but tends to concentrate on projects within a CAG (Civil Affairs Group) domain, which is usually geared to metropolitan areas. For example, in Anbar Province, Iraq, the ePRT at Ramadi worked closely with the Ramadi city council and MNF-West CAG for Ramadi, while the ePRT at Fallujah similarly worked with the Fallujah city council, local tribes, and CAG there. Both coordinated projects and resources with the provincial PRT. Reference also is made, as discussed in Chapter 7, to enhanced PRTs (also referred to as ePRTs), which add more depth and robust capabilities to those on-site initiatives focusing on rule of law, improved governance, elections, and related kinds of institution building.

As suggested in several places within this text, command structures continue to evolve, region by region and theater by theater. This flexibility has become a hallmark of PRTs and a significant operational advantage. PRTs are better able to accommodate adjustments by both the Chief of Mission and the military head of operations, in large part because of the "ready mix" of civilian and military resources made available to them. Owing to the recent escalation of hostilities in Afghanistan, as well as staffing challenges within the Foreign Service, some PRTs operating in Afghanistan (most notably those headed by NATO military personnel) have chosen to employ a direct command structure slightly different from that being used in Iraq.

Using this terminology and structure, PRTs were first instituted in Afghanistan in 2001. There appears to be greater humanitarian/SSTR outreach capacity with this model and its variants. It mimics civilian constitutional authority over military operations, with "command-and-collaboration" becoming the theme. That PRTs and ePRTs are designed to be short-term is a plus. That they are backed by both local and international military units and can include civil affairs specialists, civilian police advisors, and civilian representatives of various U.S. government agencies such as USAID also is a plus.

According to our expansive definition, a PRT or an ePRT is a kind of country team or subteam. Along with CAGs, PRTs face a number of challenges that REA (as discussed in the preceding subsection) can address. PRTs require accurate ethnographic information, and, when viewed innovatively, these teams can afford participants the opportunity to address ethical issues associated with the conduct of fieldwork. The ethnographic techniques can allow greater insight into the local "humanitarian space." The premises and methods of REA are highly inductive and empirical; they are less dependent on deductive and theoretic assumptions. REA is issue-driven rather than hypothesis-driven; that is, it readily can be targeted to already-identified or emergent problems within a community. As Schwartz, Molnar and Lovshin (1988) stress, it can accommodate any number of specific methods and can hone in on any number of projects, services, and/or systems, time and resources permitting. REA can provide information that all parties can openly discuss, since it is (ideally) presented in straightforward terms devoid of jargon. It therefore can reduce duplication of community outreach efforts; village leaders often ask both NGOs and PRTs for the same assistance when these various external change agents are not in sync data-wise and not presenting options clearly and crisply.

THE COUNTRY OPERATIONS PLAN

An in-situ preliminary assessment can lead to the development of a country operations plan, as noted in Chapter 2. Such a plan receives its imprimatur at the highest level, which in the case of DoS activity, occurs at the mission/ embassy level, in concert with input from the desk officer and representatives of other affiliated agencies, such as USAID. By contrast, in those instances when the United States has a long-standing presence in the country in question, an in-situ preliminary assessment will not factor into the plan's development. Its development will rely more heavily on previous field data, earlier in-house reports, and mission/embassy staff member updates. Economics, human rights, agricultural, communications, and other subject matter experts (SMEs)—working both on and off site—will contribute key material.

Country operations plans vary in scope and content but have a number of features in common. In addition to DoS, the plans are developed by agencies as diverse as the African Development Bank, the Islamic Development Bank, and the UNHCR. All states that are members of the G8 (Group of Eight Forum) use country plans or the equivalent, as their foreign offices engage in overseas, country-specific operations. (Some of these plans target such regions as Central America, rather than specific countries such as Honduras.) Major NGOs, such as Catholic Relief Services, World Vision, and Merlin, also develop and utilize similar documents. A synthesis of common features includes:

- *Country overview,* including ethnic and religious composition of the population and other essential demographics. For example, the most recent DoS plan for Iraq (not surprisingly) provides details on Sunni, Shi'a, and Kurdish demographics, including internal movements and displacements. Late-breaking news about the "country's pulse" also is featured here. (This subsection of a country plan sometimes includes in-depth ethnographic analyses.)

- *Economic operating environment,* including key indicators such as GNP. In some cases, these are calculated by in-house staff; in other cases, these are extracted from reliable publications such as the annual IBRD *World Development Report.* For example, a recent U.S. Embassy/ USAID plan for El Salvador relied heavily on indicator statistics developed by other agencies. (Socioeconomic factors or issues affecting the business climate sometimes are included in this subsection.)

- *Political operating environment,* including current issues involving political parties' structure and function, political participation, and political constraints or breakdowns. Information usually is referenced on pertinent national laws and any legal breakthroughs. Judicial concerns are cross-referenced. For example, a recent plan developed by UNHCR for Timor-Leste noted the lack of a proper legislative framework to deal with issues of land ownership; this in turn negatively affected foreign investment. (Security and protection issues, defined broadly, sometimes are referenced in this subsection.)

- *Sectoral analyses/emphases* are included as necessary. In general, these most often are drawn from among the health, education, social service, employment, and agricultural sectors. For example, ways to enhance food security were stressed for Indonesia in a recent plan developed by the Islamic Development Bank.
- *Operational goals* are featured. These usually are framed so as to be congruent with the mission's, agency's, or nongovernmental organization's mid-range goals for the country. For example, in a recent UNHCR plan for Bosnia, the enhancement of civil society was featured. Ways in which the UN's overall country team could be helpful, as the UNHCR (as a specific unit) phases down its work with IDPs, were noted.

Again referring to Timor-Leste, one of the bellwether nations often referenced by those associated with the Humanitarianism and War Project, it is instructive to review the UNHCR country operations plan for 2006. Its format and content are appropriately illustrative. As with all the UNHCR's annual plans, key indicators were cross-referenced, but the emphasis was more qualitative/conceptual than quantitative/statistical. In the first section an overview of the protection and socioeconomic operational environment was presented. For Timor-Leste (as a new democracy free of Indonesian rule), issues of political instability, as these have been constraining socioeconomic development, were stressed. The security situation was covered next. Issues of localized rioting and protection of IDPs, as well as refugees in West Timor, were emphasized. The needs of returnees also were covered. Operational goals and the potential for durable solutions were dealt with next. For this country such goals as the development of mechanisms for asylum law and assistance for separated children were stressed. Such country operations plans emphasize more the "what" than the "how."

We stress that specific military goals usually are not referenced in such plans, even those of the DoS. DoD goals usually are presented in separate documents. Ironically, the country operations plans of corporations (such as Chevron, which produces detailed ones) are rarely noted in the country plans of the governments doing business in the countries where the corporations do business.

Preliminary Assessments and Humanitarian Interventions

Humanitarian intervention, as noted in Chapter 1, can be defined as coercive measures employed by outside military forces to ensure access to at-risk civilians and/or enforcement of a population's rights without permission of their state. Military personnel, in many instances working with civilians, assist persons being targeted or attempting to recover from complex humanitarian emergencies or (in a small percentage of cases) disasters. Country teams can be in direct service or advisory positions. The disasters in question can be hurricanes, floods, or volcanic eruptions, or disease-related, such as cholera outbreaks. Famines, although often linked to droughts and adverse meteorological conditions, are considered to result from a combination of human-caused (read: political) and natural factors. Political factors, whether analyzed as causative, corollary, or resultant, always are involved in CHEs and disasters. Political factors, usually framed in military terms, always are involved in humanitarian interventions.

In-situ preliminary assessments often are used to determine what tactics should be used in a humanitarian intervention. Since 2007, Van Arsdale has been part of a team sponsored by the nonprofits Africa Today Associates and Africa Action and funded by the Ford Foundation, dealing with the crisis in Darfur. Four consultations have been held in Denver, Colorado; Abuja, Nigeria; Nairobi, Kenya; and Washington, D.C. Data obtained from preliminary assessments in Darfur and adjoining areas have been incorporated. Recommendations have been made regarding on-site and off-site strategies; information has been shared with the office of General Scott Gration, President Obama's Special Envoy to Sudan, among others.

Retired General Ishola Williams of Nigeria, now serving as a consultant on humanitarian affairs in Africa, contrasted two forms of intervention as the problems in Darfur were being discussed in the fourth consultation, held in Washington, D.C, in January 2009. "Military humanitarianism" involves both civilian and military actors, and incorporates a greater amount of "hard power" (that is, formalized military strategies, might, and matériel). An example was seen in East Timor in 1999. By contrast, "humanitarian intervention" involves both military and civilian actors and relies more heavily on "soft power" (that is, diplomacy and negotiation, sometimes accompanied by economic boycotts and sanctions). It also incorporates the expertise and advice of African experts who themselves are African. The African Union must be involved, including a substantial number of its peacekeeping troops. Williams recommends this second approach for Darfur. So do a majority of the others being consulted.

Any humanitarian intervention in Darfur will benefit from the type of in-situ assessment conducted by one of our colleagues, who wishes to remain anonymous. Addressing the issue of gender-based violence since 2004 from the perspective of her former role as an agency official, she stresses the value of participant observation, first-hand interviews, and active attendance at service provider meetings as threats are being considered. Roadblocks are many; avenues for change are few. A persistent advocacy on behalf of Darfur's female IDPs is essential. A persistent effort to get the myriad of service providers to cooperate also is essential. Discussions with, by, and for the country team representing UNHCR proved challenging in this case.

THREAT, RISK, AND VULNERABILITY ANALYSES

In nonpermissive and semipermissive areas of operation, people involved in the implementation of, training for, and research on country operations must have the skills to analyze the interrelated topics of threat, risk, and vulnerability. Analytic skill must be transmogrified into response skill when complex humanitarian emergencies arise. If and when threat analyses made the daily papers before September 11, 2001, they usually were buried in the back pages of the international section. Analysts at think tanks such as the Brookings

Institution and Cato Institute provided them. The 9/11 attacks changed that. Such assessments, especially those associated with suspected or anticipated terrorist activities, now figure prominently in front-page news coverage. Analysts are being asked to brief responders more extensively than previously. Symbolizing the transformation, and the challenge, is the color-coded advisory system developed by the U.S. Department of Homeland Security in consideration of terrorist threats. It provides a news-ready, albeit overly simplified, form of national threat assessment: Green = low, blue = guarded, yellow = elevated, orange = high, red = severe. Responders are learning how to translate "orange" into "high degree to readiness, on site." (In July 2009 government analysts reported that this system likely would be revamped.)

Traditional threat analyses relied more on experiences with natural disasters and disease pandemics. The 9/11 attacks changed that. Analyses now build more substantially on understandings of warfare and longer-term political strife. Our approach to threat, risk, and vulnerability analyses follows those suggested by Mary Anderson and Peter Woodrow (1998), as well as the late Fred Cuny (1999), while also considering the approach more recently presented by Irwin Redlener (2006). These authors build on their first-hand experiences with natural and human-made disasters, emphasizing CHEs. In earlier work, Peter Van Arsdale took a more traditional approach (Van Arsdale and Holland 1986). From the viewpoint of current analyses, these experts concur that field-based empirical data must stand at the core, case-by-case comparisons must be used, and continual re-evaluations must be conducted. The voices of those affected must be incorporated.

Threat Analysis

A threat is best considered from the perspective of a risky environment or vulnerable population. A threat involves force and/or intrusion, intended through human agency or unintended through natural or human-caused events. Perception of danger is key. Damage, injury, or death can be anticipated. Safety and security are jeopardized. Threatened people—and those who are aware of that threat—always use (whether consciously or not) a kind of calculus, weighing better known and lesser known factors as decisions are made concerning actions to be taken or not taken. It is accurate to refer to a threat as perceived (for example) by a PRT working in a drought-stricken region, a group of homeless people facing a cold night on the streets, or residents of a small town standing in the path of an approaching tornado.

FEMA, the U.S. Federal Emergency Management Agency, broadly considers twenty kinds of emergency to be threats, from those associated with natural hazards (for example, tornadoes and earthquakes), to those associated with technological hazards (for instance, hazardous materials incidents and nuclear power incidents), to those associated with terrorism (for example, explosions and biological threats) (2004). Different lists are employed by military operatives, the police, NGO/IGO analysts, public health officials, and others.

"Threat anxiety" is a term used by Redlener (2006: 199) to describe the emotions and the sense of possible doom the citizenry might have as news of an amorphous threat—such as a hurricane forming in the eastern Caribbean or the whispered prospect of an al-Qaeda attack—is floated. Some analysts believe that anxiety and fear levels tend to be higher when purposeful human action—ominous intent—is anticipated. When (in advance) specific data are made available by officials, actual scientific study results are presented, and/or accurate journalistic reporting is shared, threat anxiety can be reduced or eliminated.

Threats can have primary, secondary, and tertiary implications. The first array are termed "human" and usually involve questions of safety. For example, a military threat associated with the activities of al-Qaeda in Iraq will have primary human implications (for the safety of U.S., Iraqi, and allied forces), secondary human implications (for the citizenry in neighborhoods where fighting is occurring), and tertiary human implications (for relatives in distant towns). The second array are termed "matériel and infrastructural" and involve questions of resources. For example, the same al-Qaeda activities will have primary matériel implications for the arming of the troops fighting them, secondary matériel implications covering support equipment and field supplies, and tertiary matériel implications for those providing back up at distant bases. Threat assessment therefore must be intimately linked to tactical and strategic planning.

Risk and Vulnerability Analyses

Risk and *vulnerability* are sister terms. They stand in correlation, qualitatively. Risk is the probability that exposure to a hazard will lead to a negative consequence (Redlener, citing Ropeik and Gray 2006: 198). Whereas risk more appropriately can be conceptualized "in the environment" and in *actions* anticipated or taken—by perpetrators, project beneficiaries, or those assisting or intervening—vulnerability more appropriately can be conceptualized "in the cohort," in the *circumstances* of potential or actual victims. (Of course, victims often become beneficiaries.) Vulnerability refers to those factors and conditions that make life tenuous. It can be defined along any number of dimensions (military/logistical, ethnic/cultural, health/disease, socioeconomic, psychosocial, and sociopolitical, the last dimension being featured later in this subsection). Military/logistical factors are exemplified in Chapter 5. Ethnic/cultural factors include those associated with breakdowns in value structures, religious disruptions (including those linked to violent social movements), cross-ethnic clashes, and forced assimilation. Health/disease factors include those associated with exposure to pathogens, often in the context of sociopolitical disruption of society. Socioeconomic factors include those precluding or constraining sustainable livelihoods, such as household disruptions associated with civil war or famine. Psychosocial factors include those associated with disabilities and mental illnesses, as well as those stemming from posttraumatic conditions such as those experienced by survivors of the World Trade Center disaster, Hurricane Katrina, and the Srebrenica massacre in Bosnia.

"Science, technology, and experience have drained a lot of risk from our lives" David Von Drehle (2007: 15) stresses as he discusses life in the twenty-first-century United States. Yet this is not the case for those in battle zones, residing in areas prone to natural disaster, and/or struggling to survive in urban or rural areas throughout much of the developing world. Over one-third of the global population is regularly at moderate-to-high risk. Persons who are vulnerable therefore are said to be at risk in terms of certain criteria and also (depending on the type and the degree of human agency) to be "socioeconomically marginalized," "culturally marginalized," "psychosocially marginalized," and so forth. Their capabilities to respond to crises are reduced or compromised. Their access to key resources is limited. Their stances relative to other members of society are altered. Their chances for viable survival are reduced.

The classic adaptive responses to socioeconomic marginalization include (but are not limited to) out-migration for work, economic readjustment through changed employment practices, and economic readjustment through modification of family resource strategies. Barbara Thomas-Slayter (2003) provides excellent examples of these responses, based on work in Central America and elsewhere. Adaptive responses to cultural marginalization—many of which are similar to those for psychosocial marginalization—include value adjustments, shifts in attitude, suppression of the opinions of others, and even (over time) major shifts in belief systems. Anthony Marsella and colleagues (1994) provide solid examples of these, based primarily on their work with refugees.

Of greatest interest to us, in the context of country operations, is sociopolitical vulnerability. Power differentials are paramount. Disruptions of civil society and the legal order and juridical system, and the abuse or abridgement of human rights, are indicative. In severely disrupted or chaotic environments, such as those associated with terrorist attacks, famine, or warfare, sociopolitical vulnerability is among the first topics that must be addressed. Whereas those defeated in battle can be said to be politically marginalized, so, too, can those whose policies failed or whose strategies—on site or behind the scenes—did not work well.

Key adaptive responses to political vulnerability and marginalization are not exclusive of those mentioned earlier (for example, out-migration). They also can include party re-affiliation, new alliance-building, retreat, and retaliation. Smith saw all four processes at play in Anbar Province during the last part of the 2000s.

Capacity Analysis

To bring this analytic approach full circle, a risk analysis should be complemented by a capacity analysis. As Anderson and Woodrow (1998) note, capacity refers to those resources that can be brought to bear to assist those at risk. As we use the terms, *capacity* refers to what an organization can offer; by contrast, the term *capability* refers to what an individual can offer. Capacity is calculable along several dimensions. Social capacity refers to what an organization can offer (for example) toward assisting with community dynamics of the displaced. Economic capacity refers (for instance) to the ability to offer assistance in the form of improving local markets. Psychological capacity refers (for example) to an organization's ability to offer mental health counseling to victims of conflict. In each domain, the ability to achieve redundancy is essential; that is, personnel must orient their work such that multiple means ("back ups") are available to react and respond.

Political capacity is the focus here. It refers to what can be accomplished through legislative means, primarily internal to a nation, and what can be accomplished through diplomatic means, primarily external to a nation. The ability to create policies that aid the citizens of one's own nation, as well as the citizens of another (through trade, military assistance, relief activities) is a reflection of political capacity. As we define their operations, country teams work primarily to augment, to reinforce, and in certain instances to refocus, political capacity.

Military capacity, as we define it, is a subset of political capacity. Traditional explanations have focused primarily on such factors as troop strength, number and type of armaments, military organizational structures, and strategic planning ability. As country operations make clear, increased emphasis is being placed on networked organizational functions spanning military units, military contractors, cooperating civilian agencies (including NGOs), and intergovernmental organizations. As the situation in Iraq exemplifies, from the perspective of the United States and its coalition allies, capacity must be determined via networked communications, intelligence gathering operations, and transnational information feeds. To the degree to which tensions are reduced and peaceful conditions are enhanced, capacity can be said to have been translated into a beneficial outcome. Battle-site reconnaissance assessments, pre-action briefings, and after-action "hot wash" reports provide localized and relatively rapid updates.

Salvadoran Water Resources

As the civil war in El Salvador raged during the mid-1980s, Peter Van Arsdale was asked to serve as Chief-of-Party for a country team contracted to conduct a two-month assessment of the agro-related water resource needs of—and institutional incentives and constraints facing—small holders (that is, small-scale farmers, most of whom had not previously owned their own land) (Figure 3.3). These individuals were being assisted by a new government office, and so part of the assignment focused on the effectiveness of its operations, as a type of capacity analysis. Sponsored by USAID, this field reconnaissance team (FRT) consisted of an applied anthropologist, a social worker specializing in cooperative development, an agronomist, an agricultural engineer, an agricultural economist, and a specialist in Latin American sociopolitical development. These personnel were matched on site by skilled Salvadoran scientists, serving as counterparts, three of whom had extensive experience with small-farm water systems.

Disruptions owing to the civil war, in concert with agricultural resource shifts and opportunities being created by recent land reform processes, had placed small holders in a state of flux. The new government office had been created in 1978, yet nearly two years elapsed before it was clear whether the Ministry of the Interior or the Ministry of Agriculture had ultimate authority. (It proved to be the latter.) Both exciting and complicating the process for small holders/farmers was the fact that land reform was intended to benefit cooperatives as well as individuals. Expropriation of land from large estates was moving forward, with 20 percent of the nation's arable land included in the first phase alone. A number of haciendas literally were being turned over to people who, until the day before, had been non-landed farmers or laborers.

A number of findings and associated recommendations resulted from the FRT's assessment. Among the most important was that water resources for agriculture tended to be adequate but that knowledge of how to manage them tended to be inadequate. Few previously "non-landed farmers," now "landed farm managers," had received any training in how to manage such properties. People with previous experience with cooperatives did tend to fare better. Better clarity regarding obligations, negotiations, and appropriations regarding land and water rights was needed on the part of the government office. Better skills in farm administration were needed on the part of the small holders (Applied Social Science and Health Consultants 1984). (Several of the project's field methods, and the specific ways in which they were tweaked, served as precursors for those techniques selected a quarter-century later for the Ethiopian project reported earlier in this chapter.)

FIGURE 3.3   A farm family responds to questions about irrigation resources during the mid-1980s land reform transition in El Salvador (photo by Peter Van Arsdale).

Benchmarks

Threat, risk, and vulnerability analyses often are associated with the use of benchmarks. These are not the type of benchmarks that the Bush Administration linked to the war in Iraq and that caused so much consternation in Congress during the summer of 2007 as "progress toward definable objectives" was evaluated. Rather, these are thresholds or markers that are used by first-, second-, and third-responders to quickly evaluate the progress being made in complex humanitarian emergencies to assist those in need/at risk.

In New York City, on September 11, 2001, one of many first-responder benchmarks was attained with the successful deployment at the World Trade Center of 18 firefighting rigs within 15 minutes of the first tower being struck. One of many second-responder benchmarks was attained with the successful implementation of Red Cross assistance, including temporary shelters, within 24 hours of the event. One of many third-responder benchmarks was achieved with the coordination of health professionals representing more than 220 organizations through the Greater New York Hospital Association. As Redlener (2006) notes, the organizations were represented by specialists who met during the weeks that immediately followed the tragedy, aiding the delivery of services as diverse as trauma care and nursing home care.

Program Evaluation

An area of fieldwork that has been overlooked by many specialists in the delivery of humanitarian assistance, as well as other work at the military-civilian interface, is that of program evaluation. Although not a topic of this book, it is worth noting briefly in this chapter. Some U.S. country teams are moving to better incorporate an evaluation process, but much work remains. Those readers interested in more details, from complementary anthropological vantage points, are encouraged to consult the volume edited by Mary Odell Butler and Jacqueline Copeland-Carson, *Creating Evaluation Anthropology* (2005).

As program evaluations are considered, we return to the work of Charles Erasmus (1961), whose evaluation efforts were briefly noted in Chapter 1. Innovations in the field of development again prove key to the field of humanitarianism. His early work proved seminal. Working as a development specialist, he was among the first during the post-World War II era to identify the roles that social scientists could play as "social cost accounting" was undertaken. He advocated the evaluation of all major technical assistance efforts in which Westerners (especially Americans) were involved in introducing social change, either through development programs or—in those instances when they were classified as distinct—through foreign aid programs. He stressed that the weighing of costs and benefits should involve both quantitative and qualitative methods, with qualitative measures being pre-eminent.

Tapping understandings derived from both economics and anthropology, Erasmus stressed that social cost accounting must not focus on standard Western capitalistic indicators. An indigenous business that expands owing to an influx of external capital and improves owing to an influx of external ideas should not be evaluated primarily by criteria that feature increases in profit margins and the timeliness of loan repayments. Although economic considerations are important, socioeconomic considerations often are more important. Such qualitative indicators as social mobility, social capital, and entrepreneurial independence should be featured as evaluations are conducted. Nearly a half-century later, country team evaluators would do well to heed these admonitions.

It is worth noting that, via a few twists and turns, Erasmus's "social cost accounting" evolved into "outcome-focused program evaluation" within the development field.

Kofi Annan's Lessons

Kofi Annan is a leader who frequently has espoused the value of in-situ or empirical assessments, particularly in "hot spots" worldwide. On retiring from his post as United Nations Secretary-General, Annan presented an address at the Truman Presidential Library in Independence, Missouri (2006). He discussed five lessons he has learned while serving in this role.

The first lesson has to do with shared security. He believes that the security of each person is linked to that of every other person. No nation can make itself secure by seeking supremacy over other nations; shared responsibility for one another's security ultimately rests with individuals working through established institutions. Thoughtfully conceived military operations, particularly those involving multilateral forces operating under the UN flag, were noted as important venues for actualizing this lesson. The second lesson has to do with shared welfare. He believes that consideration of issues associated with the global market economy—with attention focused on disparity reduction— lends itself to what others might term a socioeconomically responsive stance. He spoke robustly on behalf of the UN Millennium Development Goals, to be reached, it is hoped, by 2015. These include such goals as reducing by 50 percent the proportion of people worldwide who do not have potable drinking water.

Annan's third lesson has to do with the relationship between security and development. He believes that both ultimately depend on respect for human rights and the rule of law. Taking a more traditional stance, he went on to state that both foreign investors and a country's citizens are more likely to engage in productive activity when their rights are assured. He sees a continuing strong role for the United States here, as long as it "remains true to its principles," including the fight against terrorism. As states interact, they need to "play by the rules."

His fourth lesson follows closely on the third. He believes that governments must be accountable for their actions in both the international and the domestic arenas. His position as a systems thinker becomes clearer in this regard, because he also addresses the roles of such non-state actors as for-profit corporations, charities, lobbying and pressure groups, and universities. When properly constituted, these have the capacity to influence the political process at both international and national levels.

The consummate politician, Annan concludes with a fifth lesson that derives from the first four. He says: "We can only do all these things by working together through a multilateral system, and by making the best possible use of the unique instrument [of] the United Nations."

Annan's views stand in contrast to some of those expressed in the so-called Baker-Hamilton ("Iraq Study Group") report, issued in December 2006. Tackling the question of U.S. involvement in Iraq from a bipartisan perspective, James Baker, Lee Hamilton, and eight colleagues offered a number of diagnoses, some very hard-hitting. The report offered somewhat fewer long-term strategies and very few recommendations that could be considered "humanitarian." The challenge of doing this type of work within conflict zones remains extreme.

We believe that cooperation among civilian and military personnel, well-coordinated and well-versed in humanitarian principles, offers a powerful parallel. The paradigms and methods associated with "country operations" can serve as innovative tools as field activities are engaged. As this book demonstrates, so-called country teams can offer expertise in applied research, civilian-military cotraining, and actual field operations.

PART II

ON SITE, IN ACTION

CHAPTER 4

TRAINING AND EQUIPPING FOR DEPLOYMENT

PERSONAL PREPAREDNESS

Although we live in a world of bureaucratic morass that seemingly controls aid and assistance programs, as well as a sea of checklists and administrative overhead that don't seem to help feed a single person or build a single dwelling, there is certain logic to such routines in both preparation and deployment. In fact, systematically working through what often are tedious steps in planning for training and equipping for deployment can help a country team member "get into the game," to become more organizationally sound and more emotionally and mentally prepared for the challenges of an overseas mission.

The cardinal rule of training and field preparation: your safety is your concern. If you are reliant on someone else to guarantee your safety, you must make sure that person is up to snuff. If a country plan has been provided, you need to make sure that it is understood and that associated threat, risk, and vulnerability analyses are adequate. As Irwin Redlener (2006) stresses throughout his work, professional preparedness must be primary in the face of emergencies. If you get captured or otherwise victimized, you will be helped little by saying after the fact: "The other team members didn't do their job!" The bottom line is that a team member ultimately has no one else to guarantee the bottom line. Security does not reside in "the Other." Even if troops, personal security details (PSDs), escorts, local police, or paramilitary personnel are present, it is your ultimate mistake if plans, protocols, or procedures prove inadequate.

This chapter presents a variety of checklists, training considerations, and suggestions for detailed preparation. Such materials must be reviewed before undertaking a mission. Not every checklist will be needed, nor will every detail be applicable in every instance; ultimately, the country team and each individual member must prepare their own mission-specific checklists. But, with these guidelines, a member will be better prepared to go into the field, accomplish the mission, and return safely. The training also should be based on the latest intelligence, analyzed and applied in advance of deployment. One's personal kit (that is, immediately accessible field supplies and equipment) and bug-out bag should always be tailored to the environment of each project. Even an easy weekend hike in the wilderness, as discovered in 2009 by an aid worker in the Philippines, can end in disaster.

Health Care and Medical Preparation

Health examinations are vital. Plan medical appointments well in advance of deployment, making certain that they are age specific. Vision and dental checkups are of equal importance. Because many aid workers and country team members are "young and in their prime," it is easy to overlook high cholesterol levels, blood sugar swings, heart valve issues, and breast lumps. A minor scratch can lead to a major infection. The standard array of vaccinations will serve most personnel well. A quick review of additional precautions (including vaccinations, prophylactic medications, and preventative practices) attuned to the theater in question will also serve well. Some vaccines (such as that for Hepatitis series B) can be administered in three separate shots over a 6-month period. Hepatitis series A, as we both discovered on independent trips to Sudan, required two shots separated by 6 months. A typhoid vaccination equivalent is now available in oral capsules; immunizations for polio, measles, mumps, rubella, and yellow fever all must be considered. In some areas HIV/AIDS testing is required before deployment can be authorized.

Proof of all immunizations usually is required for country team members. The record card should be kept with the passport and copies of earlier medical records in one's "important papers file." The well-known yellow card, International Certificate of Vaccination as Approved by the World Health Organization, is commonly used and accepted worldwide.

Therefore, one must travel with a "synopsis" of one's essential medical documentation. The up-to-date vaccination card in one's possession should be backed up by a photocopy kept at the home base. Family members also should have access to copies of key records. That some medical records now are being encrypted and made available to authorized personnel online is a useful convenience. Information retrieved from *http:/travel.state.gov/travel/ travel_1744.html* is also useful, as is that obtained from the websites of such major relief and aid organizations as World Vision. Predeployment discussions should be held with available veterans from the specific AO (area of operations). It is best to get one more piece of information, one more shot, one extra prophylactic treatment, if there is any doubt. Missing a malaria prophylaxis is an unforgiving error. Sound prevention and early detection are the obvious watchwords.

The DoS offers a series of medical examinations to establish a "Class One Medical Clearance," which is required for many overseas hardship posts and virtually all danger-pay unaccompanied sites. (Types of rural and urban sites are discussed in Chapter 6.) Family members also need to be cleared, should they be accompanying the team member. Annual blood workups; blood pressure, heart, and stress tests; and eye, ear, nose, and throat examinations usually are mandated. Joint and podiatry exams are recommended. A review of family history can yield valuable information on one's vulnerability to diabetes and renal, bone, breast, or prostate cancers, and can provide clues to hypertension, elevated cholesterol levels, and hearing or vision problems.

Assignment at a remote fixed site for a 2-year stint will preclude detailed examinations; the chance for survival should a severe trauma or disease occur will be enhanced to the degree that predeployment medical reviews and precautions have been taken. Waiting for R&R leave to take care of problems is not recommended, but updating one's exams and following up on problems during R&R is recommended.

In advance of deployment, as well as during R&Rs, it is a good idea to collect relevant late-breaking medical information. Websites such as that sponsored by the Mayo Clinic are useful. A lingering toothache or a seemingly insignificant nuisance such as an ingrown nail can mushroom into larger problems; R&R is the time to address these. All necessary prescriptions and shatterproof eye glasses, with backup pairs kept in separate locations, are essential. A rule of thumb is that overseas assignments of 6 months duration or more should mandate duplicate/backup gear in all essential medical areas.

Although the country team will have a large kit for general use (including gear such as stretchers), each team member should always travel with his or her own medical kit and know how to use it. (Additional information on this appears later in this chapter.) Knowledge of backcountry first aid, combat first aid, EMT guidelines, and related medical protocols is vital. Our students have benefited from Red Cross training, which we arranged.

As we have experienced in settings as diverse as Papua Province, Indonesia, and Anbar Province, Iraq, an American deployed in a remote setting might be the closest thing to a doctor that the villagers recently have seen. Peter Van Arsdale has bandaged a man whose foot was partly severed by an errant axe blow, helped reset a boy's dislocated elbow, and treated a man suffering from gonorrhea. Derrin Smith has treated a wide variety of infections and aided perinatal mothers and their babies. We both have encountered people injured by camels (Figure 4.1). Although unlicensed, we had to step in. (Of course, if at all possible, one should radio for trained medical assistance. In contemporary

Figure 4.1 Camels are commonly used as secondary means of transport by country team members working in the Middle East (photo by Derrin Smith).

conflictive environments, an air ambulance often is available should medical transport be required.)

For team members on a regimen, for example, of Lipitor for cholesterol problems or morning baby aspirin to reduce the risk of stroke and who are on a long assignment, the preceding rule of thumb applies: a 6-month minimum daily supply must be secured before departure. For some prescriptions, pharmacies will require a letter from the country team's sponsor before supplying a large order. Certain orders require as much as 4 weeks advance notice. One cannot always trust the labels of medicines that are purchased in developing countries; counterfeit and substandard chemicals are a constant risk overseas.

We recommend a "continental perspective," that is, focusing on the region of deployment but considering disease and health threats at a broader "continental level." A threat in Tajikistan might become a threat in Afghanistan; a threat in Uganda might become a threat in Sudan. This approach also enables consulting doctors, dentists, and nurses to advise more broadly in advance of the deployment.

Hygiene Issues

One lighthearted slogan has a good deal of merit: "floss early and often." Good health is complemented by good hygiene. Basic hygiene in the field is invaluable in extending tours to completion, avoiding absenteeism, and aiding physical fitness. If good hygiene becomes routine, it also can be a morale booster and serve as a trigger for (or lead-in to) outreach programs to local residents. (Most recently this was demonstrated by a University of Denver, Jomo Kenyatta University, Rotary Club team working in the Kibera slum of Kenya.) At its most basic, good hygiene is a guardian against disease. A minor gum or tooth infection can have serious consequences when the team member is stationed at a remote fixed site. Unfiltered water and poorly maintained sanitation systems (exemplified by latrines) can lead to infections such as cholera, which remain leading killers in developing countries worldwide. Good hygiene equipment is inexpensive, sensible hygiene practices can readily be implemented, and resultant health gains can easily be tracked. Hygiene is preventive, not curative.

A "field kit" for good hygiene can metaphorically and literally be constructed head to toe. It can see a team member through the dirtiest extended remote tour. For the hair and scalp, head lice, boring worms, cradle-cap infections, psoriasis, and sunburn can be major problems. A Franciscan monk who became a trusted ally of Derrin Smith during the unrest in Kosovo and Bosnia would tug a baseball cap hard over his bald head, the cap inscribed with the words "Gee, I miss you, wish you were HAIR." He would then head out unarmed to face every hardship with a smile and a prayer. Sunburn was the greatest threat to his exposed and well-polished scalp, but lice from the street children and war orphans he assisted threatened him time and again. A container of hair lice remover is worth packing. Short hair can be a defense against some parasites and scalp infections, but not every culture is ready to accept an aid worker with a Marine-style high-and-tight shaved haircut. (A relaxed civilian style that is culturally appropriate can have the benefit of removing a cultural barrier, however slight, that might result from military-style hair appearance. In some parts of the world, the wrong haircut or shave can get a person into trouble. It is important to learn the norms of dress, clothing, and style in the region in question.)

In certain Middle Eastern cultures, women find that following the social requirement of wearing the *hijab* or a head scarf over their hair offers the benefit of enhancing cleanliness and protecting hair from dust. Another seemingly minor dust problem is often overlooked: vehicles kicking up nasty bacteria-laden dust that can penetrate deep into the scalp, eyes, and ears, resulting in infections. (Major convoy problems are covered in Chapter 5.)

Teeth and gums can deteriorate rapidly on long deployments, owing to a combination of unfiltered water, strange food and bacteria, tooth-grinding at night from frustration or stress, and reduced attention to general hygiene when things get hectic. Normal oral hygiene practices often slip in the field. Subsequent infections can affect the health of the entire body (and personnel down for a sick day for any reason can throw off the work schedule of the entire team). Dental floss is a must, both for oral hygiene and for durable equipment repairs. The stitching strength of dental floss is remarkable. Derrin Smith still carries a Wenger "Swiss Army" backpack as a bug-out bag that had a near-fatal tear on the carrying strap. A quick repair job on the shredded strap with dental floss, a touch-up with black magic marker to match the bag's color, and four years of hard use and abuse later the repaired strap is holding up perfectly. (The dental floss repair job has survived Iraq, Afghanistan, and eastern Europe.) Ingenuity in the field and creative measures to "make do" will serve the team well in ways that extend far beyond personal health and hygiene.

Remarkably, even body odor can make a difference. Members of some communities in Africa, the Middle East, and East Asia are not shy in commenting on the "strange-smelling foreigners" they encounter. The use of deodorant may have no effect whatsoever; locally available herbal-scented powders can be helpful.

The feet can be a breeding ground for bacterial and fungal problems. Athlete's foot is only one of several types of infection that, if untreated, can become severe. Clean, dry feet are essential. It is a good idea to keep at least one cheap pair of shower shoes available for the shower or bath area. Depending on the residential toilet arrangements, a "latrine pair" may also be required. Each team member should have extra socks that are changed regularly, use foot powders with antifungals, and maintain precise toenail hygiene to avoid unnecessary, painful, and potentially dangerous infections. A predeployment consultation with a doctor regarding any podiatric medical conditions or foot discomfort will pay dividends in the long run.

Physical Training

Prospective team members, especially rookies, often begin with the notion that their inadequate physical fitness can be upgraded once they arrive on site. Although improvements indeed can be made once there, team members must arrive fit. To say "I run 2 miles three times a week, swim laps, hit the gym. . ." is not always enough. In reviewing team after team, at site after site, even in military organizations, we see overweight members struggle. Even 5 or 10 extra pounds can prove detrimental. Being a step too slow during an escape up a mountainside can prove tragic.

Team members must take steps to increase endurance. Strength training, endurance walking or running, weight training, yoga, and/or martial arts (covered in detail in the next subsection) are recommended. If you are going to be deployed to the field, be in shape. If in good shape, get into better shape. It is essential to consider the region where the team will be working and to make a plan for fitness and diet and weight control that matches the incentives and constraints offered by that setting. It is all too easy to add weight in a foreign environment. The internet provides a number of ready references to diet and weight control (which are invariably easier to read than to apply). We recommend several of the "how to" manuals that are regularly referenced in *Track & Field News* and *Runner's World Magazine.*

One must research the options, develop a reasonable plan that will work, and then stick to it. The field plan should complement a general health plan. First and foremost, don't smoke. Not only does smoking compromise one's health, it can compromise one's security if emergency medical care is needed. We have been surprised at how many of our graduate students were smokers; several of them lacked "that extra breath" needed to complete a field exercise in the sessions held in Romania and Colorado (reported in Chapter 6). In addition, paradoxically, something as innocuous as a fancy Zippo engraved lighter resting on the dashboard at the wrong time at the wrong checkpoint has been known to initiate an action by outsiders that had dangerous consequences.

Each team member therefore should have established his or her own standard of physical fitness. It is then possible to track one's readiness and compare oneself on a regular basis to others. Derrin Smith (a former Marine) has used the Marine Corps Physical Fitness Test for several decades, and it works well. Several other tests also are available, as referenced in such publications as *Runner's World Magazine*. By mastering the test and referencing it regularly, corrective action can be taken early if necessary. Age-adjusted performance ratios are incorporated into most measures, although insurgents who might be encountered in some types of field operations don't bother to account for these. One tried-and-true set of measures (the First Class Personal Fitness Test, included in the Marine test mentioned above) sets thresholds as follows: a 3-mile run in 18 minutes, 20 pull-ups to a cadence count, and 80 bent-knee sit-ups in 2 minutes. To protect the lower back, abdominal curls are preferred to full sit-ups. For a 50-year-old person, a superior First Class PFT measure is exemplified by a 3-mile run in 21 minutes.

A team member cannot wait until deployment to discover that carrying a 20-, 30-, or 40-pound pack is draining energy levels too low. Sophisticated gym equipment, spring-loaded weight machines, and medicine balls are not required to conduct effective workouts. An open space and regimented "plan of attack" suffice. Despite the value espoused—and nutritional gains often demonstrated—by those following vegan diets, these can prove difficult to follow in many field settings. We recommend studying the Body for Life™ regime for diet and exercise. Good nutritional fitness, strength, and endurance literally can be the difference between life and death in conflictive and postconflictive environments.

Martial Arts Training

A regime of martial arts is good for fitness, good for confidence, and good in times of real danger. This perhaps surprising recommended preparation can improve alertness and aid the immediate analysis needed when encountering a vulnerable victim or an intruder on site. More traditional forms of exercise and nutritional fitness are a given for fieldwork; martial arts can be viewed as exercise with another benefit in that the physical, mental, and emotional rewards can go far beyond just lowering blood pressure or reducing the waist line. Derrin Smith (Figure 4.2) prefers relatively traditional *karate-do* ("empty hand technique") and *kobu-do* ("weapons technique"); other styles suit other preferences.

Some team members prefer sport styles, some more basic combat or law enforcement techniques of self-defense. There are grapplers, boxers, and Tai Chi artists, and even dance forms that are based on self-defense principles. Each has merit; selection depends largely on personality, previous experience, and (to a much lesser extent) place of deployment. A traditional style that engages an experienced, credentialed teacher is recommended. (See the website of the All Okinawa Shorin Ryu Kenshin Kan Karate and Kobudo Federation, *www.kenshin-kan.com* for specific details.) Martial arts, complemented by a dedication to the spirit embodied

FIGURE 4.2   A martial arts regimen can serve as an important component of fitness training, as Derrin Smith demonstrates (photo by Derrin Smith).

in the particular program chosen, can lead to an activity that is practiced and fine-tuned on a continual basis. While team members are deployed, it can serve as an unusual diversion, a fitness regime, and a method of spiritual enhancement.

The art and practice of self-defense can open other doors. Derrin Smith became certified as a Police Self-Defense Instructor a quarter-century ago. It could not then have been anticipated how—in conjunction with vital communications—these skills would help open avenues into government, security, military, and law enforcement academies in the countries where he has subsequently been deployed. Not only was an avenue of secondary employment opened; teaching seminars were also created that led to unusual network connections, and initially surprising relationships developed with personnel in positions of authority. These contacts remain important today.

Equipment Needs and Checklists

Before deploying, check with the personnel being replaced. Whether in person, by phone, or by e-mail, a discussion must take place. First-hand information on what they carried into the field, what they needed and did not need, and nuances associated with adjusting to the new (temporary or permanent, fixed or semifixed, rural or urban site) location is step one. Service and operational sites vary greatly, and equipment lists need to be tailored in three ways: (1) to location, (2) to assignment goals and objectives, and (3) to personal expertise.

Survival Kits and Basic Gear

In general, whether one is working out of the mud-and-brick buildings at Firebase Anaconda in Afghanistan or a small room near the town of El Fasher in Darfur, the primary survival *cum* work kit should always be "a quick grasp." Typically, the team member's daypack carries a laptop, a charging and communications device, day-papers (annotated current assignment sheets), and mobile office supplies. A humid climate mandates that day-papers be tucked into zip-top plastic bags. Tucked into one zipper daypack pocket is a small, commercially available survival kit (including water purification tablets or a battery-powered water purification wand using ultraviolet light); in a second pocket is a batch of basic traveler's first-aid supplies (including Neosporin ointment), and in a third pocket is extra cash in mixed denominations along with some LRP (long-range patrol) energy rations and protein bars. These supplies do not add much extra weight and are not conspicuous; a minimum of fluids, gels, and metal materials helps team members avoid delays during airport security screenings.

The "space blanket" in the survival kit provides protection against hypothermia, yet weighs less than 3 ounces. The food bars provide some energy while one is awaiting personnel rotation (or rescue if an emergency occurs). A signaling device, often no more than a highly reflective mirror, can help in rescue work. The antibiotics included with the first-aid supplies help keep small problems from getting bigger while one is working or awaiting relief in the bush. All in all, these small things provide much security and comfort.

We encourage experimentation with field gear. Peter Van Arsdale wears a fly-fishing vest and uses every one of its twelve pockets to carry miscellaneous items that are not in the backpack or bug-out bag. Remember that many supplies have a designated shelf life, so a list of such items should be created, maintained, and reviewed regularly. Indeed, the entire travel inventory should be recorded, item by item. This helps not only in replacing items stolen in transit but also in packing for the next assignment. In our experience, seemingly insignificant—yet ultimately vital—toiletries, batteries, and extra socks are the items most likely to be overlooked. One checklist should be maintained for general gear (usually packed in a duffle bag), one for the survival kit (including mobile office supplies), one for the bug-out bag discussed in the next subsection, and one for any items shipped separately.

The same pouch or pocket should be used for the same item each time. Only when the item has been stowed should it be checked off its respective list. Interestingly, checklists not only work practically, but they also have the additional psychological effect of "getting your head into the game," which goes with assembling, inventorying, and packing according to a list. All considerations that can be covered in advance must be covered in advance. As both of us have discovered on multiple occasions, something as small as a caribiner attached to the belt can come in handy if a person must be lowered from a helicopter on a winch (Figure 4.3) or cross a flooded stream on a small

FIGURE 4.3   A helicopter winch is used to lift a student at a Romanian Land Forces training base in the Transylvanian mountains, part of the University of Denver's 2004 program (photo by Shannon C. Smith).

make-shift boat. A team member's equipment suite must be regularized and ready, yet adjustable and adaptable.

Bug-Out Bags   A sturdy, nondescript minidaypack or fanny pack/ carry-all that is equipped so that the team member can survive a few days "on the run" or while hunkered down awaiting rescue is referred to as a *bug-out bag*. A small nonbreakable water bottle, an old-fashioned compass, waterproof matches, water purification tablets, a multipurpose knife, band-aids, and a space blanket constitute the seven "magic" items the bag should contain; duplicates of some other of the small items included in the survival kit also can be considered.

For university students still in training, it is worth considering the same kind of pack that is used to carry miscellaneous items to class. A bug-out bag often attracts the attention of outside observers. Simple colors should be chosen; fancy bangles and logos should be avoided. It should be packed so as to be quiet when one is walking, running, or working. As a test, we recommend shaking the packed bag hard while listening for any sounds of tinkling metal or noisy plastic.

Some fabrics even make loud rubbing noises when a person is moving quickly. A simple solution involves taking cloth electrical tape, or other non-shiny binding adhesive tape, and isolating any metal or plastic zipper handles, clasps, buckles, hooks, and loops. Once the pack is ready, employ the "kangaroo test": jump up and down with the pack tightly strapped in place. The less sound, the better the packing and the more efficient the bug-out bag for actual fieldwork.

We have seen joggers, field researchers, and country team members with bug-out bags of every style and size. We have seen them in the parks of Washington, D.C. and in the streets of Sarajevo. People who are seasoned professionals often can be observed testing and retesting their packs, shaking and then readjusting them, even when not "on assignment." Preparing a properly equipped and efficiently packed bag becomes second nature. It is a priority for every overseas professional.

CLOTHING   Clothing should be climate-, culture-, and work-specific. For remote tropical or desert areas, however, one complete "generic" back-country outfit purchased from one of the better sporting goods/sportswear chains is invaluable. Jeans and typical American casual wear might suffice for assignments in less remote and less rigorous Western settings, but personnel should strongly consider local culture and climate when choosing apparel for assignments in East and Southeast Asia, Central and Southwest Asia, the Middle East, and sub-Saharan Africa. In our experience, Latin America and the Caribbean are less of an issue. For example, despite being comfortable to wear in a place such as Darfur, Bermuda shorts on men are not appropriate. In all cases, avoid conspicuous fashions and jewelry. Also, in cool climates, multiple layers of light clothing are preferable to a single layer of heavy clothing.

At the end of a deployment, we donate some of our clothing to locals who have been of assistance and have a demonstrated need. This usually is easier—and more culturally appropriate—for male team members to do than for female team members. Also consider purchasing some local fabrics and outfits in the local markets; spending money that goes into the pockets of local entrepreneurs can help build relationships, and local clothing may feature dyes and styles that work well for one's deployment. In no instance, however, do we recommend "going native." It is highly inappropriate to attempt to take on the attributes or cultural characteristics of people with whom one is working. An egregious example is seen in a documentary film by Napoleon Chagnon, who spent years working among the Yanomami of Venezuela. The data he and his colleagues collected, although in some ways controversial, was informative

---

Operation Jaque

An insignia can make the difference, for better or worse, in some overseas operations, as the following account describes. (As Robert Wyllie noted in a classic article published in 1919 in *The National Geographic Magazine*, modern insignia and medals—including those presented by dignitaries to soldiers and sailors for acts of bravery—can be traced to the reign of Queen Elizabeth I. In 1588 she presented a medal called "Ark in Flood," presumably to naval veterans.)

As Javier Womeldorff (2009) summarizes the case, in the summer of 2008 Colombian government operatives rescued 15 prisoners from the FARC (Revolutionary Armed Forces of Colombia). The operatives posed as other FARC soldiers, NGO representatives, and journalists. The rescue targeted four high-profile captives, including Ingrid Betancourt and three employees of Northrup Grumman, one of two U.S.-based corporations leading efforts at drug eradication in this South American nation. The employees had been held for several years. Even though over 700 hostages still remained in FARC control, the raid initially was hailed as a major success.

It later was learned that one of the Colombian operatives had been wearing a Red Cross emblem. Unauthorized use of this insignia violates Geneva Conventions by "feigning . . . protected status by the use of . . . emblems." Pictures taken before the rescue was launched show a variety of different emblems on the clothing of the operatives and the aircraft. One belonged to the supposed "Misión Internacional Humanitaria" of Spain, a group whose existence could not be confirmed. The Red Cross issued a statement stressing that it had, in no way, been engaged in the effort. President Álvaro Uribe of Colombia stated that the Red Cross emblem had been used "mistakenly and contrary to orders."

The release of prisoners on other occasions had been facilitated by negotiations among the Red Cross, President Hugo Chávez of Venezuela, and FARC. A number of media and political analysts expressed the opinion that Operation Jaque had jeopardized the possible future release of other hostages and the hard-won image of the Red Cross as a neutral agency.

(cf. Van Arsdale 2001). Yet, in one scene he can be seen naked with only a few feathers and loincloth, mimicking the style of local warriors—spear and all.

Always pack light. Take fewer clothing items and a little extra money to buy more as needed. Do not use clothing to identify oneself, other than when special clothing and/or insignias are required. In some instances, we have cut the name brands and tags out of our clothes to make the Western brands and American logos less obvious. Such labels can be red flags to members of some insurgent groups. However, such "sanitizing" has become less necessary in today's globalized world.

To summarize, it is essential to have at least one complete, high-quality generic outback outfit suitable for the local environment; to be sensitive to local cultural customs and styles; to acquire some items on the local market; to "sanitize" one's wardrobe for additional safety; and to pack light. Personnel cannot neglect handkerchiefs, sturdy socks, high-quality undergarments, and clothing that withstands jungle rot or the grit of desert dust. It is worth considering the newer fabrics with SPF ratings as well, to minimize the effects of exposure to the sun. Army/Navy Surplus, U.S. Patriot, U.S. Cavalry, 511 Tactical, and other retail outlets stock high-quality field gear and clothing for professional use; team members who do not have essential gear provided for them by a sponsoring agency should shop two months in advance of deployment and wear and otherwise test all new gear (including unusual types of clothing). In our experience, special sale items should be avoided. The detail and construction of all garments should be checked: every seam, zipper, and button should be inspected, because these are the potential "weak links."

FOOTWEAR   The issue of footwear is extremely important—and very often overlooked. In an era of clogs and flip-flops, the wearing of quality footwear might seem to be dying out. However, there is no item of gear more important than footwear, and, among footware, no item more important than field/workboots. (Sandals, athletic shoes, and house moccasins are useful in their own ways.) Two pairs of high-quality boots are needed: one pair to be worn; one pair to be drying after fumigation and treatment with antifungals. Such rotation, on a 3-, 5-, or 7-day basis, will dramatically increase boot life and improve foot hygiene. Wearing a thin pair of cotton socks inside a thicker pair of socks (reinforced in the toe and heel) can minimize blistering.

The varieties of bacteria, fungus, and mildew that will settle into boots and socks can be amazing to the field newcomer. Even sturdy mountain boots can dissolve and rot under the attack of desert or jungle environments in as little as 3 months' time. Starting with a high-quality, laced, knobbed boot, the upper surface should be covered with ample applications of Sno Seal or a similar sealant. Even a bit of simple Kiwi shoe polish, if generously applied, can dramatically improve the serviceable life of a pair of boots. (To anyone who doubts the value of this critically important piece of gear, we recommend a simple test: put on a pair of flip-flops and run as fast as possible through a thistle patch. Then do the same thing with a pair of boots. Lesson learned.)

A wide range of boot brands are available. A military airborne colleague referred to running, hiking, and going cross-country on foot as the "Corcoran Express," in honor of his Corcoran paratrooper jump boots. At any site, at any time, personnel might be required to move quickly via the "Corcoran Express." Both feet and footwear must be ready.

TRAINING PROTOCOLS

Country team members bound for overseas deployments are strongly encouraged by the DoS to read a DoD publication entitled *Country Handbook: A Field-Ready Reference Publication* (2003). Although tailored specifically for Iraq, the information it contains is widely applicable. Another publication of value is *Guide for Participants in Peace, Stability, and Relief Operations* (Perito 2007). Both illustrate key practices and effective training regimens that experienced personnel have demonstrated in several domains. Indeed, there is an important distinction between education and training, as stressed earlier. Most novice country team personnel (who have not also received military educations) have been educated in their specializations in more or less traditional university settings and in many instances already have participated in some form of overseas research-, study-, internship-, or service-learning-based opportunity (see Chapter 6 for details). An increasing number have participated in the Peace Corps. Among the traditional disciplines well represented among older-generation country team members are anthropology, economics, sociology, political science, agricultural science, law, and civil engineering. These disciplines are also studied by newer-generation personnel, but they increasingly are being complemented by specialized subjects involving human rights, humanitarian assistance, development, intercultural communications, conflict resolution, security, international administration, and nonprofit/NGO management.

This type of education, usually resulting in an M.A. or M.S. degree, ideally should precede the types of training covered in this chapter. It should be complemented by attendance at seminars, the publishing of articles, briefs, or op/ed pieces, and participation in appropriate short courses. Education in this sense is more dependent on review, training in this sense more dependent on practice. A true specialty—saleable to those recruiting for a country team— emerges from the synthesis of university education and field training.

Field training, as we are defining it, consists of three primary kinds of protocol. First is the kind that also is practiced behind a desk, such as the specialized study (and possibly the rewiring) of a communication device. Second is the type that is practiced on site; this also is referred to as "experiential"— training by doing the assignment—and it ideally has repetitive elements built in. Mentors are engaged whenever possible. Navigation training and communications training fit here and are covered below. Third is the kind that enhances one's fitness, details of which were provided earlier. Exercise is the core. Studying topics spanning diet, physiology, and physical therapy can augment this, as personal preference dictates. In our experience this third type, exercise—as simple as it seems—is the most difficult to consistently inculcate in and carry out with country team members.

At a broader and more diversified level, there also is a fourth type: auxiliary training. Supplementing the first three, this can take many forms and cover many subspecializations. "Auxiliary" does not mean "less important"; it is meant to imply that not every team member requires it. Logistics/Supply chain development, outback cooking, escape/evasion, interrogation resistance, countersurveillance, and counterthreat training are good examples. Public speaking for effective presentations, dialectic immersion-language practice, and mass casualty/disaster preparedness exercises also fit here. Tactical and security driving training, and, more recently, weapons safety training, are among those auxiliary trainings we have found to be the most important; they are covered below. Receiving a one-time certificate in a formal training regime like this is a noteworthy achievement, but keeping it current with repetitive exercise and field experience creates a more robust proficiency.

Certainly, decision cycles and processes differ in humanitarian, development, and intervention operations—being more consensus-driven than hierarchical-chain-of-command-driven, for example—but core training regimes usually are similar. Country team members ideally will have common skill sets complemented by individualized, specialty skill sets. Team leaders will call on team members to tap their skills as needed. Once the basic skills have been mastered, and experience has enabled team members to be fine-tuned through several deployments, it is possible for them to consider becoming certified instructors in one or more categories. There is no better way to prove mastery of any skill or art than to be able to teach it well.

None of these four types of training protocol rely extensively on theory, yet all are effectively complemented by the theories, concepts, and operational premises we lay out in Part I and Part III in this text. All contemporary training protocols engage both standard and emergent technologies. Such technologies are a means to an end, to be used judiciously and in respect to local conditions and customs. Country teams need members well trained in the ways technology and culture intersect, not mere "tech jockies." CALL (Center for Army Lessons Learned) is one appropriate resource; documents are available online that cover such issues as the intersection of culturally appropriate training protocols and small-scale field technologies useful in a setting such as Iraq.

Navigation

Improving one's navigation skills often can prove worthwhile. Most people go through life operating on the assumption that they can navigate reasonably well, at least in familiar local environments. Yet virtually everyone gets lost at one time or another, as frequently in an urban as in a rural setting. When an appointment is missed or family members are left stranded, we are reminded of the need for navigation skills. Both of us—veterans in the use of faint trails in remote lands—have been reminded of this on those occasions when an obscure but essential marker was missed and a wrong turn was taken. Navigation is an under-valued skill, and in the field it can be a life-saver. Consequently, scheduling basic navigation courses for all personnel is an important field requirement. All of our University of Denver students who are training for future deployments study navigation. At its best, the training is experiential.

Every member of the team should be trained in compass use. Each should have an old-fashioned pocket compass tucked into the bug-out bag; an orientation compass with good azimuth sights should be tucked into the survival kit. Map interpretation and intelligence is a discipline unto itself, but each team member should be taught (at a minimum) the basics of symbol and contour interpretation, direction setting, and distance/line-of-sight plotting. Linking a mapped landscape feature to an observed landscape feature is a core skill. GPS devices have been improved and are recommended, but not at the expense of the basic interpretive, hands-on skills noted here. A two-hour introductory course in the use of such devices is recommended as a supplement, particularly if taught by a geographer. GPS devices, like all others that depend on batteries, can go dead in a downpour. A simple rule of thumb: for every electronic device in a kit, have available at least one analog, manual back-up method. Electronic maps must be augmented by paper maps and charts for the region in question.

Many manufacturers of navigation devices offer owner training courses. Outdoor/Sports equipment retailers such as REI also offer courses. Orienteering is a popular (and healthy) outdoor sport that uses the most important overland navigation skills. A weekend spent with a local club, predeployment, can help team members develop life-saving skills. SAR (search-and-rescue) training can be valuable. In some overseas preparation programs, navigation skills are combined with escape/evasion and survival training as an integrated course. Participating in a professionally run program such as this, together as a team, has the added benefit of creating team spirit, improved morale, and a more unified sense of purpose. Mission focus and shared hardship during a rigorous training program are key elements of all special operations groups, as well as of many country teams.

Communications

The subtleties of communications practices and equipment usage, much like navigation, are sometimes overlooked when preparing personnel for overseas deployment. Radio protocols, wireless communications use, and basic device maintenance are taken for granted. Technical details are covered in Chapter 5; however, here we note courses of instruction. A formal course of instruction on mission-specific communications, such as intra- and interteam contact, medevac protocols, emergency extraction, air and sea deliveries, and convoy communications, is a nuts-and-bolts element of predeployment training. In preparing communications equipment, a specialist with adequate on-site knowledge of the local and regional networks—the communications operating environment—should be consulted. A combination of landline telephone, wireless/cellular telephone, and radio and satellite communications (as available in the AO) will provide adequate redundancy. If one system fails, another can be brought online.

For short-range line-of-sight communication, the seemingly lost skills of mirror and flag signaling still have a place. Even Morse Code, used through the second half of the nineteenth and first half of the twentieth centuries, can have a place in an emergency at a remote facility. The classic "SOS" emergency distress signal can be traced to the electrical "dots" and "dashes" code operators tapped on their telegraphy pads. (Peter Van Arsdale learned the basics of Samuel Morse's code from his great uncle, who had served as the code operator for the Colorado Fuel and Iron Corporation during the 1920s and 1930s.) At the most basic level, a signal as simple as an arrow composed of rocks and branches, trampled brush, or smoke from a fire can help lead rescue personnel to one's location. Participation in Boy Scouts or Girl Scouts as a youngster has contributed to this type of skill development for many of our colleagues.

At its best, communications training also is experiential. A series of well-established protocols exist. The appendix features a number of useful pointers.

Tactical and Security Driving

The topic of tactical and security driving deserves special consideration. Many people in the United States have taken defensive driving courses or informally practiced all-weather, all-terrain vehicle driving skills on their own. Although these can be enjoyable skills to learn to do well, they are important in their own right. These skills are directly transferable for those deployed in nonpermissive or semipermissive operating environments. The best way to practice emergency driving skills is on a closed, professional course with certified instructors. Almost every state has a driving school offering tactical, pursuit, and personal-security driving courses. With teams always being reliant on ground transportation, even in hostile areas, it is worth the time and money for one member to acquire training certification through a qualified program.

In one "crash and bang" course that Derrin Smith took before a remote deployment, trainees encountered and responded to a wide variety of ambush, chase, and checkpoint scenarios under the watchful eyes of professionals. One tactic required each trainee to smash through another car at an "illegal road-block checkpoint," using a particular technique to most surprise the "checkpoint bandits" and provide the best avenue of escape. Other tactics were much more benign but equally useful. Close-to-real-life simulations are used in most of the best tactical driving schools. The practice is repetitive. With luck, personnel will never need to apply these skills in the field. Furthermore, with enough dedicated training, a team member might reach the pinnacle of tactical driving: the ability to handle traffic in Italy and survive to tell the tale.

Weapons Safety

Just as vehicle skills once reserved for certified drivers and escorts are now being acquired by other members of country teams, there is an even newer appreciation for weapons safety training—and not just skilled marksmen and infantrymen need this. The emphasis now is on safety—not target practice, military assault practice, or other traditional field weapons skills; not only action, but reaction. Issues associated with "friendly fire" or simple tragic accidents in Iraq and Afghanistan have, in part, driven this change. (U.S. Army Ranger Pat Tillman's death in 2004 in Afghanistan under originally opaque but later sadly transparent circumstances produced newspaper headlines for several months.) Further, even in relatively peaceful regions where a country team might be providing humanitarian services, the team may encounter child soldiers, lightly trained local militia, poorly trained police agents, or other NSAs carrying a variety of combat arms. These groups are but another aspect of the "new wars" discussed in Chapter 2.

Understanding how a weapon works is the starting point. Beyond this, a team member's ability to take possession of a weapon and render it safe and possibly even inoperable is yet another practical field skill that can be acquired only through hands-on training. Practice should be attempted only at a professional range, with certified instructors, preferably with experience in handling a wide variety of common military and civilian weapons. Even in the relatively peaceful, diplomatic culture of the Department of State, such weapon familiarization ("famfire") programs are made available to personnel before overseas deployment. In certain settings the Regional Security Officer (RSO) at an embassy maintains a firing range for security personnel and will offer safety and familiarization courses to others. Professional shops and associations also have safety and familiarization courses. Since team members commonly encounter AK-47 assault rifles and other sophisticated weaponry in remote overseas sites, a certified professional safety and "famfire" program is the best way to prepare for this aspect of field operations.

Self-Doctoring Kits and Medical Training

Nonmedically supervised emergency trauma care, backcountry first aid, and SAR assistance are not adequate or recommended replacements for the services of professionally trained medical personnel. However, immediate intervention (for minor wounds and sprains to more serious illnesses) can be necessary; while awaiting the medical staff or the evacuation of the injured team member, the application of basic skill may be required. Basic antibiotics, antiseptics, wound bandages, and sutures—and the knowledge of how to use them—are vital to the safety and well-being of any backcountry operation; they constitute a "self-doctoring kit."

We recommend the short courses offered by the American Red Cross. Those students who participated in the Romanian operation detailed in Chapter 6 were required to take three, covering various aspects of emergency first aid (see Figure 4.4). One of the instructors had extensive overseas and military experience. He was able to cross-reference specific incidents as part of his instructional regimen.

Immediately on arrival on site, identify those members of other teams working in the vicinity that have professional medical training and, equally important, identify local professionals with similar expertise. There are remarkably large numbers of qualified doctors and nurses in such places as Iraq and

FIGURE 4.4   Building on training offered by the Mile High Chapter of the American Red Cross, students learn about first aid in simulated conflictive environments (photo by Derrin Smith).

Bosnia, although few in such places as Sudan and Ethiopia. Once located, they should be contacted and provided details about one's operation. The abilities and humanitarian dedication of such people should never be underestimated. (After a severe accident in the field in 1997, Peter Van Arsdale was assisted mightily by such local personnel.)

In most foreign countries, access to many medicines is less restrictive than in the United States. Although precautions must be taken, since some inferior medications may have been dumped on local markets, a reasonable supply of local high-quality drugs and pharmaceuticals can be created. A good supply of oral antibiotics, in particular, can prevent minor ear/nose/tooth/throat/wound infections from becoming life-threatening conditions. Good antiseptic practices—applied immediately on a tear in the skin—will ward off the so-called "Snows of Kilimanjaro" rapid infection/burn syndrome.

In both Afghanistan and Iraq, Derrin Smith's overland convoys had clearly identified "Combat Life Saver" emergency medical personnel accompanying them at all times. Most were simply soldiers and civilians who had completed a rigorous emergency medical training (EMT) curriculum, which gave them more robust emergency medical skills than were normally available outside the canvas confines of a mobile army surgical hospital or field clinic. Since most soldiers and civilians wounded in an IED attack or small-arms ambush have a high likelihood of survival once they reach a military medical care center, the DoD and DoS have come to concentrate greater medical resources in making certain that adequately trained medical personnel accompany the convoys. Basic care and stabilization of injured personnel, immediately rendered, dramatically improves survival rates. Humanitarian, relief, and reconstruction organizations similarly can benefit by positioning robust interim-medical-care capabilities with each remote team. Doctors Without Borders offers valuable protocols that can be studied. The combination of redundant communications, close-in emergency medical care, and a more aware staff that is treating even minor injuries early can improve performance, morale, and accident/death data for country team operators.

LEGAL CHECKLISTS

Birth certificates; marriage certificates; high school and university diplomas; tax records; automobile, life, health, and home insurance records; and investment records constitute the basic non-employment-related portfolio of the well-organized American citizen. A checklist of these key materials must be created. The checklist, along with the materials themselves, obviously must be maintained in a safe place while a country team member is deployed overseas.

The *Personal Affairs Record Book*, published by the Council for Court Excellence through its Probate Council for Court Excellence, is a useful resource. This is a workbook that systematically guides the reader as information is assembled in five checklist-friendly categories: (1) personal and family information; (2) employment; (3) assets; (4) liabilities; (5) other information. Data can conveniently be updated annually. Whether using this book or another of the guides available online, access to the information should be made available to a trusted family member, lawyer, and tax accountant. Such records protect not only the country team member but also his or her family. In this sense they should be viewed as reciprocal, not unilineal, documents. Attention also must be given to unusual events such as divorce, bankruptcy, or the death of a close family member. The book itself becomes an asset; its very existence offers peace of mind to its owner while on assignment.

Special attention must be given to the issue of a viable, up-to-date will. We are aware of several persons who had been assigned overseas who had not taken this critically important document into account, died intestate, and left bereaved family members to wrestle with a number of hard financial and family decisions. No one likes to confront his or her own mortality, and perhaps that is why "death planning" is among the least popular courses for members preparing for overseas deployment. Yet several kinds of short course and seminar are offered and are well worth considering for those without a will. At the same time, it is wise to select a respected person who can be vested with limited Power of Attorney. Last wishes also should be discussed with loved ones, including issues surrounding organ donation.

CHAPTER 5

TRANSIT OPERATIONS, COMMUNICATIONS, AND SMART TECHNOLOGIES

TRANSIT OPERATIONS: ALWAYS NECESSARY, OFTEN CONTROVERSIAL

Transit operations are at the heart of expeditionary diplomacy, aid and reconstruction projects, and most humanitarian initiatives. The majority of personnel injured, victimized, or killed while participating in country team operations overseas suffer their fates while underway. The casualty events range from random crimes of opportunity by bandits to well-orchestrated attacks by insurgent and terrorist groups. Whereas in past years an emblem from an aid or humanitarian relief organization was a shield that could help protect personnel, that shield has since become a target. Kidnappings for ransom, grisly attacks for shock and media value, revenge killings of aid personnel as a political statement or to avenge some perceived wrong by the host nation have become so common as to rarely be reported by the international media. The majority of such targeted crimes, from robberies to rapes to torture and homicide, go unpunished. In many cases, arrests that are made are either politically motivated or done for public show. Successful prosecution or imprisonment is a rare outcome.

This chapter, primarily featuring the type of country team that supports military outreach in conflictive areas such as Iraq and works in embedded fashion, examines transit operations by land (with only brief references to those by air and sea), threat environments and associated assessments, and requisite communications support capabilities. Technological innovations are highlighted. "Best practices" are noted.

Convoys

Of primary importance are land convoy operations, since every overseas endeavor "at the civilian—military interface" includes some land transit capability. This also is statistically where the majority of the casualties occur (Welch 2009: 14). Although aircraft or ship fatalities tend to be more dramatic, land movement involves a disproportionate share of risk and casualties owing to ease of interdiction by hostile forces and, sometimes, a lack of care in planning and execution due to an overconfident familiarity. Moving through remote territory, even in peace time, can leave a team vulnerable to the whims of the local populace. Crimes of opportunity are common. Transiting remote territory that also is experiencing hostilities dramatically multiplies the risk factor. No preventive measures are completely fail-safe, but to fail to plan is to be vulnerable to the worst possible scenarios.

The civilian population also is at risk. Iraq is a case at point. It is incumbent on the country team member to engage in transit practices that are tuned to the local threat environment while also being tuned to the intersection of ethical "rules of engagement" and military "rules of engagement."

No mission is so important that its route cannot be adjusted or its vehicles turned back, or so imperative that innocent lives are needlessly endangered. In an important book entitled *Collateral Damage: America's War against Iraqi Civilians* (2008), Chris Hedges and Laila al-Arian decry the ways in which many innocent civilians have been caught up, and caught in, the turmoil in the Middle East. In the chapter entitled "Convoys," these authors detail what can go wrong. Rules of engagement can be misconstrued by soldiers, to civilians' detriment. Although some specific rules are classified, there are no general uniform rules for convoy operations in Iraq. Specific locales and circumstances allow specific commanders to fine-tune and modify operations as they see fit. This often works to the benefit of civilians, but at times does not. Innocent bystanders get fired on, trapped, and sometimes killed. The pre-emptive firing of warning shots, to thwart attacks, can help clear an area; this procedure also can backfire. Some civilians on foot have been run over as a convoy passes on a roadway (2008: 18–19). Michael Massing states: "When a U.S. convoy runs over a car, it usually just keeps going" (2007: 82). As indicated in Chapter 3 herein, innocent lives were lost in the tragedy associated with Blackwater's Raven 23 convoy in September of 2007. Tragic accidents can lead to compensation ("condolences payments") for the victims' families by the U.S. military, but not in all instances and at times in very small amounts (Von Zielbauer 2007).

At times employing hyperbole and exaggerated theatrics, several veterans of Iraqi operations have published books covering their exploits. Not surprisingly the excitement, frustration, fear, and machismo accompanying convoy operations have been featured, as John Geddes' account (2008) exemplifies. As a self-described "mercenary soldier" and former British SAS warrant officer, he describes his time in Iraq protecting and ferrying engineers, financiers, diplomats, and media representatives on "the highway to hell." He reports that the "tariff" on the highway includes IEDs (improvised explosive devices), suicide bombers, rocket attacks, and machine gun fire. It is also counted in bodies representing both sides. He claims to have killed Iraqi militants during the course of his duties guarding members of the press while in transit. Whether or not exaggerated, such accounts provide food for thought.

Convoys are the "arteries," as Hedges and al-Arian state (2008: 9). Their protection is complicated, especially when vehicle maintenance becomes an issue. Rules of engagement also are complicated. Once a convoy is attacked by insurgents, a degree of chaos is interjected into even the best-run operation. Heightened tensions in turn can lead to misunderstandings on both sides, especially at checkpoints. Country team members engaged in this type of support activity ideally should be among the best trained and most experienced in the AO.

Land Transit Operations

Figure 5.1 helps to illustrate how easily security measures can be ignored when the unexpected strikes. In this case, the point vehicle suffered an overheated engine, and the entire convoy limped to a standstill on the dirt shoulder of a divided highway in Iraq. Correct procedure would have been to remain on the paved portion, which is much more difficult to mine effectively. This scenario is familiar to almost every humanitarian assistant, relief worker, and country team member with extensive experience in backcountry road travel.

FIGURE 5.1   Crippled convoy in Iraq (photo by Derrin Smith).

Whether because of an engine over-taxed by heat, poor maintenance, or burdened with too heavy a load or too many years of hard service, vehicle failure is a virtual guarantee in the course of any sustained operation. Antivehicle and antipersonnel mines remain long-term residual and recurring hazards along all regular convoy routes in conflictive and postconflictive areas. The threat from mines in Bosnia and Ethiopia, where Peter Van Arsdale worked during the 1990s, and in Iraq and Afghanistan, where Derrin Smith worked in the 2000s, has been a major issue. For example, some 48,000 mines of all models and descriptions, manufactured in numerous countries, were recently secured from the facilities near Diwaniyah, Iraq, alone. The discoveries (both actively deployed and in armory inventories in munitions bunkers) were made when U.S. and coalition troops were preparing the site as a major military staging area in Multi-National Division Central South. Insurgent forces and terrorist groups have had significant access to mines and the matériel to build IEDs in recent years. Overall, mines remain a real threat from Southeast Asia through the Middle East and across Central America. They are found in much of Africa and residually in the Balkans. As recently as August, 2009, UNIFIL estimated that up to one million land mines and elements of UXO continue to litter agricultural fields and public areas in south Lebanon, a constant reminder of the 2006 war discussed in Chapter 2. Specially trained country teams have the opportunity to tackle this problem in these locales.

Analysis of the same stalled convoy reveals other problems. Figure 5.1 shows that there is no security on top of the point vehicle. An abandoned helmet rests on the roof beside the heavy weapon. No one with binoculars or a spotting scope is scanning traffic patterns or the horizon, or assessing immediate threats to the stopped vehicles. This was a large convoy, but no Point Security is on the roadway to look for possible attackers. A group of civilians and military personnel can be seen talking in the roadway, near a large cargo truck that also was transporting munitions boxes and several guards. An IED or well-placed rocket-propelled grenade (RPG) igniting the munitions would therefore generate maximum human casualties. It turned out that the driver and two escort personnel in the point vehicle discovered that they had no additional bottles of coolant to replenish the boiled-over radiator. While the driver sat in the shaded seat, the others wandered down the stalled convoy line, in search of coolant and a screwdriver to repair the damaged radiator hose and restart the convoy. In the interim the entire convoy was exposed, vulnerable, and only partially guarded, while some personnel did not even bother to put on their helmets. After over an hour of delays, the point vehicle was rendered functional, and the convoy again moved toward a secure destination. Breakdowns occur during transit, unexpected stops happen, nothing goes precisely according to plan. It is imperative in transit operations to maintain a strict protocol to address these and other unanticipated problems. Maintaining ready-repair route kits in every convoy vehicle is a key best practice. Fortunately for this convoy, the insurgents were asleep at the switch and missed a golden opportunity to fire on a sitting duck.

In 2008 during a Marine convoy to pick up the Anbar Province's governor for transport to an operating base for meetings, a military Hummer simply died on the main boulevard in a decidedly Red Zone. While the governor and Derrin Smith waited, and the driver rotated through his immediate action protocol to restart the engine, two escort vehicles established a hasty perimeter. The governor, a high-value target for insurgents and terrorists at that time, shuffled through his papers and made a few jokes at the expense of the U.S. military. (The escorts were not amused.) A second Hummer attached a tow bar and towed the first Hummer to a known side street where the military security team perceived there was better cover and concealment while others dealt with the problem. The team's communications specialist had immediately alerted the tactical operations center (TOC) to the predicament—stranded in a Red Zone with a VIP and country team members aboard—and the forward operating base therefore promptly dispatched another team, with a MRAP multiple-passenger armored vehicle and two more Hummers, to assist. Suddenly, the engine turned over and the convoy quickly resumed transit, back out to the boulevard. However, within about two blocks, the engine again died. The communications specialist again notified the TOC, a security perimeter was set up, and the driver resumed his checklist to deal with engine failure. No luck in restarting this time, so the convoy commander quickly escorted Smith and the others to another functioning vehicle, poised for a hasty exit in event of hostilities. Nearly 40 minutes had passed. Not only was the team in danger of missing its meetings at the FOB, more than enough time had passed for nearby enemy fighters to begin to respond to the convoy's predicament. When the convoy commander confirmed that the support MRAP and Hummer were approaching, the driver swung the operational Hummer around and seamlessly slipped into the line of vehicles as they motored past. Marines promptly reconnected the tow bar to the failed vehicle and also swung into line, to follow the dust of the convoy.

Although the vehicle failure left the convoy exposed and vulnerable, the rapid and professional response of the Marine Corps escorts mitigated the danger. They kept a flexible security corridor, maintained constant communications with the TOC, secured help from the FOB, and quickly got all concerned out of harm's way. In spite of this, the convoy commander was not satisfied. "Number one," he explained to Smith later, "that vehicle never should have failed. Number two, we should have had you and the governor cleared from that site within minutes. It was totally 'unsat.'" The term stands for "unsatisfactory" and is, in fact, among the most graphic words used to describe a negative operation or situation, short of an expletive. The convoy commander then took corrective action—from his supply and logistics procedures to his team's immediate response plan—and for the remainder of Smith's time in Anbar, the team had a 100 percent mission success rate.

Surveillance, as illustrated in Figure 5.2, is a key to protecting convoy assets. Early warning of suspicious activity or impending assault dramatically improves survivability of personnel and assets. Surveillance is such a vital element of transit operations that it should begin well before the first vehicle hits the road; it should be conducted along convoy routes on a continuous basis; it should continue after vehicles have been secured in the destination compound. In the current context of transiting hostile territories, complementary technology permitting near-real-time imagery of convoy operations (as broadcast to remote monitors) can make the difference between success and failure.

In many cases, land transit operations have a scheduled program of stops, either to deliver cargo or accomplish tasks at particular points along a route or, on longer convoys, to provide comfort breaks for passengers. The

FIGURE 5.2   Remaining vigilant. Constant surveillance and reporting dramatically improves convoy safety and success (photo by Derrin Smith).

final approach to a programmed stop can be hazardous, especially if a routine has been established or the mission was unknowingly compromised in advance. During a DoS convoy on a Middle Eastern peace mission, personnel were lost midway during a visit in the Gaza Strip to deliver Fulbright scholarships to Palestinian award winners. Doctors Without Borders lost personnel on a remote roadway in Afghanistan. Southern Baptists working on a charity program were kidnapped from their vehicles and killed north of Baghdad. As previously noted, in the post-9/11 era a UN humanitarian aid worker who is employed in overseas food distribution or water sanitation work has a greater statistical likelihood of dying in the line of duty than a New York City police officer. Transit operations are inherently dangerous. Making mistakes in the execution of these missions can result in irreversible losses.

An act as casual as parking incorrectly at a scheduled stop can lead to disaster. As illustrated in Figure 5.3, military vehicles are parked at a curbside in a small Iraqi village, in front of a school where engineering inspections are being conducted by military personnel. As a general proposition, as

FIGURE 5.3   Convoy parallel parked at school in Iraq (photo by Derrin Smith).

noted earlier, military convoys are conducted in accordance with well-defined protocols. Detailed checklists—including parking requirements—leave little to chance. Once out of the Green Zone, however, even a minor oversight can leave convoys and personnel vulnerable. In an otherwise well-conducted mission, the five vehicles involved (three being visible in the photograph) were parallel parked on the dirt road in front of the school. The nose-to-tail parking would prevent a rapid egress or redeployment of the vehicles in the event that hostilities broke out. A jam could occur. Instead, all of the vehicles should have been parked diagonally facing away from the curb toward a traffic lane or "escape path" that is unobstructed. A nose-out escape mode is a best practice. The driver should be able to start the engine, slam it into gear, and accelerate rapidly onto the road in event of attack. On the plus side in this instance, all personnel are appropriately wearing body armor and protective head gear, security personnel are alert, and vehicles and cargoes are guarded. Civilian activity on the pedestrian walkway is being closely observed by the gunner on top of the HumVee. Traffic activity and the buildings across the thoroughfare also are being watched by well-armed security personnel.

A standard route security practice for convoys includes having an unmarked scout or reconnaissance vehicle (such as the small white truck in Figure 5.3) run several hundred meters ahead of the convoy, checking the route for hazards, congestion, and other problems. The scout vehicle is in radio communications with the convoy commander, reporting on any hazards encountered and potential threat conditions. In the event that a problem is spotted, the scout vehicle can report and the convoy can take appropriate evasive action, including moving to alternate routes or (at the extreme) abandoning the mission. At no time should the unmarked scout vehicle and on-board reconnaissance personnel be associated with the rest of the convoy, as was mistakenly done (while parallel parked) in the preceding case. This compromises route surveillance and can place reconnaissance personnel at greater risk, since they generally operate with minimal security and at some distance from additional protection resources.

However, during a number of missions "outside the wire" with Derrin Smith embedded, this particular convoy team consistently maintained good security and movement best practices. What are the elements, then, that characterize a successful land transit operation? Primarily, it is the delivery of personnel, goods, and services in accomplishment of the mission at hand. Getting the vehicles, the cargo, and the personnel safely from Point A to Point B is key. Secondarily, it is demonstrating a "peaceful presence" to the local populace and indicating that, despite hostilities, a region is secure enough to permit some business-as-usual activities by country team personnel, as well as the indigenous residents. (One of the most important indicators of this in Iraq is the ability to keep the neighborhood bakery operating, as Tavernise stresses [2006b].) In the best of circumstances, transit operations also can be used to improve relations between the local population and country team members. On a 2005 convoy from Camp Echo in Diwaniyah, Iraq, north to Victory Base South near Baghdad, the team took care to wave and exchange greetings in Arabic with pedestrians; left water, hygiene products, and foodstuffs for the local inhabitants at each stop; and sought to minimize disruption to local traffic patterns. One ambitious sergeant made it a point to toss candy treats, water bottles, and prepackaged foods to clusters of people near intersections or other choke points when the convoy was moving slowly enough. Although analysts might debate the wisdom of throwing articles at pedestrians from moving vehicles, might suggest that such actions reduce security by encouraging citizens to approach convoys for hand-outs, and might criticize a seemingly blatant "win 'em with gifts" approach, one thing was clear on that particular day. The smiles on the faces were genuine and the gifts were welcomed by the men, women, and children who had been struggling. For this sergeant, the controversial slogan "winning hearts and minds" was perceived as genuinely meaningful. No wonder other convoy members called him Santa Claus.

Land transit operations therefore are as necessary as they are dangerous; they represent an unavoidable logistics necessity for relief, reconstruction, and humanitarian operations in any region where country teams operate. Those conducted by air and sea can involve similar risks and rewards but are not dealt with extensively here. NSAs (ranging from NGOs to insurgents) increasingly influence the ways these operations play out. What are some of the other elements that help ensure safe, secure, and successful convoys?

PLANNING FOR THREATS: OBVIOUSLY NEEDED, OCCASIONALLY IGNORED

Few things get country team members in greater trouble, more frequently, than rushing to satisfy new mission demands. Regularly, for those working at the civilian-military interface, orders come down the military chain of command that mandate immediate action. At these times, it is valuable to take a few extra moments to make certain that nothing is overlooked in the planning phase of the transit operation. If a mission is urgent enough to require "expedite" or "rush" attention, then it is also important enough to warrant an additional review of the mission plan. This also will help assure that innocent civilians are not placed in danger.

Preplanning, that is, maintaining a constant state of mission readiness for convoys, helps to minimize the delay between receipt of orders and execution of the mission. Checklists are vital to avoid oversights in preparation and deployment, helping to overcome those momentary memory lapses that occur under stressful field conditions. Our field experiences lead us to recommend that each organization establish its own set of convoy operations, in concert with mission guidelines, with specific checklists that not only are tailored to the regional AO but that also can be adjusted to ever-changing daily threat conditions. Our students at the University of Denver are tasked with developing such checklists as they prepare for simulated relief missions, an exercise that has proven exceptionally useful for them.

Certain threat, risk, and vulnerability issues are often encountered by transit and land convoy teams. As noted in Chapter 3, the terms *risk* and *vulnerability* are related. We believe that the former is best conceptualized "in the environment," the latter "in a cohort" of people. A threat involves force or intrusion, purposefully intended or unintended, with the possibility of damage, injury, or death. There is a perception of danger. A threat can be "lodged" behaviorally in the simplest and most benign setting. Crossing the street to the coffee shop, riding an elevator, driving the kids to school—even these seemingly mundane day-to-day activities are imbued with a potential threat element, which often can be quantified. Knowingly or unknowingly, we react to our local threat environment daily, taking preventive and corrective measures even in common circumstances. One can act on vulnerability; it can be evaluated, measured, and sometimes reduced. (In a fundamental risk equation, the threat environment multiplied by the vulnerability component provides the risk evaluation: $T \times V \sim R$.) Risk management disciples, such as insurance actuaries, are adept at detailed quantifications and policy premium projections; "coverage" and "liability" are two of their bywords.

For the purposes of country team operations, however, one can look at the risk environment and vulnerability of personnel, mission by mission, in order to establish or reaffirm best practices while minimizing the likelihood of casualties during project activities. Such assessments are often more qualitative than quantitative. The threat environment is frequently dynamic and can vary wildly in a matter of hours or minutes. A peaceful demonstration outside an embassy can suddenly become chaotic as mob-think and instigators of violence take over, quickly influencing a crowd. Even in relatively tranquil overseas posts, such as Mexico City, the situation can become dangerous on short notice. The visit of President George W. Bush to Mérida in March of 2007 prompted activists to engage in a peaceful protest march in Mexico City, down the Paseo de la Reforma. The official marchers remained focused on speeches and a left-wing pro-Communist protest message. However, instigators assaulted the police barricades, and after a couple hours of rock and Molotov-cocktail throwing, the previously patient police responded with tear gas, pepper spray, and arrests when the defensive barriers were breached by youth armed with basic street weapons (Figure 5.4).

No country team operation (including those with no military connections) is conducted in a vacuum or an all-protective safe haven. There is always risk, whether delivering schoolbooks to children (as Derrin Smith in Iraq) or assisting with IDP camp evaluations (as Peter Van Arsdale in Timor-Leste). Risk must be acknowledged and evaluated rapidly. A threat assessment can be constructed using a checklist *cum* protocol on a single sheet of paper; it

FIGURE 5.4   Instigators breach protective barriers at the U.S. Embassy in Mexico City, March 2007, in protest of U.S. presidential visit (photo by Mihaela Biliovschi Smith, reproduced with permission).

does not have to be lengthy and complex. Risks are listed in the left column, vulnerabilities in the central column, tactics/mitigations in the right column. A summary statement then can be derived, covering one's exposure that day to the most dangerous factors within the operational environment. More broadly, with the help of other team members, an array of threats can be prioritized. Resources are allocated accordingly, to maximize security. Such an approach is integral to proper planning.

During the Mexico City incident, Derrin Smith and his colleague (a research journalist/photographer) witnessed how a threat unfolds into a hazard. The potential became the actual. Lives were at risk. (Interestingly, organizers of the peace protest and speeches went to great lengths to distance themselves from the violence, even going so far as to relocate their sound system, small stage, and rally area down the block, away from the embassy.) When the security barriers protecting the embassy finally were breached under the sustained assault, the resultant violence was in full view of the press cameras. The extent to which this breach occurred expressly because of the media attention—or because the instigators were hired—could not be judged. Yet another lesson regarding the planning process, especially where potential threats to civilians are concerned, is that a media presence is likely to help shape an event's outcome. Long ago, John Prendergast reminded humanitarians that press coverage of tragedy and travail can be a big, and influential, business (1996: 4–6).

Particularly for those engaged in transit operations, updated threat analyses are essential. Threat tends to be greater when teams and matériel are in motion than when they are stationary. Although most country team movement occurs over land, transits involving aircraft and ships can be more difficult to plan. (This was confirmed for our University of Denver students engaged in Romanian-based training operations in 2004.) The threat environment has become increasingly fast-changing in large part because NSAs (both those who are friendly and those who are not) have become increasingly adept at changing their tactics. A rule of thumb is that, whether the country team is working in a modern Western society or a remote Eastern territory, "potential violence is only a stone's throw away."

Ubiquitous Threats

There are many different kinds of threat that should be addressed by the wary country team operations professional. Some are environmental in the most literal sense of the word. Is the team operating in an earthquake zone? Are wild fires a seasonal problem in the region? Might flash floods or seasonal flooding be encountered? Are hurricanes, tornadoes, or other kinds of violent weather (including lightning strikes) an issue? Volcanic eruptions, mud slides, dust storms, white-out blizzards, marauding animals, rampant rivers, or devastating droughts might characterize the territory during any given season. The compilation of a clear, detailed documentary history of such threats is a good first step in getting a handle on best practices for a country team's AO. Similarly, sanitation and hygiene issues, toxic ground water, and diseases such as HIV/AIDS, cholera, malaria, typhoid, smallpox, dengue fever, and certain rare debilitating ailments such as Asian bird flu and hanta virus can characterize the local threat environment. The more a team works and moves with the local populace outside the Green Zone, the greater the likelihood of encountering infection and disease. Convoy operations and rural outreach programs usually result in up-close and personal exchanges in the AO, with the potential for a single carrier to infect an entire team. Prophylactic protections and countermeasures for the environment must be part of the preplanning and planning processes. A detailed empirical picture of the threat environment leads to planning, which leads to protection. (A brief threat assessment guide is provided in the appendix. It is intended to be only illustrative. Every region has unusual considerations; every operation will face a distinctive mix of threats. An off-the-shelf, pre-existing checklist will not cover all eventualities.)

Transit planning benefits greatly from the type of demographic, social, economic, and cultural data that applied anthropologists and economists are adept at collecting. Understanding literacy rates, poverty levels, economic dependencies, religious messages, local infrastructure, levels of government control, and politically disenfranchised segments of the society can help country team operators better document and predict likely threats. Operational security (OPSEC) is necessarily dependent on thoroughly understanding local crime patterns, insurgent activities, and the availability and types of weaponry in the local market. Common banditry or focused terrorist activity are both capable of disrupting convoy operations or killing team members.

Countermeasures and protective plans should be designed to focus on the securing of needed resources and their tactical applications. Operators must understand which threat is the most active and urgent in the theater. An angry mob with machetes represents one level of local threat, but the same mob armed with RPGs, assault rifles or even surface-to-air missiles, such as man-portable air defense devices (MANPADs), represent a very different threat and mandate different countermeasures.

Convoys are especially vulnerable to IEDs, as previously noted. These run the gamut from low technology, cobbled-together weapons of opportunity to sophisticated conical-focus armor-piercing high explosives capable of destroying the most heavily armored tanks and vehicles available in modern military inventories. Some types of IED require a local spotter to manually detonate the device as the targeted vehicles enter the kill zone. The weapons used to attack the DoS personnel delivering the Fulbright scholarships, noted earlier, were this type of local-line-of-sight, wireline-detonated device. Remotely triggered devices using cellphones, radio-controlled triggers, or timers are also commonly deployed against convoy targets, for several years in Iraq and more recently in Afghanistan. Suicide bombers also have invaded convoy operations, with vehicle-borne improvised explosive devices (VBIEDs) being used frequently. VBIEDs are even being used with devastating effect against fixed sites and reinforced Green Zone facilities. One popular tactic is to drive the VBIED down a thoroughfare, searching for targets of opportunity. When an oncoming convoy comes into view, the VBIED suicide-driver veers across the roadway into the highest value vehicle target, perhaps a tanker-truck loaded with flammable fuel, to maximize collateral damage. Troop carriers and large buses also have been targeted. To counter this latter possibility, country team leaders should spread several large buses throughout a convoy, curtains drawn or windows blacked out, with most traveling empty and only one surreptitiously carrying the bulk of the personnel. Spreading out targets and providing dummy targets during convoy operations is one way to counter and confuse the VBIED attacker. Low-value targets must be interspersed with high-value targets. Paradoxically, providing a single well-armored and well-guarded vehicle for the entire country team, as was done by USAID for Peter Van Arsdale and his colleagues during the height of the El Salvadoran civil war, can actually be counterproductive; the targeting risk is increased.

Hardening vehicles is another example of a countermeasure against armed attackers. There are different levels of hardening against attack, with benefits and drawbacks to each. In the case of expedient hardening, which may be effected rapidly, simply lining a troop-carrier truck bed and walls with sandbags offers additional protection against blast and small-arms fire. Surplus body armor (which in our experience is rarely available) can be set against doors and windows to increase protection of passengers. Lining the floors of a passenger bus with sandbags, placing passengers only in aisle seats away from windows, and reinforcing walls and windows with sandbags or Kevlar inserts similarly increases the safety of passengers. According to the concepts of threat and vulnerability, in this passenger-bus example the threat has not changed—there are still the same number of VBIED bombers or armed bandits cruising the convoy routes. However, the vulnerability has been reduced by expedient protective measures—sand bags and Kevlar inserts have made the passengers less vulnerable in the event of an assault. The total risk, therefore, also has been reduced in favor of the country team members. Operations personnel and passengers are always to be considered as the number-one cargo to be protected during convoy operations. Goods and matériel are replaceable. Human lives are not.

In addition to expedient hardening, which is recommended in any dangerous field environment to tailor convoy vehicles to the local and immediate threat elements, there are professionally designed and installed protective devices. Personnel working under General Stanley McChrystal, appointed in 2009 as the new U.S. commander in Afghanistan, have lobbied for improvements in this area.

COMMUNICATIONS

Fast Information and Security Assistance

In the previous section, we discussed at length land transit operations, which utilize pathways known generically as "lines of communication" (whether they be roadways, waterways, or air flight corridors). This and the following sections cover communications in the more literal sense: standard radio, satellite, cellphone, landline analog telephone, digital transmission, microwave transmission. There are nearly as many ways to collect information remotely, communicate over considerable distances, and call for help or survey a changing situation as there are ways of getting into trouble. And this is a good thing.

Trouble is going to find you, sooner or later. As history demonstrates, differences in interpretation and intent regarding communications can create problems. In the mid-seventeenth century, as Oliver Cromwell strove to strengthen the British at the expense of the Dutch, segments of fleets representing both nations encountered each other in the Straits of Dover. A storm was brewing, and the winds were increasing. Each side was confused about the other's intent; the system of communicating by means of flags and sail position had yet to be fully developed. Under the so-called Navigation Act of 1651, enacted by the British Parliament, protectionism was the watchword. Only British ships were to be allowed to deliver goods to British ports in the channel. A subclause stated that foreign vessels sailing in the area had to lower their flags in salute. Dutch authorities had determined that their commanders would do no such thing. As eloquently described by Russell Shorto (2004: 247–248), two legendary naval figures—Robert Blake for the British and Maarten Tromp for the Dutch—were at the helms of the lead vessels. A tremendous battle ensued, sparked by Tromp's failure to lower his flags in salute. Forty-two Dutch and twelve larger British ships fired on one another over a five-hour period; some of the assault occurred at point-blank range. Shortly thereafter, in July of 1652, the Dutch Republic declared war on England.

Events indeed unfold unexpectedly. Looking at the track record of remote-post and embassy evacuations in recent years, one can only with difficulty predict which overseas assignment is going to put a team in harm's way. It may be "a remote," such as Juba, Sudan, where the United States recently opened a DoS consular presence, or a well-known site, such as Mexico City, where anti-establishment demonstrations during a 2007 visit between President Bush and President Calderon of Mexico brought a wide variety of protestors into the streets, as discussed earlier: antiwar, antigovernment (including

New Age anarchists), antipolice (possibly including professional instigators), pro-union, antichurch, pro-Communist, pro-Fascist, and anticapitalist (while the vendors worked the crowd with an unbridled passion for capitalism). But, barricades were breached, tear gas was fired, several combatants were hospitalized, and spectators were mugged—all in line-of-sight of tourists and locals dining at the hip-spots of Zona Rosa. Derrin Smith and his colleague were in the middle of eating an Argentinean steak (having just photographed the protestors and running street battles) when a stampede of harried combatants and hangers-on came racing by the restaurant terrace, eyes aglow with the energy of street action (or gleaming from tear gas). Buses and subways attacked in Great Britain, a church targeted in Georgia (USA), a school in the Balkans terrorized. The fact of the matter is that trouble often finds a country team. Readiness is the watchword.

A team member's best friend is a communications tool. In a survival situation it may be as simple as a shard of glass or a mirror to reflect sunlight (surprisingly effectively) toward a rescue aircraft. It might be a 9-feet-tall inflatable neon-orange-colored tube to summon a ship, a whistle in the woods, a bell in a church steeple. In a number of old world districts, low-tone bells broadcast the time, a higher tone series of bells announces services and weddings, and a separate series issues civil defense or natural disaster warnings. In some cases, all ring at the same time, furiously. Wherever a team is assigned, they must learn and promptly recognize the local signals. (Sirens for tornado activity? Bells for approaching hostile militia? Flashing headlights for illegal checkpoints, radar traps, or washed-away roadways?) Local residents can be consulted regarding communications standards. In one remote Iraqi village, where Derrin Smith's team was supporting a feeding program for an indigenous tribe experiencing food shortages, there was a local burro (nicknamed Algebra after the one of "Our Gang" comedy fame). Every night, spot-on at 9:30 P.M., Algebra would trot down the middle of the dirt lane, braying loudly, to announce to residents the end of day and that all was well. Algebra's presence, night after night, became a comforting beacon to the team on assignment there. No matter what the local signals and communications standards might be, they must be learned. They may save a life.

Modern technologies have brought more diverse and sophisticated ways of communicating (and, ironically, ways to waste monumental amounts of time). There are significant pluses and minuses. The correct selection of technology can provide hand-held navigation through Global Positioning System (GPS) tracking and plotting devices, which can pin-point locational communications almost anywhere on the face of the globe; our training simulations with University of Denver students utilize this system. However, certain technologies have important shortcomings. For example, some satellite signals, such as Yridium, suffer blocking by "urban canyon syndrome" in city environments. Some devices cannot receive signals at all without clear line of site to the sky. A SatPhone (see next section) might need to be used from a doorway. Other communications tools, such as cellphones, require proximity to a tower network and are useless outside an operational "cell" structure. Landlines are easily disrupted by severe weather or natural disasters (flood, fire, earthquake), hostile militia activity, or simple theft, owing to the local populace taking cables and clamps for other purposes. A team might encounter palm-frond roofs held together by strips of fiber-optic cable that have been pilfered from the local hybrid fiber-coax broadband communications infrastructure. A team might encounter a Bedouin tent with a Honda generator powering a sky dish and cable television. Being remote no longer means that the team—and the local populace—do not have a window to the world. Communications technology is therefore changing the complexion and the complexity of almost everything done on remote assignments. Reporting itself can be immediate, real time. Data collection, security assistance, and logistics requests can be almost instantaneous. An emergency extraction can be effected rapidly. While recognizing the constraints, with the right communications tools in the field one's life can be easier and safer.

Radio

Radio communications continue to be a mainstay of every bug-out bag and every transit team, and are the backbone of local security coordination. Embassies rely on them. Police, fire and ambulance services, militia units, and military security escorts do, too. Personnel from missions all over the world engage weekly (or at least monthly) in radio checks. The base station, "control," will announce the call signs of the members of the network. Members will key their mikes, responding with their call signs in response to the signals from control. In the event that disaster strikes, each harbor site, panic room, and embassy vehicle theoretically is capable of relying on radio communications— using standard frequencies—to carry out virtually everything from routine missions to emergency evacuations.

Consequently, radio skills are a must. Having played with walkie-talkies as kids, most team members already have some of the basic skills. We employ walkie-talkies in most of our training exercises. Channel selection, the proper use of prowords, line-of-sight communication, and evacuation protocols (for example) all can be practiced. Citizen band radios (CBs) were a craze in the 1970s and remain a mainstay in vehicle-to-vehicle communications for many civilians on duty in remote territories. However, with these systems a mission and its security can be compromised entirely; unless team members are talking on a military-encrypted network, the broadcasting is "clear," and the signal can be readily heard and copied by anyone tuned to the same frequency. It is omnidirectional. There is no privacy in general radio communications, and in a crisis situation in which stealth may be an issue, hostile forces can home in on a signal and triangulate onto one's location with remarkable precision.

Despite the minuses, radio communications are cheap, networks are easy to deploy across remote regions, and the equipment is sturdy and simple to use. There are minimal infrastructure requirements. In only a few minutes of training with air-ground radios, our students in Romania in 2004 were vectoring helicopters safely to drop zones and helicopter landing areas (HLAs), and signaling pilots as to where to lower cargoes.

There are a few simple rules: radio comments must be concise. Nobody likes a blowhard on the radio, and as long as a microphone is keyed, everyone on the "net" can hear every whistle, wheeze, and wise-crack but cannot broadcast (for instance) their urgent request for medical evacuation. Precise enunciation is vital. Smaller words are better in broadcast than multisyllabic ones. Don't say "gigantic" if "big" will do. Phonetics are linked to the transmission of letters. "Alpha" (preferred) or "Adam" for "A," or "Zulu" (preferred) or "Zebra" for "Z," will work. Team members must become comfortable with a standardized phonetic alphabet and use it routinely. Practice makes perfect.

Consistent courtesy is required in radio discipline. If someone needs to jump onto a channel—for example, Channel 3 (on a Motorola handheld) or Channel 18 (on a CB)—one must wait for a pause and say "Break, break 3 for a radio check" or "Break, break 18 for a report from Remote Alpha." This "break" allows everyone on the network to be silent for a moment, to enable a broadcast to control. In the event of a lengthy report, control must be alerted to "squawk" to a different channel; then others can resume their communications. It is important to "break" politely, establish one's purpose, use short sentences, and emphasize prowords (see appendix). The word "over" is the single most important proword.

SMART TECHNOLOGIES AND ELECTRONIC INNOVATIONS

The Presidential Mandate

Since 2004, a series of presidentially mandated "spectrum policies" and related studies have been released. Wireless technologies are essential in supporting federal agency missions perceived as crucial to national security. They also enable commercial and nonfederal public safety operations that support economic growth and safeguard lives and property. As changing government missions increase demands for mobility and security, and private-sector uses continue to expand, a set of spectrum policies has been deemed a critical asset. To ensure that the United States in the twenty-first century continues to effectively harness the power of the airwaves "to meet federal mission requirements and enhance prosperity," President George W. Bush issued an executive memorandum in June of 2003, this leading to formalization of the Spectrum Policy Initiative in 2004. The goal remains: a comprehensive set of initiatives that will foster economic growth, ensure homeland security, maintain U.S. global leadership in communications technology and services, and satisfy other vital needs in areas such as public safety, scientific research, federal transportation infrastructure, and law enforcement (DoC 2004, FCC 2005).

"Smart" Technologies

The rapid increase in innovations associated with "smart" technologies reflects an extension of the Information Revolution in Euro-American warfare analyzed by Max Boot (2006), as noted in Chapter 2. Radio communications are at the core. Many agencies plan to implement "smart" radio technologies such as software-defined radio (SDR) to improve adaptability and flexibility within an operational environment. Ultimately, these and other technologies will provide more rapid access to needed frequencies, wherever and whenever needed. Through automatic reprogramming, an SDR device can transmit and receive on a wide range of frequencies and readily operate pursuant to changing technologies and service standards. "Cognitive" radios are programmed to "perceive" and "learn" their radio environment. By tracking and adapting to their electromagnetic environment, cognitive radios can dynamically use whatever spectrum is available at a particular moment and at the same time prevent interference from co-existing systems. The National Telecommunications and Information Administration (NTIA) is monitoring the development of such spectrally efficient approaches and encouraging additional technology developments, particularly in the area of dynamic spectrum access. NTIA is looking to both the government and private sector for assistance and support in devising the necessary plans and strategies that will allow evolution of the spectrum-management system to support use of these technologies and minimize human-directed processes, as the Spectrum Policy Initiative indicates.

Most country teams require a variety of information and communications systems to accomplish their missions. Some host countries will have a spectrum plan, much like the one referenced above, to allow sophisticated radio communications without talking over the bandwidth or interfering with the channels of other users. The available bandwidth is generally partitioned, segmented in the higher frequencies for government users and offering a broad band of common channels for civilian and personal radio users in the lower frequencies. As noted earlier, standard radio frequency (RF) communications remain among the most common and practical for remote operations. Their relative ease of set up and use, as well as relatively low cost and low infrastructure requirements relative to other systems, indicate that RF communications will remain a part of the tool kit for years to come. For more robust and long-range RF systems, licensing by the national host government often is required in accordance with its national frequency allocation plan.

Very high frequency (VHF) systems that allow reasonable encryption protection and longer distance broadcast capabilities in all weather conditions generally require this type of registration. Law enforcement, emergency first responders, military and local security units, and other government organizations may already employ VHF communications systems. The country team must therefore work with appropriate government offices before procuring and installing radio communications to support in-country operations, whether urban or remote. Encryption and other specialized systems offer tremendous security benefits with enhanced broadcast capabilities and longer transmit/receive ranges but also significantly complicate authorization, integration, and operation. The price can also be very high, and in some cases licensing is required for the initial purchase and export of such equipment. To avoid running afoul of local, national, or international laws and radio communications regulations, consultation with an expert is necessary. Generally speaking, the more robust, expensive, and capable a communications system is, the more it makes the team an attractive target for interdiction, banditry, and victimization. In some instances in Africa and Southwest Asia, host government organizations have confiscated equipment for their own uses. The environment (technical, operational, environmental, human) must be known before procuring and shipping information processing and communications systems.

Satellite Communications, Terminals, and Telephones

SatCom, SatTerms, and SatPhones have become more widely deployed globally as services and equipment, previously available only to governments and official agencies, have advanced and been commercialized for general civilian applications. Significantly more expensive than everyday RF hand-held equipment, the benefits of global reach and digital data streams often justify the investment. Instant remote internet-based voice and data communications may be available via very small aperture terminals (VSATs) such as those offered worldwide by Hughes Network Systems. Even remote base-station operations can employ high-speed voice and internet, as long as they have clear line of sight to a satellite or a repeater antenna.

SatPhones offer global reach, although building-block and environmental interference may cause signal problems for operators at inconvenient times. Encryption features for both voice and data tend to be relatively easy to use and more robust than those intended for RF and landline analog telephone systems. System-entry prices vary dramatically, as do licensing and export-control requirements; due diligence is needed before investing. A training and familiarization course for the latest-generation information processing and communications systems (I&CS) is strongly recommended for country team personnel. Fundamental debugging and trouble-shooting knowledge is invaluable for team members, since tech support is generally not accessible from remotes, especially when the system is down. With Provincial Reconstruction Teams (PRTs) in the Middle East, Derrin Smith had the benefit of highly skilled military signal corps personnel, as well as an embedded civilian I&CS expert; yet even with these resources network problems were not insignificant. Information transmission is the lifeblood of humanitarian, emergency response and remote diplomatic operations outside the Green Zone. Satellite capabilities are increasingly affordable and accessible, as are secure alternatives for I&CS, but licensing requirements, life-cycle costs, import/export permits, and training/operations requirements need to be carefully addressed as part of an integrated communications plan (ICP) for the country team.

Wireless Telephone Voice and Data Capabilities

Thanks to aggressive marketing and infrastructure build-out by major international providers of voice and data services, cellular systems offer ever more remote capabilities. The level of sophistication of services varies from basic voice only to fully integrated data and internet capabilities. This is almost entirely dependent on host nation infrastructure and the national and international licensing and marketing agreements that are in place. Even remote tribesmen and nomadic herders can be found using cellphones these days, so locale-specific research is needed before selecting a service provider and hand-held unit. In some markets with strong internal infrastructure and inter-provider competition, service bundles can be found at a relatively low price. For our international travels, a Blackberry with global edition software and a major international service provider has satisfied many of our voice and data needs. Combined with a local radio system for regional transit and point-to-point voice communications, as well as emergency applications, we have adequate redundancy and reliability. If we need to reach out and touch the world at any particular time, we have a good likelihood of making contact.

In both Iraq and Afghanistan, over the course of several years, Derrin Smith witnessed a transition in communications with clients. It is akin to a "fourth wave," following on the "third wave" popularized years ago by Alvin Toffler (1980). The team progressed from military radio communications and SatCom during the early phase of engagement, into a phase using satellite phones in the hands of tribal leaders and key governmental contacts, to a phase involving rapid deployment of hand-held cellphones serving as the local cellular communications as networks were built out by national and international carriers. For daily deployments, the team would have a combination of systems on board for any given mission, including vehicle radio communications (VRC) with full encryption, hand-held radio units with limited encryption for each team member, and cellphones linked to the local network, which was used for voice conversations in "the clear," with full knowledge that hostile groups were possibly hanging on every word and movement. Very rarely, over nearly four years of operations, did Smith's team members find themselves stranded without robust communications; even as one type of system failed, the others could immediately maintain contact with base support and security personnel.

Such redundancy and robustness should be established as part of the ICP for all country team operations. Security training and established communication protocols are a must for all team members. Targeted communications can save one's life in a jam; they also can be exploited by hostile forces to target team personnel. But exploiting the advantages and avoiding the pitfalls requires practice.

Security, Encryption, and Authentication

For many years, national governments and federal agencies—including those in the United States—have fought to have exclusive purview over secure communications and encryption. Advances in technology and the availability of data and voice encryption for the general citizenry makes interdiction, monitoring, and law enforcement much more challenging today. Terrorists, insurgents, and organized crime organizations and drug cartels (such as that based in Medellín, Colombia, as noted in Chapter 7) benefit from secure communications. Since the 1970s, advances in secure voice and data communications technology have challenged government organizations to rush to keep pace with commercial developments (Banisar 2002). Currently, all the major American telephone and internet service providers have agreements in place with the National Security Agency and law enforcement organizations to help combat crime and protect national security. Although first responders, humanitarian operations, and remote diplomatic missions have legitimate needs for robust secure communications, host governments and international law enforcement groups have higher-priority national security mandates. Public key encryption, basic email security software, and voice terminals with basic signal encryption benefit the country team in much the same way as locking the doors and windows of one's house help deter common crime. Digital transmission and microwave transmission technologies, once augmented, will allow still greater capabilities within this arena. Take away the easy crime of opportunity and it is possible to remove the vast majority of the threat from interdiction, direction-finding, and the compromising of a team's voice/data communications.

Along with an integrated communications plan, more than technical functionality and operations need to be considered. Each organization and team leaves a footprint in the local community. The safety of team members and security of the organization usually are closely intertwined with the image and the message of the mission. Information processing and communication systems, as well as personal interactions and public relations, need to be mutually reinforcing. The I&CS equipment provides a tool for country teams to use in communicating their message. Defining the message, as well as choosing the best means of disseminating it, is also vitally important to mission success (as discussed in the next section).

MESSAGE DISSEMINATION AND PUBLIC RELATIONS

Military units and some governmental organizations actively deploy psychological operations (PsyOps) capabilities to help create favorable public opinions of the operations within an area, as also suggested in Chapter 7. This involves technical systems supporting public messages in the community to explain to both the general populace and decision makers the need to accept and support the actions or interventions of the team. From providing education about elections, to distributing information to help catch bandits and criminals, to explaining the nature, extent and location of aid available to the local population, effective and ethical outreach are vital to securing citizen support for country team presence and projects. Diplomatic missions use the term Public Diplomacy (PD) for their information outreach programs; government entities and large NGOs and IGOs frequently have a Press Affairs Office or Public Affairs Office (PAO) to provide a point of contact for professional media inquiries or for dealing with questions from the general public. Government officials frequently have press secretaries and other media professionals to handle this interface, as well as to smooth the movement of program information into the public domain. Public fund raising for missions can similarly be enhanced with the correct media message and public outreach, internationally as well as locally. The current global network of information and communications systems allows a remote diplomatic outpost or NGO-run refugee camp to access global resources and outlets for information, fund raising, and reporting. Important operational information, from local, regional, and national threat data to weather forecasts and environmental data, can be made available to team members and leaders with a few clicks and screen pops. Every country team should consider its public diplomacy approach, its media presence, and its local and national information outreach programs. These requirements may actually drive the selection of I&CS equipment suites.

The use of night vision, in concert with other advanced digital technologies, has introduced a factor both intriguing and troubling into the equation. What once was seen by day is now also being seen by night, with sometimes unexpected results. Visual technology enables penetration of the murkiest battlefield environments. In the hands of reputable military analysts it contributes to the tactics chosen. However, a still-murky interface is evolving among military, television broadcast, and electronic/video game environments. A blurred reality is emerging as the actual battlefield is transmogrified into a virtual battlefield. In the case of television, networks such as CNN are utilizing advanced technologies to introduce an "edited modification" into what is transmitted to the viewing world. In the case of games, such as those being designed for Xbox (for example, "Call to Duty: Modern Warfare 2"), sister technologies are forcing a blend between fact and fiction, between the "real soldier" and the "super cyborg." In sum, the relationship between the military and the experience of war, as Jose Vasquez (2009) stresses, is shifting.

The insights that Joshua Friedman (2003) shares for humanitarians working with the press are particularly useful. Some humanitarian groups are so driven to get good publicity that they attempt to manipulate the press, a tactic that rarely works. The press, in turn, often seems to be seeking stories about disasters, tragedies, and human torment. Coverage of the type of activities that most country teams engage in is exceedingly rare. Fiscal constraints have increased. Decreasing revenue streams at major newspapers, thus much smaller overseas travel budgets, as our colleague Bruce Finley of *The Denver Post* tells us, have reduced the type of on-site reporting that is possible. Finley's former path-breaking trips to "hot spots" such as Pakistan and Afghanistan are a thing of the past. Friedman's former investigative undertakings, such as when he went to cover the 1999 Kosovo crisis for *Newsday* by way of plane, car, and ferry, now are more difficult to pull off. The ability of *Newsday* (or most other news periodicals) to lavishly support a journalist on site, such as it did for an acquaintance of Peter Van Arsdale in both El Salvador and Mexico during the mid-1980s, now is a rarity.

The types of advanced communication devices discussed earlier, such as SatPhones, are used increasingly by press reporters in remote locales. Friedman believes that the technologically enhanced access and rapid news turnaround, despite other institutional constraints, can improve overseas reporting from trouble spots. But the need for "fixers," as they say in Iraq, or "people who can *urus*," as they say in Indonesia, will continue unabated. These are the local inhabitants who have a special talent for "arranging things," from locating a makeshift press conference facility, to securing a savvy cab driver, to adroitly assisting press team or country team members when the situation becomes too dangerous.

InterAction, a U.S.-based organizational coalition, has focused on media relations as it works to integrate certain of the activities and outcomes of nearly 175 private voluntary organizations. It is the largest coalition of U.S.-based international NGOs working on issues of poverty, vulnerability, and gender equity (InterAction 2007a). Its recently published guidelines to improve NGO-military interactions and communications (InterAction 2007b) are the gold standard. Even such seemingly small but significant points as the proper display of insignia are covered (to avoid problems such as those associated with Operation Jaque, covered in Chapter 4). The guidelines have been formally endorsed by the DoD.

InterAction compiles data on the impact of various NGO outreach programs, including many that collaborate with country teams, to identify best practices. Using nearly thirty working groups and committees, it tackles tough issues head on; "policy and communications" constitutes one of three major subsets. It cross-references the UN's Millennium Development Goals in the process. One of its objectives for the 2007–2009 period was advocating the establishment of a cabinet-level U.S. Department of Development and Humanitarian Assistance. InterAction effectively continues its work with U.S. government officials, including those representing the military, to instigate desired changes in the humanitarian sphere. In our opinion, because of its creative and synthetic capacity, it is among the most important agencies currently operating in this field.

The handbook in the appendix covers the specifics of field communications, including an example of a simple "hot wash" report template and other useful reporting tools.

CHAPTER 6

BEST PRACTICES FOR HAZARDOUS AREAS OF OPERATION: FIXED SITES AND FIELD SCHOOLS*

MILITARY FORTRESSES, BASES, AND CAMPS

Military bases and camps serve as the central stations/platforms for both training activities and military operations, at home and abroad. So-called fixed sites can be understood from both logistical/strategic and sociological/tactical perspectives. This chapter provides a brief overview of several types of sites. A special civilian-military training site, established in Romania in 2004, also is featured. Modern-day Provincial Reconstruction Team (PRT)

---

*Parts of this chapter regarding the Romanian field school are adapted directly from Van Arsdale (2008).

sites, as they have been implemented since 2002, are an interesting combination of military bases and encampments. To some extent they also incorporate features of formidable fortresses needed to protect foreigners and locals alike in nonpermissive and semipermissive areas of reconstruction and development, some associated with humanitarian interventions.

Military bases and encampments are common in the history of both Eastern and Western powers. As an example from ancient Egypt, the town of Kysis in the Sahara's Fayum region had a fortress and encampment that sheltered an agricultural community at a trading crossroads (cf. Clarysse and Thompson 2006). Kysis merchants, craftsmen, and establishments that catered to the various needs of both soldiers and trade caravans from all points of the compass flourished until about the fourth century c.e. The fortress provided regional security from its 250-foot high point, although most of the commerce and town was spread across the hillsides. Both the fortress and the townspeople were highly dependent on a series of underground wells that were engineered into a sophisticated potable water/irrigation system. These life-giving water resources deep in the desert were quite possibly of even greater importance than the fresh oasis produce. Situated at a southern point on the vital trade route of Daarb el-Arbahin, the military installation protected the crossroads but also provided the necessary muscle and firepower to resolve disputes and prevent banditry. In spite of its vital importance from a security perspective, once the wells dried up, archaeological evidence suggests, the site was abandoned. This fate underscores a fundamental tenet of fixed sites: basic needs such as water, food, and safety dictate the sustainability of the operation.

In the centuries after Kysis was abandoned to the sands, concepts for fortresses, military encampments, and expansion of trade under military protection evolved in lockstep with the weaponry that defined conflict and commerce. Towering vertical castles represented the state of the art of fortresses in the medieval period, but as these succumbed to sustained assault from ship cannons and artillery, the science of fortification progressed. The geometric and sloping structural designs of the sixteenth century, meant to absorb artillery attacks while maintaining a defensive artillery position that could target virtually all avenues of approach, helped merchant firms with military support to spread globally with their trade on an unprecedented scale. The movement of an army in and of itself insured some commercial opportunities for locals and camp-followers alike. In general, crossroads enjoyed reinforced fortresses, and trade routes were speckled with monitoring outposts sharing the lines of communications with smaller fortresses to provide command, control, support, and logistics across vast trading distances. Fortresses built within artillery distance of sea lanes and choke-points attracted settlements that flourished within the protective reach of the military, but outside the gates and walls of the hardened sites. Often the most highly protected elements of a fixed site were those related to local governance, administration, and the chain of command to control security forces. Internal warehouses, reinforced underground storage, garrison facilities, and bunkers enabled both troops and political administrators to survive even prolonged sieges. Thus, through the 1600s and 1700s, European fortresses were a major enabler of colonialism and European hegemony and were a linchpin for commercial expansion on an unprecedented scale. Merchant ships could travel from Europe to the most distant points in Asia, sailing from reinforced fortress to reinforced fortress, dramatically accelerating the flow of goods, services, and people in both directions. The ever-growing fleets of trade ships accelerated the competing trade of piracy, which in turn prompted nation-states to pursue more powerfully lethal means to protect both fleets and fortresses.

In many respects, these characteristics might not be so different from humanitarian interventions or reconstruction and development initiatives today, in semipermissive zones of operation. With enough local security attached to the fixed site, most local powers and threats are effectively mitigated. In many cases, local actors who might otherwise attack and overpower the interlopers become trading partners, participants in activities and initiatives; some even become "distant eyes and ears" of the fixed-site inhabitants. The security forces provide the environmental stability, which in turn attracts all manner of human enterprises, good and bad. The early fortresses, fortified way-stations, controllers of maritime choke-points, and the command, control, communications, and intelligence that followed land and sea trade routes essentially constituted the first worldwide web.

However, webs can be broken, and no fixed site is invulnerable, no matter how well designed and operated. Consequently, in the design of fixed sites to support humanitarian assistance and stabilization operations, the objective is to engineer to mitigate immediate local risks to enable activities within the designated area of operations. Threats against the site of greater force or effect require evacuation of the country team. In some politically sensitive withdrawals, these evacuations may instead be referred to as "assisted departures," for either public relations or diplomatic reasons. Every fixed site must have plans for departure, whether rapid or stately in nature. From a six-month disengagement in transition and turnover to local authorities to a hastily executed "bug out" with a moment's notice, plans must be formalized and practiced, and all staff must be intimately familiar with their responsibilities and actions under the plans.

The withdrawal of the Dutch in 1662 from the island that is now modern-day Taiwan is an example of a successful departure from a conquered fixed site, when the fall of the Fortress Zeelandia to the troops of General Zheng Cheng-gong ended thirty-eight years of Dutch colonial rule there. The Dutch were defending Zeelandia with a minimal security force of only 2,000 troops, besieged by General Koxinga's attacking force of over 25,000 troops and 400 warships. The Dutch held this superior force at bay for nine months. Only when the Chinese finally captured an elevation that allowed their artillery to rain fire down on the fortress—with the defenders having run completely out of fresh water—was a surrender executed. In exchange for leaving the fortress infrastructure and properties intact, the surviving Dutch political and military personnel, as well as all civilians, were permitted to leave with their personal belongings and adequate supplies for the short term. Arguably, the conquest of Fortress Zeelandia by the Chinese could have had graver consequences for the survivors had the forces of Koxinga not obeyed the letter of the surrender treaty (cf. Davison 2003: 6–16). That the Dutch East India Company continued to exert disproportionate leverage in the Far East, in a kind of "Dutch-Javanese-Chinese triangle," must be noted (Kohn 1999: 246).

In the modern era, there no longer seems to be a reasonable guarantee of safe exit or passage in many of the areas where country teams and remote field teams operate; treaties and departure agreements seem all too easily ignored. Thus, modern fixed-site operations necessitate a rapid-exit plan—generally air-mobile extraction, as discussed later in this chapter—when local security conditions deteriorate to the level of imminent danger to managers and staff. For those who hesitate, prison or death is too often the result. Incarceration may or may not be the preferred outcome, as history illustrates.

Ominous military prison camps, remembered for their brutality, also are well known historically. The POW camp at Cabanatuán was established by the Japanese during that nation's occupation of the Philippines during World War II. Many of the camp's prisoners had arrived via the Bataan "death march" and indeed were among its last known survivors. They were freed in January of 1945 during a remarkable raid led by American and Filipino special forces. One reason for the raiders' success was their knowledge of military camp layouts and logistical operations (Sides 2001). Known variously as "POW," "concentration," or "torture" camps, during the twentieth century most of these were run by state militaries. Peter Van Arsdale has written elsewhere about the Serb-run camps of Omarska and Foča in Bosnia, operative during the civil war of 1992–1995 (2006: 73–77). In the former, torture of (primarily) men was an every-day occurrence; in the latter, rape of (primarily) women also was an every-day occurrence. Although they were not liberated in the dramatic fashion of Cabanatuán, they were forced to close as military and civilian pressure—including that by research journalists—mounted.

The most remarkable military POW camp established on U.S. soil was that at Andersonville, Georgia, during the civil war. As many as 400,000 soldiers, representing both Union and Confederate forces, were detained as POWs at a number of sites during the conflict. The facility at Camp Sumter, located near Andersonville, came to epitomize the worst. Some 45,000 Union soldiers were imprisoned, and approximately 13,000 died during a 14-month period. Disease and sanitation issues were the biggest killers (Van Arsdale 2006: 169). Little known but also of importance in understanding the role that military camps have played in U.S. history is a prison that once operated on a small island in Lake Erie, Ohio. The Johnson's Island Civil War Military Prison was used from April, 1862, through September, 1865. As Trudy Bell (2006) notes, it was the only one of 32 prisons used by Union forces during the Civil War built specifically to be a prisoner of war camp and the only one used exclusively for Confederate officers. Although overcrowded when housing over 2,800 men at one time, as was sometimes the case, the practices employed there were innovative and humane for that era. The pharmacy was relatively well stocked, the hospital provided the latest in care, and the cafeteria provided decent meals. Correspondence with loved ones was encouraged; mail was delivered regularly. Although the late stages of the war brought resource constraints, and some 800 officers eventually died, the encampment was in sharp contrast with those located elsewhere in Union or Confederate states.

ROMANIAN MILITARY CAMPS AND OPERATIONS

We helped develop, and then engaged in, an innovative civilian-military training exercise—a special kind of field school—in Romania during the summer of 2004. One key element was development of a fully functioning camp. The University of Denver (where we both were on the faculty) provided the students. In many ways this epitomizes core principles laid out in this book: the importance of recognizing the value of armed forces work in postconflictive and noncombat field operations; the significance of field-ready and site-specific training for humanitarian intervention; and the value of stabilization and reconstruction operations at the civilian-military interface, particularly as partnerships are developed that genuinely integrate the ideas and expertise of soldiers, outside civilians, and the indigenous populace. Insights into country operations from the perspective of a U.S. ally and new NATO member are substantial.

Romanian Military History

Background on the Romanian military enterprise is necessary to understand how a summer-long, integrated university-military training program could be implemented in such a seemingly unusual place. Military engagements in this part of the Greater Balkan Peninsula conjure fact, legend, and myth. Key historical points have been summarized by Călin Hentea (2007). Among the earliest engagements, the famed Persian king, Darius I, mounted a campaign against the Scythians, north of the Danube River, in 514 B.C.E. Macedonians and other regional forces engaged in various battles over a several-century span; Alexander the Great passed through. The Dacians constituted a significant "pre-Romanian" ethnic population, so identified during the early centuries of the Christian era. The defeat of the Roman praetorian consul Fuscus by the Dacian king Decebalus, in 87 C.E., was a benchmark in early Romanian military history. However, two subsequent campaigns involving Romans proved ominous, and in apparent despair, Decebalus committed suicide (Kohn 1999: 141). Rome ruled Dacia from 106 through 275 C.E.

In subsequent centuries what can be called Romania and Moldavia were penetrated by Avars, Slavic tribes from outside the Carpathian Mountains, and Hungarian tribes. Warfare was instrumental in shaping the landscape. The "end of the creation process" for the Romanian language—a relative of Italian—and its peoples is dated to the tenth century, as Hentea notes (2007: 2). Subsequent Tatar invasions and the obviously significant Ottoman invasion into Wallachia in 1369, though by no means smooth, as the Turkish force subsequently spread, can be seen as the defining historical foundation—in point/counterpoint fashion—for the type of often entrenched yet at times proactive and innovative militarism that evolved. For over 500 years, through the nineteenth century, provincial powers acted and reacted, often violently, to opportunities in "the Danube," "Wallachia," "Moldavia," and "Transylvania," as if these regions had taken on mythic status. (As our recent work there suggests, in some ways they had.)

During the late nineteenth century, and especially as the Ottoman Empire came to be repulsed, Romanian military activities took on an altered look and stratagem. Modern military history in the country is traced by some to the 1860s, in concert with a re-emergent "national idea" (Hentea 2007: 82). Although "the Hungarian question" continued unabated, a transprovincial consolidation was afoot. Two examples: In June of 1913 Romania declared war on Bulgaria; within two months, after a peace conference in Bucharest, it had gained additional territory. In April of 1918 a delegation from Transylvania visited Washington, D.C., to update the American government on the situation in Romania and the desire of Romanians living in the region occupied by Austria-Hungary to join a united Romania. The following year the National Romania League was created in Washington to follow up (Hentea 2007: 14–16).

Subsequent decades saw increasingly strong Soviet and communist influence. The Romanian Communist Party gained strength through World War II, taking power within the Parliament of Romania in November of 1946. King Mihai I, a constitutional monarch, was forced to abdicate the next year; the country was then proclaimed the Popular Republic of Romania. Pressures among Yugoslavian/Tito and Soviet/Stalin factions only exacerbated Romania's precarious position; by the early 1950s the latter had prevailed, and various Soviet military models (for example, regarding central command structures) were being more formally incorporated. Since the late 1940s, however, "educators" had been inculcating the armed forces with communist doctrines. In 1965, as Nicolae Ceauşescu came to power, the country was renamed the Socialist Republic of Romania.

The oppressive Ceauşescu regime lasted from 1965 through 1989. It summarily ended with his execution, as well as that of his wife Elena, on December 25. Yet, a few days before that, the military had renounced the role of "the people's butcher" (Hentea 2007: 174). The tide had begun to turn toward yet another (very Western) military model, one that—once refined—persists to the present day.

From a Warsaw Pact cofounder in 1955 to a NATO member in 2004, during half a century Romania's military transformation was in one sense profound yet in another sense not. A baseline for modern country operations was indirectly being created. As our colleagues with the 10th Land Forces Division told us in 2004, the foundation of a solid, diversified, well-trained, humane military organization long had been forming. A strategically beneficial friendship with the United States could be dated to the 1919 founding of the National Romanian League, but broader Euro-American sociopolitical ties were deemed essential. Membership in NATO was deemed essential. Eventual full membership in the European Union also was deemed essential.

The three branches of the Romanian military are the Land Forces (that is, army), Air Force, and Navy. Contemporary peacekeeping and humanitarian interventions involving the military have been summarized by Hentea (2007) and, additionally, shed light on the special joint training operation we mounted in 2004. Although certainly intended to help others, these operations also have been conducted strategically so that Romania's place in the Western panoply of transnational actors could be strengthened. During the past decade reform has occurred at the strategic command level with the organization of the armed forces into battalions, brigades, and army corps. An interoperability process also was launched with the armed forces of the NATO member states. By 1997 the units designated for peacekeeping missions had become operational. Immediately thereafter, the General Staff and its services were organized according to NATO-like modular structures. Yet, even before this, Romanian humanitarian outreach to conflict zones had begun. Three examples: In 1994 military doctors took part in UNOSOM II, in and around Mogadishu, Somalia; some 75,000 sick and injured persons were assisted. Between 1995 and 1999 hundreds of personnel were deployed in Angola through UNAVEM III. Personnel participated in patrols, built and set up camps for UNITA, escorted convoys, searched camps and cleared them of mines, and staffed a field hospital. This operation proved to be Romania's biggest overseas peacekeeping challenge, and after 1999 unarmed officers continued to participate as military observers. Immediately after the cessation of fighting in Bosnia, in 1996 an engineering battalion was deployed through IFOR (Implementation Force for Bosnia), in complement to NATO mandates. Personnel built and maintained roads and bridges, and again worked with mine clearance. Following IFOR, the battalion participated in SFOR (Stabilization Force for Bosnia).

Peacekeeping efforts have encompassed Albania (through Operation ALBA) and Kosovo (through KFOR). PsyOps were included with the latter. The Romanian-Hungarian Joint Battalion was established in 1999 and will serve in future peacekeeping operations. On the combat front, a military police platoon was deployed to Kabul, Afghanistan, in 2002, followed by an infantry detachment deployed to Kandahar as part of the U.S.-led Operation Enduring Freedom. Romanian troops also engaged in Operation Iraqi Freedom. During the past decade military observers have been posted in locales as diverse as Georgia and Ethiopia. As Hentea notes, with approximately 112,000 military and 28,000 allied civilian personnel, effective NATO integration remains at the forefront of the country's military mandate (2007: 200).

The timing of our civilian-military training program *cum* field school in 2004 therefore was ideal from the perspective of the Romanian military. Public relations opportunities abounded. If the University of Denver's Graduate School of International Studies (in 2008 renamed the Josef Korbel School of International Studies) could recruit fifteen top-flight graduate students and fund about 15 percent of the total cost, the Romanian Ministry of National Defense would recruit leading Air Force and Land Forces trainers and cadets, and fund the remaining 85 percent. In concert with senior Ministry of National Defense administrators, Derrin Smith devised, planned, and (with the assistance of Peter Van Arsdale) implemented this first-of-a-kind effort.

The Romanian Field School

The following two examples indicate just how energetically the field school *cum* camp that we established in Romania engaged its participants:

> The machine gun fire rattled our brains. The gunner was only a few feet away, and the sound was deafening. Our convoy ground to a halt. The walls of the narrow mountain valley seemed suddenly too close. The drivers jumped out and ran into the forest. A burly, ominous-looking man with a bandanna wrapped around his forehead and ammunition belts draped over his shoulders ran into the road and waved his AK-47 in our direction. "I am Dracul. We are taking over!"

> "Get out of those trucks, now!" Dracul shouted. He waved his gun in the direction of our students, riding in the cargo bays, and then added: "You'll be sorry if you do not move." Other militia men and women, following their leader's command, converged around the rear doors of the three convoy vehicles and herded the students off. Some stumbled, since they'd been forced to put on black hoods a moment earlier and couldn't get their bearings.

The militia lined the students up near a small stream. "Put your hands behind your heads, spread your legs, and shut up," one yelled. "Keep those hoods on," another screamed. Female militia then began patting down the female students; male militia began patting down the male students. "All clear," one woman stated in a matter-of-fact fashion.

"You do not have authority to enter our territory," Dracul said. "Did you think you could bring these trucks in without our permission? Did you think you could help those refugees without going through us?" He poked his gun at one of our students, a young man who himself had been in the military, and said: "Did you?" "No, sir," our student replied. "Then get out of the way. We are in charge here. I only have two friends—my knife and my gun."

With that, Dracul and his ten colleagues jumped into the trucks, turned them around, and drove them back down the valley. Our students, seemingly dazed, also turned around and began the journey back on foot, trudging the five kilometers to where they had begun their relief operation hours earlier.

This was a simulation. It included all the "bells and whistles." Dracul and his militia colleagues in fact were Romanian troops in training, members of the elite Romanian Land Forces Academy (similar to the U.S. Army's West Point). They were enacting a simulation that our staff, in concert with Romanian officers, had concocted days in advance. The fifteen students who were "captured" had no idea that this would happen but had been well versed in country team operations, had been working alongside Romanian soldiers, and had been preparing for unusual and realistic scenarios. As the summer of 2004 went on, they encountered a number of other difficult situations in the Transylvania mountains (Figure 6.1):

Our convoy of trucks and military equipment lumbered through a small valley and up a rough dirt road. Although part of a military

FIGURE 6.1 After a staged ambush, University of Denver students are captured by "insurgents" under the command of "Dracul" during a 2004 training exercise in Transylvania (photo by Derrin Smith).

reservation, it was littered with rocks and potholes. The Transylvanian forest enclosed us on all sides. As our first vehicle crested a steep rise, it suddenly came to a halt. There was smoke and fire dead ahead; it appeared that a jeep and small truck (traveling on a separate, crossing road) had collided just prior to our arrival. Two people lay in the road, seemingly covered with blood and severely injured.

Having trained with the Mile High Chapter of the American Red Cross to assist the injured in such emergencies, five of our students sprang from their truck and rushed forward. The other ten remained back, along with their Romanian military colleagues, awaiting further instructions.

The first five were in for a surprise. Masked militia men and women charged from behind a nearby grove of trees and surrounded them.

Dracul appeared, ordering the students to the ground, face-first. "You let this little accident we staged distract you! Tell the others to stay away; we're armed and won't hold back if they attempt to trick us." Radio communications were engaged and the others retreated to safety, back into the small valley.

"There's an abandoned farmhouse nearby. We're taking one of the women there as a hostage," Dracul shouted. "The other four can go. We'll relay you our demands shortly." One of the female students was bound, hooded, and led away by two armed militia women.

For half an hour, there was silence. No militia could be seen, no sounds could be heard. Then a single masked man appeared. "Dracul is ready to negotiate. You can have the woman if we can have one of your trucks. Meet him in the farmhouse, half a kilometer to the west." The remaining students walked cautiously there, accompanied by their Romanian colleagues. They found the student sitting on a stool in the corner of the living room, still bound and hooded. A gun was pointed at her head. The room itself was filthy.

"Do we have a deal?" Dracul asked. "One truck for one woman, a more-than-fair bargain." The students huddled, discussed the offer, and told him he had a deal. The woman was released; the simulation ended. All totaled, about an hour had elapsed.

Although other types of field school, service learning, and study abroad programs exist, as summarized by Iris (2004) and Van Arsdale (2008), the one described here represents an extreme outlier. Likely the first of its kind, at least as far as the partnering of a Balkan and non-Balkan nation are concerned, our program was built on the notion of country team operations. While incorporating some of what Iris (2004: 11) describes as a "grand tour," with site visits throughout the country, the Romanian field school also was extremely focused. The notion of "building the civilian-military interface" was central.

Built in part on service learning principles, the country team operations model incorporates training exercises, scenarios or simulations, and on-site study and guest lectures. It is maximally experiential. Although not aimed at community service per se, it is aimed at cross-cultural community integration, manifested through jointly planned and jointly implemented exercises. It employs a type of cooperative learning. A formal, contractual partnering is undertaken. Our version, sponsored jointly by the University of Denver and the Romanian Ministry of National Defense (as noted previously), focused on humanitarian assistance and intervention that could benefit refugees and IDPs.

The initial plan for the project was conceived by Derrin Smith. His extensive work in Romania during the previous decade had opened a number of communication channels and a number of transnational training opportunities. His previous service in the U.S. Marine Corps, coupled with his recent contractual work with defense agencies, had enabled him to develop expertise in an array of field operations. One of his contacts reached to the office of the Romanian presidency, another to the highest levels of that nation's defense ministry. Several senior administrators expressed interest in the possibility of working with a foreign university on joint training operations. This complemented the Romanian president's vision of expanded military cooperation with NATO, which his nation was about to join when the planning for this exercise was initiated. It also complemented his aides' vision of expanded educational cooperation with the United States.

The Colorado Field School Antecedents

On the U.S. side, preparations for a summer of training operations in Romania began with a five-credit, campus-based, graduate-level class entitled "Country Team Operations: Theory and Training." We offered this during the spring quarter of 2004. Best practices associated with matériel deployment, refugee camp operations, recovery operations, and field communications were featured. Also featured were ways to write predeparture reports, field assessments, event-specific briefing papers, "hot washes," and related after-action reports. One of Van Arsdale's specialties is theory and praxis associated with humanitarian operations and the roles of NGOs, so two 3-hour lectures featured this. One of Smith's specialties is field deployment and recovery operations under military supervision, so two of his lectures featured this. Three lectures covered operations of the American Red Cross; these were complemented by all-day certification exercises in which our students learned CPR, techniques of basic medical assistance, and ways to construct and use stretchers. Case-based examples of emergency preparedness planning and emergency operations worldwide (including some associated with natural disasters) rounded out the classroom lectures.

The class ended with a set of carefully crafted field exercises. These took place near the small mountain town of Creede, Colorado, located near the headwaters of the Rio Grande. Activities spanned a 3-day period during mid-May, 2004. In addition to us, our professional field staff consisted of three non-university-based professionals. Two had extensive military experience. Students were responsible for planning all basic logistics. Five teams were assembled, each headed by an administrative officer. Supplies were requisitioned in the same manner that they would be in an overseas operation. Convoys were set up, so that students could travel by car from Denver to Creede—a distance of 300 miles—in organized fashion. On arrival in the field, tents were set up and supplies distributed. One student was assigned responsibility for overall site coordination, another for radio communications, still another for field logistics. Each team contributed to cooking, cleaning, and site maintenance.

Field exercises focused on two primary missions: (1) to conduct a search and rescue (SAR) mission for survivors of a 16-seat aircraft accident, and (2) to observe and report the local conditions affecting internally displaced persons (IDPs). Since these in fact were mock operations, built on scenarios the staff had created, a mock nation also was created. The "nation of Anstravia" therefore became the seat of operations. It was deemed to be "under siege" and students/field operatives/humanitarians were deemed to be operating under a medium-to-high threat level (Fontaine 2004).

As the exercises unfolded, students were able to engage several areas of emergent expertise. In addition to convoy operations, these included the conduct of site surveys, with an emphasis on map interpretation and intelligence.

Compass work over rough terrain allowed them to hone their skills. A type of orienteering was employed as they sought clues to the "downed aircraft." Work with threat assessment was complemented by the establishment of security perimeters for our camp, as well as logistical protocols and security practices, which ultimately assisted them as they completed local conditions reports benefiting "Anstravian IDPs."

The Colorado-Romania Interface

All these skills again were utilized when the students arrived in Romania several weeks later. During the first phase of our trip, a kind of "grand tour," we were primarily aided by officers of the Romanian Air Force and were billeted at the equivalent of that nation's Air Force Academy. Several guest lecturers gave presentations. During the second phase of our trip, a targeted "on-site training," we were primarily aided by officers and advanced cadets of the Romanian Land Forces Academy. We were based at one of their primary training camps and shuttled 30 miles west to one of their primary field camps.

The process of entrée to the Transylvanian field camp site was designed in such a way that students were divided into two teams, each charged with mapping out a route, arranging a convoy of military vehicles, loading and transporting supplies, and coordinating radio communications. One team took the "high route," through hills and low mountains. The other took the "low route," through a system of valleys. It was on a follow-up relief operation through the "low route," after both teams had joined, that they were "captured" by Dracul and his band of militia (as summarized in the first example, above).

A complete relief camp was built, literally from the ground up and centered on large military tents, in a gently rolling field about a mile from the academy's primary field base. Outhouses were constructed and latrines installed. A small communications command post was set up on an adjacent hilltop. A generator-run electrical system was installed. In short, we established a camp that would serve as the center of field operations and as a base to assist "refugees" and "IDPs" whose arrivals were anticipated.

During the next few days, and following some scenarios that had been scripted by members of our team in conjunction with the Romanian officers and cadets, a number of difficult situations unfolded. At the ready and working 24/7, our students were variously confronted by "irate peasants" from a "neighboring village," who claimed that our camp's new operations were upsetting the local political situation; the same group, who came again on a subsequent day, claiming that we had inadvertently but thoughtlessly constructed our camp over several community gravesites; "IDPs" who required nighttime medical assistance based on a protocol and triage system we previously had practiced (with Red Cross assistance) in Denver; "guerrillas" who attacked our camp at midnight; "refugees" who needed to be evacuated; and the "hostage situation" reported earlier (in the second example).

These exercises illustrate both the realism that our mock operations engendered and the financial costs that our program incurred. The "refugees" were evacuated on Romanian military helicopters. We had access to these for two days, including training in flight operations, the loading of supplies, care of the wounded, and radio communications. The woman's capture was preceded by a battle that included the use of training explosives, dummy mortars and gunfire, and the mock automobile/truck accident already noted. We had six trucks, two ambulances, and ten senior Romanian military officers at our disposal throughout this set of field exercises. We had eight helicopter crewmen at our disposal for two days, including one of the country's senior flight instructors.

Best Practices, Lessons Learned

The initiative allowed master's candidates from a wide range of concentrations, all within the University of Denver's now-renamed Josef Korbel School of International Studies, to work together. It also allowed a modified version of the field project to continue at the school through the present day. This originally included students focusing their studies on homeland security, human rights, international development, and international administration, and since 2007 it has expanded to include those focusing on humanitarian assistance and conflict resolution as well. It has afforded students whose political views are conservative to work alongside those whose views are liberal. It has afforded students who have had military experience to work alongside those with no such experience; indeed, some in the latter group had been vocally outspoken against the military before joining our program. Of equal importance, it has afforded students the opportunity to merge theory with practice in an ethical context—our definition of praxis—and to hone skills essential to careers involving on-site work in refugee camps, civil-military relief operations, or disaster assistance activities. Best practices and lessons learned were featured (see Tables 6.1, 6.2, and 6.3). Some participants will eventually become members of country teams.

Table 6.1   Students participating in the Romanian field exercise were presented with these best practices and derived these lessons learned. For comparative purposes, these same best practices are reiterated in Chapter 7, in the box "Best Practices, Lessons Learned #3," with lessons learned derived from actual field operations in Iraq.

Best Practices #1	Lessons Learned #1
• Establish entrée and rapport	• Entrée essential, but deception likely where cross-ethnic tensions exist.
• Promote personal relationships	• Even with adversaries, personal relationships are beneficial; use them judiciously.
• Work shoulder to shoulder with others	• On-site work on humanitarian tasks can take precedence over office-based initiatives.
• Perform careful reconnaissance	• Geopolitical reconnaissance essential before establishing relief centers; maps a key.
• Perform careful route assessment	• A "route" includes the surrounding terrain; diversionary entrapments are likely.
• Perform careful site assessment	• Perimeter assessments must precede camp-specific wet-up and logistical maneuvers.
• Maintain situational awareness	• Attacks can serve as diversions, as "requests for aid," or as actual assaults.
• Respond based on assessments	• Refugee relief is as much responding to local villagers' concerns as helping refugees.

Through country team training operations in Romania in 2004—including the preparatory work in Colorado—students learned disaster relief planning (including refugee camp development and maintenance), mass casualty aid (nonmedical), emergency first aid, triage needs assessment (nonmedical), techniques for maintaining site security and the fixing of perimeters, the process of threat assessment, the process of personnel deployment and task assignment, map interpretation and intelligence, and radio communication. These are field skills of direct use to those who move on to careers in practicing anthropology, overseas development, NGO outreach, and many others. A student practicing on- and off-loading of supplies with a helicopter in Romania is authentically preparing for assignment to the most challenging of field situations.

This program also enabled our students to improve their writing skills, specifically in ways that are useful on site, under stress. Students maintained daily logs of specific activities, these tied to the administrative and service components of the program. The writing of briefs, issue papers, and field reports summarizing "key learnings" and "best practices" were essential. The "hot washes" and after-action briefings produced by students enrolled in the project—even though derived from simulations—are precisely the kind of briefings they will have to produce should they find themselves working in a refugee camp in Kenya or a hurricane relief encampment in Louisiana.

Table 6.2   Students participating in the Romanian field exercise also were presented with these best practices and derived these lessons learned. For comparative purposes, these same best practices are reiterated in Chapter 7, in the box "Best Practices, Lessons Learned #2," on Iraqi helo-diplomacy and emergency tactics.

Best Practices #2	Lessons Learned #2
• Emergency action plan (EAP)	• Plan developed with input of American citizens (i.e., the authors) and Romanian military personnel. Key elements: identification of ingress and egress routes, use of non-encrypted radio communications for land and air movements, and assignment of roles to facilitate rapid camp evacuation.

(*continued*)

Table 6.2   (*Continued*)

Best Practices #2	Lessons Learned #2
• On-site security	• A hasty perimeter, established on arrival, was followed by establishment of fixed-site perimeter. Hasty security perimeter removes "soft target" vulnerabilities otherwise inherent in unplanned delays, breakdowns, and logistical difficulties. Radio communication and field observation post established on nearby hill overlooking camp. Later, site map developed, pin-pointing all proximate terrain and infrastructural features.
• Automatic response	• Training in Colorado preceded deployment and simulations in Romania. Emphasized in rank order: principles of teamwork, logistics, and geopolitical environment. In Romania, students began to develop automatic level of teamwork in triage activities and mass casualty responses, as well as in security overruns and bug-out situations. A "practices fluidity" eventually emerged.
• Physical fitness	• Importance of physical fitness cannot be overstated. Problems such as diarrhea, fatigue, and mental duress, as well as injury, likely will occur. Integrated strength/endurance regimen enable coping as activities continue. 35-to-50 lb. pack transport ability required.
• 24/7 action	• Students engaged 24/7 in the field, with little down time to "catch a breath." From students' perspectives, expected/ unexpected training activities and simulations could—and did—occur at virtually any time. Lead team trainers (a U.S. diplomat and a Romanian colonel) paid close attention to warning signs of possible fatigue or burnout.

Table 6.3   Insights gained from cultural and medical anthropology proved especially important with this set of "best practices" and "lessons learned." For comparative purposes, these same "best practices" are reiterated in Chapter 7, in the box "Best Practices, Lessons Learned #1," with lessons derived from three actual cases.

Best Practices #3	Lessons Learned #3
• Cultural sensitivity and sociopolitical awareness	• Students confronted scenarios, such as "graveyard incursion" and "village protest," requiring cultural sensitivity— gained through class work, on-site discussions with team, and interchanges with "villagers." Gestural/Haptic communications included.
• Knowledge of local authority structures	• Students had to negotiate with leadership of nearby "village" once they made the mistake of appearing to interfere with local elections, the consequence of a misunderstood comment by a student "aid worker." A rethinking of the role of religion in power politics also was required.
• Medical mission familiarity	• Students built on ICRC training to perform simulated medical emergency responses for "refugees," complemented by land (ambulance) and air (helicopter) transport. Triage, bandaging, and stretchering featured.
• Writing, reporting, radioing	• Daily logs maintained by each student. Teams prepared daily pre-exercise briefings, in-situ analyses, and post-exercise "hot washes." Intracamp radio communications used for postings and updates.

The Romanian initiative incorporated elements of what we refer to as "pragmatic humanitarianism" (Van Arsdale 2006), discussed in more depth in the concluding chapter. Tied to an emerging theory of obligation, this notion of humanitarianism features hands-on training with at-risk populations. It respects rather than castigates humanitarian intervention. It engages the simple liberal premise that what one person does, within one grassroots agency or field site, makes a difference. Through what are termed "obligated actions," the materially possible (for example, a network of service providers) is linked with the morally possible (for instance, institutional accountability).

We believe that virtually all the students who participated in the Romanian exercise benefited greatly from their experiences. Several used their experiences as "springboards" to other university-based overseas opportunities, some of these also in the Balkans (for example, Bosnia, Croatia, Albania). Several followed up with master's theses or major research papers that dealt with topics of humanitarian intervention, international security, disaster relief, and refugee affairs. Career-wise, some of the students subsequently went on to work for IGOs and NGOs. One serves as a specialist with the American Red Cross. Another serves as an analyst with InterAction. Still another works with the U.S. military.

FIXING PERIMETERS, ESTABLISHING SITES, AND SECURING OPERATIONS

There is no one-size-fits-all formula for local and regional security plans, or for the types of fortifications and perimeters that might define the fixed site. This is one of those areas where experience counts, and intelligence on the local security and threat environment is vital. As a general proposition, resources will be limited, and it will be necessary to badger higher-ranking authorities for enough to get the job done. There will rarely, if ever, be surplus. Sometimes the only definition given to the initial perimeter of a fixed site is a small fence of local reeds and grasses, or a stand of shrubs with some hand-lettered signing posted. This was the case with our camp in Creede, Colorado. In other more nomadic operations, such as reconnaissance to select a location for a fixed site, or short-term missions such as civilian medical assistance exercises (CMAXs) that might be conducted out of the backs of Hummers situated near rock walls, the "perimeter" might be a few armored vehicles with tough men sporting big guns on top.

Once the team decides to establish a more permanent presence, however, design of the fixed site begins with attention to the regional security situation and the perimeter. Basic survival needs include protection from hazardous elements, clean sustainable water supply, terrain features suitable for defense in event of attack, and terrain features suitable for an air-mobile evacuation if escape or emergency medical evacuation is required. All of these have served as the foundation for military encampments and fortresses since Kysis and before. Securing the closest highpoint for a communications relay and security observation post, as well as to prevent an encroaching attacker from firing down into the fixed site position, is another "first on site" checklist priority. On a CMAX mission in Kandahar, Afghanistan, Derrin Smith's armored convoy had barely stopped when the first fire team began moving in all haste to secure the nearest highpoint. These men were the first to deploy and the last to rejoin the unit immediately before departure. Upon movement out of the site, the team revised its return route to an alternate in order to avoid interdiction by insurgent forces. Although it returned without incident to its base, Smith later learned that a supply unit following the original route that afternoon had been engaged in a fire fight. Changing routes and not establishing externally discernible patterns or habits can be a life saver.

On initial arrival at a site that has been prescreened for establishing a more permanent fixed site, two things should happen. First, the accompanying security team should establish a hasty defensive perimeter while the team leader radios geo-coordinates and arrival data to the main base. The hasty defensive perimeter includes securing the highest point overlooking the site; establishing observation posts (OP) for surveillance of all approaches to the site; and quick deployment of concertina wire or available fencing materials—even wood slats, rope, or twine on stakes at waist-high level—to limit access to the perimeter to a single control gate. Owing to the potential, especially in humanitarian interventions or disasters, to be quickly overwhelmed by the local population you are there to serve, starting with a somewhat smaller perimeter and gradually expanding the dimensions to a larger area and buffer zone provides better control. Second, the target population should be directed into a queue at the main "gate" in order to begin processing them. The worst case security situation is to be surrounded on all sides by a crush of people. Relief convoys frequently encounter the onslaught of crowds, even panic and stampedes, when they roll to a stop in an uncontrolled area and desperate citizens are able to simply rush the trucks. Aid workers also must be protected. Thus the first steps must always involve controlling a small patch of earth, as well as any intended beneficiaries.

Even in very remote regions, word of a team's presence will spread amazingly quickly. Emergency relief workers tell stories of rolling into remote sites unannounced and within hours being overwhelmed by incredible surges of local people seeking assistance. (Surge control, although not a subject of this text, is standard in the training of emergency managers at home and abroad.) During our civil-military training exercise in Romania, we made sure that our graduate students faced this challenge. As their convoy approached the fixed site that the students had selected from their earlier field reconnaissance and site survey, we instituted a surge of "casualties" and "disaster victims." After a short while one of our students approached in frustration, objecting: "This isn't fair, we aren't set up yet!" In their planning, the students had carefully allocated tasks to all team personnel to set up the clinic, food distribution, and facilities; no one was left to process the "victims" that flooded their site. Team leaders quickly got the message and re-organized on the fly. A fluid situation was unfolding on the ground.

The first phase of establishing the fixed site can easily be the most dangerous. Acceptance by the local community and the corresponding militias or political leaders cannot be guaranteed; desperate populations may in turn victimize the humanitarians, their military counterparts, and auxiliary personnel. The team is most vulnerable to the crime of opportunity or whims of unscrupulous local actors if security and control have not been adequately established. In a worst-case scenario where control cannot be established and the team is at high risk, the bulk of the supplies should be left with representatives of the local population and personnel should be evacuated. It is not uncommon, as aid workers have recently discovered in Darfur, for transport vehicles to be in such high demand that the mere presence of trucks, Jeeps, and other vehicles transforms the relief team into a high-value target.

Permanent Urban Facilities

Not every fixed site starts in a dusty desert or patch of swampy earth during monsoon season. Many new missions commence with establishing a fixed site in an urban center, and, during conflict and immediate postconflict environments, site planning can literally be the difference between accomplishing a mission and experiencing abject failure. Mission failure and death at times go hand in hand.

Urban centers in nonpermissive and semipermissive areas of operation run the gamut from a vibrant, teaming metropolis, such as Beirut, to a dirty, sweltering site, such as Kandahar. Dense populations, political seats of national power, crowded international airports, and busy ports and/or transit facilities are just a few of the characteristics of most such urban centers. Permanent facilities for the country team typically include both offices and residences. In more "rustic," less developed nations, especially in conflict zones, one commonly finds residences joined with the office operations. Even in relative peace and security in newly emerging economies such as China during the 1970s and 1980s, it paid to be creative. In China during those two decades it was generally more convenient to rent fully equipped hotel suites for both office and residential purposes. Advantages for headquarters (HQ) operations include more modern conveniences, better security and logistics, access to government offices and commercial centers, and flexibility regarding occupation and exit dates. Paradoxically, yet seemingly by design, such hotel-office facilities afford a significant buffer between the occupants and the local population. No advisor can see ordinary Cuban neighborhoods, abject poverty, and side-alley misery from a luxury hotel in Havana. This is the case in nearly all countries of operation, so although modern conveniences and logistics may help country teams get established in urban centers quickly and flexibly, the trade off is difficulty in "culturally accessing" the target/beneficiary population and, certainly, the near impossibility of that target population gaining access to the team's services. In some conflict-riddled urban centers, such as Ramadi, Iraq, and Jalalabad, Afghanistan, humanitarian relief, aid, and development groups often prefer to rent offices with apartments in local neighborhoods, thus being closer to the target populations. In virtually all cases, however, the fundamental logistical considerations for the country team are the same.

Urban Offices and Services

Basic office facilities, rented on the local market, may or may not offer running water, indoor plumbing for toilet facilities, or even electricity. If electrical power is available, it might not be from the public grid but from diesel-fuel generators, which range from small, garage-style gasoline-fueled models to much larger and higher capacity diesel versions with power backup, current modulators, and failover to uninterruptable power supplies. Other office and residential buildings might have a connection to the national power grid but because of frequent outages have failover to diesel generators. Before signing a lease and taking occupancy, team representatives must observe the building, the utility grid, and the immediate neighborhoods over a period of time (which may be days, weeks or months, mission permitting).

Initial issues for the team to consider pre-occupancy include ingress and egress. In the event of emergency, whether violent protests in the street, civil war, or natural disasters such as earthquakes, do you have safe access into and exit from your facilities? This point seems fundamental, but personnel have been hunted down and killed by mobs, because they had no way out, except through the ranks of the attackers. In the event of fire, or a fire fight, what are the safe routes out? Is there an interior area that is strong enough to act as a "panic room" until help arrives if you find yourself under assault? Are there protective barriers against explosions or small arms fire? Sandbags, concrete T-walls, Hesco-barriers filled with earth, concrete bunkers, and take-cover shelters all provide protection against every-day threats in a hostile area of operation.

Considerations of "cover" and "concealment" (terms that are complementary, not identical) also are essential. Protection against bullets and shrapnel constitutes cover for you and your staff. Concealment, however, is the ability to hide, even if you are not protected against projectiles. A camouflage uniform in bushes provides concealment for a soldier, although he may not have protective cover from direct or indirect fire. Although color-matching is an important element of camouflage and concealment, of even greater importance is motion (or the absence thereof). A deer can blend into the forest easily, but a bob of the head or flick of the tail is all that it takes for experienced hunters to draw a clean bead. Movement, above all else, captures attention and draws the eyes of spotters. Sometimes, quieting one's breathing and remaining motionless in a doorway shadow is all that it takes to deceive a potential assailant. Taking a good look at the interior and the exterior of one's facility, at different times of day and night, as well as at different light angles, helps one to plan for stealthy movements in event of danger.

The urban office facility should offer some of the same characteristics of observation and area surveillance as a remote fixed site. In a conflict, one needs to be able to see and monitor the activities on the street, sidewalks, alleys, and open ground without exposing oneself. A variety of simple, high-technology sensors are available at reasonable prices to provide all-weather and all-light-level capabilities in and around the office area. Small battery-powered, radio-frequency motion detectors and emergency lights, often with built-in smoke or carbon monoxide detectors, significantly enhance occupant safety. Although current U.S. Department of State regulations do not authorize or approve rope ladders for office or residential evacuation, from lower levels (third floor or less), they can provide the flexibility of egress that makes an emergency exit possible. There are a variety of fire escape chutes on the market that can be deployed from significant heights off a balcony. For the expenditure of a few hundred dollars, such devices can overcome the shortcomings in building safety designs often encountered in urban settings in less developed nations.

Once entries, exits, emergency escapes, cover and concealment are handled, and safety and surveillance systems have been evaluated, "creature comforts" can be addressed—from electrical supplies to plumbing and toilets. We have worked in facilities where the latrine was simply a hole in the floor of a shed, or where the urinal was a fifth-story drain pipe outside a window that rolled down to the street gutter. In such cases, ordering small, portable chemical camping toilets can greatly improve sanitation as well as morale. Flies, vermin, and stench can be distracting. Furthermore, external latrines generally are located in exposed places where staff or beneficiaries can be victimized. It is not coincidence that many assaults on women at refugee camps and aid stations have occurred in the vicinity of toilet or shower facilities. Most fixed-site operations, both urban and remote, find cyalume or similar chemical light sticks extremely useful for marking obstacles, passageways, or key facilities—such as a port-a-pot—during dark hours and power blackouts. Offices in peri-urban areas also should be selected with an eye toward other facilities and resources. By situating closer to major financial centers, roadways, embassy buildings, restaurants, and market areas, staff will be less exposed when accessing key services. However, marketplaces, foreign missions, and financial centers are often the first areas to be targeted by insurgent forces, protest demonstrators, and rioters. When bombs explode in Baghdad, for example, popular market places and government centers nearly always are at "ground zero" for the blasts.

There is no single correct protocol for situating offices in an urban center. Thinking logically about staff safety, being able to see panoramically and to plan an escape—and with luck adding some creature comforts and modern conveniences—is the best a team can do. Creativity goes a long way; backyard tooling and engineering can make even stark facilities more comfortable and functional, and the simplest of conveniences can elevate staff morale. Derrin Smith's experience with the U.S. Marines, both as a Marine and while embedded with Marine Corps personnel as a civilian, leaves him convinced that "some of the world's best all-time scroungers wear Marine green." The things a motivated Marine can do with a number ten can, a stick, a pocket knife, and a few canteens of water will amaze the uninitiated: the team will have an REI-quality camp field shower in no time.

Residences

Many of the concerns mentioned for an urban office site also apply to personal residences. A rule of thumb on personal residences for staff is that they should be located close enough together so that residents can look after one another, keep tabs on one another, and be easily accessible in event of an emergency evacuation. However, too highly concentrated staff in a single location, building, or neighborhood has the disadvantage of creating a high-value target. Local threat conditions will dictate which of the approaches are best suited to a mission. In one instance, a USAID officer in Jordan had a small stand of bushes around the pathway to his front door. Gunmen were able to conceal themselves, shoot the officer to death, and escape. The officer's regular schedule, predictability, lone-target profile, and lack of personal security guards all contributed to his death, in a city generally known for its safety. Residences of foreign workers and officials are always potential targets. Having a panic room, reliable communications with redundancy (for example, a cell phone for normal use and walkie-talkies for emergency use), and reliable food and water supplies for two weeks in an emergency greatly enhance staff safety and security. Heavy-duty doors with steel bolts, secured windows, and the ability to study and observe the surrounding neighborhood are all strongly recommended.

Surveillance, by both friendly and hostile forces, is the norm. Countersurveillance training for all staff is an important tool for their personal survival toolkit. (Guidelines for this are provided in another section of this text.) Strangers should never be permitted to access one's home or personal quarters. One must be wary of local and foreign national service technicians, maid or cook services, and utilities or delivery personnel. Even acquaintances can turn out to be threats. One such circumstance cost a young U.S. diplomat his life in Addis Ababa, Ethiopia, in 2009. His murder occurred in a U.S. Department of State residential apartment complex, with all the external security and safeguards one would expect. On his birthday, he voluntarily granted access to his apartment to a person who proved to be his killer. Vehicle movements, agency schedules, and personal activities of the American staff and local personnel likely had been observed, noted, and reported by the assailant's colleagues, thus aiding his attack. Never assume that you are not being watched. To the contrary, always assume that you, your colleagues, and your vulnerabilities are being studied.

PERMANENT RURAL FACILITIES

Rural and remote sites present a full range of complementary threats. Being distant from an embassy or financial center might remove the country team from the urban target zone for insurgents but also put it out of the reach of friendly security forces or the protection of a concentrated civilian law enforcement contingent. The team's operations and safe conduct ultimately might be at the whim of local war lords, tribal leaders, militia commanders, bandits, or other NSAs. The unwary team can become a "soft target" or easy prey. Relief convoys and aid stations have discovered this in Iraq and Afghanistan—as well as in several African nations—since 2003.

For example, Robert Fowler, a brilliant Canadian diplomat and UN envoy to Niger, disappeared in 2008 while heading into one of his favorite backcountry mining regions. Although he was intimately familiar with the region and the local culture, initial accounts suggested that he was either lost or dead. According to others, he was a captive of al-Qaeda of Mahgreb, an African affiliate of Osama bin Laden's group. He was eventually freed in April of 2009.

Offices, residences, and remote "presence posts" (which often incorporate two into one, as discussed later), away from urban centers, can offer some of the most fulfilling, exciting, and valuable work that an officer or aid worker can hope to experience. Tribal settings, remote villages and encampments, presence posts surrounded by dense jungle or expanses of forbidding desert—country team personnel who embrace such assignments often are rewarded in both spirit and satisfaction. Much of Peter Van Arsdale's applied field research has been conducted in such areas. Much of Derrin Smith's career has been spent "on remotes"; he has expressed a strong preference for the austerity of distant wilderness operations, rural forward operating bases, and fire bases in desolate hostile areas. His forays into Baghdad and the Green Zone (with the pressure of almost-daily rocket attacks), while exciting, were less rewarding. The Green Bean coffee shop, convenient laundry facilities, and internet availability in the CHUs (containerized housing units)—near Saddam's infamous swimming pool—were not as rewarding as the streets of al-Chaim or the market near al-Asad.

In short, rural operations (as considered elsewhere in this text) tend to rely on small facilities in small towns or agricultural regions. They are characterized by low population densities, agrarian or subsistence living, few modern conveniences, and a significant influence exercised by local political or tribal powers. Although a major roadway might pass near this fixed site, the site still might be dozens of miles from the national capital, a major urban center, or the team's own embassy. A more robust inventory of infrastructure, in concert with greater independence to sustain operations apart from headquarters, is required. Security may rely primarily on local assets and the staff's own wits. (For example, it may be necessary to improvise so that sleeping quarters do not double as the work area where clients or beneficiaries are received.) Psychological and security considerations must proceed in lockstep.

Rural Offices and Services

One key characteristic of rural offices is self-reliance over extended periods of time. Electrical power generation typically is from portable power generators with fuel bought in the local market or the nearest small town. Water usually has to be purified on site, using microfilters, electrostatic purifiers, or boiling and chemical treatments. In certain high-risk rural sites, some combination of these treatments is necessary to maximize the chances for water purity and minimize the chances for illness. Food supplies secured through reliable local markets obviously are key as well.

Air service options must be fully evaluated in advance of the selection of a rural fixed site. Pre-arranged air-mobile evacuation services for medical or security emergencies are generally necessary. Rural offices may be too distant for efficient overland travel back to an urban center for the sick or injured. Marking a clearing with a large "H" using rocks or other distinctive natural materials can signal an impromptu helicopter landing area.

A rural office operation generally requires greater dependence on the local population for support than does an urban one. Even little things such as security against petty theft or banditry can be quickly alleviated with an appeal to the right local actor. At one remote site in 2004 in Afghanistan Derrin Smith's team had placed a small marker flag on a hillside with an antenna and a sensor array, yet the fabric marker kept disappearing. A couple of inquiries provided information that a young boy was taking the fabric to his mother, who immediately put each specimen to good use in the household. The team decided to provide fabric and food to the small thief and develop a marker protection plan, and the thefts indeed stopped. A positive local engagement, as simple as it was, solved the problem. In rural areas where subsistence living and extreme poverty are the norm, petty theft is often a great challenge. Constant, thorough inventorying and accountability of supplies are necessary. There is no worse feeling than heading to the supply room with a large group of inbound clients only to discover that the bulk of the cans and boxes have already been emptied of their contents and the containers placed back on the shelves.

Offices located in rural locations also need to have the ability to function independently from headquarters for periods of time dictated by HQ resupply schedules. Perimeter security, surveillance, constant observation of routes of approach, climate forecasts, and a warning system for such natural disasters as forest fires and monsoon floods all need to be taken into account. Establishing a well-considered rally point for staff, in the event of an emergency evacuation, is vital. In more extreme environments, such as remote posts in Anbar Province, Iraq, one must also have a "harbor site" nearby for a possible emergency "bug out;" canned food, bottled water, sleeping bags, medical supplies, and communications equipment to support staff in a concealed mode must be available until evacuation teams can arrive. Each team member should have a small backpack or "bug-out bag" with basic self-sustaining items within reach at all times, especially if security in the area is starting to deteriorate.

Residences

Team residences usually consist of existing buildings, converted as needed, or large fixed tents. CHUs are rarely used. As noted above, sleeping quarters and residences should be separate from areas where local clients are met or treated. Since country team staff are particularly vulnerable when sleeping it is necessary to maintain "fire watch" or security patrols 24 hours a day. It is never permissible to have all of the staff asleep at the same time. It is never permissible, in a semipermissive area of operations, to assign 100 percent of the fire watch or over-night security responsibilities to local, non-staff personnel. A senior staff member should cover the late night security shifts and the monitoring of local guards. As a general rule and when nighttime staffing permits, assign two team members—one on roving patrol with a radio, the second at a more secure "base" looking after the residences and sleeping quarters. The roving patrol can radio back frequently to the base, reporting any activities on the approaches to the fixed site and updating the status of key points near the perimeter. Night vision equipment, although optional, is always a benefit for "graveyard" security observations.

The practice of keeping a few members of the staff awake, alert, and efficiently observing 24 hours a day takes discipline and planning. In Anbar Province a small OP of young Marines, located near key residences, was over-taken by assailants. Two members of the fire team had decided to "catch a few winks" during the late night shift; the OP was vulnerable. The attackers were stealthy in their approach. Reports to us indicate that the one member who was awake might have been reading a magazine and wearing a headset listen-ing to music as the terrorists breached their rooftop position. The fire team was slaughtered in their sleep, stripped, and all weapons and equipment either taken or disabled. Several factors likely contributed to the tragedy in addition to the team's lack of vigilance. The rooftop observation post had been used repeatedly in previous weeks, likely alerting enemy militia to a usual presence there. Enemy surveillance might have inferred a loss of vigilance by the young Marines, as weeks passed without incident. The team probably was lulled into a sense of security by the relative inactivity in the district and relative peace on the streets. Picking the period of least alertness, which biorhythmically occurs between about 2:30 A.M. and 4:00 A.M. in most people, the assailants engaged an action that did serve immediately thereafter to alert all the forces in MNF-West to the residual threat against observation posts in Anbar Province.

If well-trained soldiers in modern combat can experience such a deadly lapse, imagine the risk for sleeping country team members after weeks of gru-eling work at a rural fixed site. Continual vigilance is vital, and, as we have said, team members are most vulnerable at their residences during sleeping hours. And militia attacks and bandit raids are often made in the hours of lowest biological attentiveness. Fire watch teams and security guards need to be constantly tested and reminded that their duty is not just an "after-hours chore" or "duty officer inconvenience." Staff and clients at the fixed site are totally reliant on their alert attention to detail. Danger, in animal or more often human predatory form, can strike under cover of darkness in remote areas.

Presence Posts

Recent movement toward the use of "presence posts" has created a debate in some diplomatic and humanitarian aid circles. A presence post is a facility, perhaps little more than a thatched-roof hut with a radio set, intended to extend some visible outreach to a more remote community. Even the term *presence patrol* has generated some discussion in the military. If the presence post or patrol is just for the purpose of being seen in an area, what else constitutes the mission and what are the limitations on the teams? Is it security? Is it law enforcement? Is it reconnaissance? Is it community outreach?

The mission of any presence post should be detailed before extending personnel and resources into harm's way. In some nontraditional diplomatic circles, a presence post to create an American presence in a remote area, featuring outreach to local communities, makes perfect sense. To give a rural community a hint of American presence and experience can represent grassroots diplomacy. By contrast, to many senior Foreign Service officers and old guard diplomats, presence post "thatched-roof diplomacy" is a distraction from the core mission of diplomacy. It is perceived as an unnecessary waste of time, money and matériel and needlessly places diplomatic personnel and support staff at risk in unstable regions. In the opinion of some Foreign Service veterans, traditional diplomacy best takes place in fortress-like embassies or bunkered and secured consulates; services are rendered from secure facilities behind blast-proof enclosures; and outreach to the local government is done in carefully orchestrated and scripted events. The American expatriate community can report to the embassy or consulate for support services, and public relations outreach is the primary vehicle to influence local perceptions of the United States. We have heard these opinions in locales as diverse as El Salvador, Bosnia, and Timor-Leste.

There are American Cultural Centers and similar facilities in many urban areas to communicate information on American culture to locals. Kicking through sand dunes or hacking through the jungles to a remote presence post may be to the liking of some officers, but to others, it is anathema to the central intent of diplomatic practice. In semipermissive environments, rarely is a presence post deployed except by specifically trained and highly skilled special operations intelligence and military personnel. Heavily armed, with instant satellite communications to contact their support and extraction units, self-sufficient and trained to live off the land for weeks at a time, remote operations field teams have a unique portfolio of proven skills for such hostile, remote environments. Examples include U.S. Navy SEALS and Army Special Forces ("Green Berets"), Marine Corps Force Recon, STA and special operations Marines; civilian personnel include national clandestine service Special Operations Group (SOG) officers and those from other similar U.S. agencies. Some members of the highly controversial Joint Special Operations Command (JSOC) also participate.

In the U.S. Department of State there is a perceived need for grooming highly skilled special operations personnel for more remote and hostile deployments. Some of these are assigned to presence posts. However, the argument over mission and culture within the department must first be settled. For example, to what extent should humanitarian imperatives be placed above battle imperatives? What is the proper balance between military and civilian personnel? How can both "intrusion" and "sovereignty" be dealt with equitably? Basic principles still prevail. Such an operative is responsible for his or her survival and for the well-being of the team. Failure to come out alive is, first and foremost, a personal failure. If a team member suffers losses yet survives, it does no good to point fingers at headquarters or those in positions of higher authority, at auxiliary/ support groups, at local security guards, or at private security agencies. If a team member suffers losses and does not survive, the whole argument is moot.

PERMANENT REMOTE FACILITIES

Fixed sites in truly remote locations are increasingly common as humanitarian needs and crises dictate intervention. Certain of the characteristics for permanent remote facilities are similar to those discussed above for permanent rural facilities. When correctly planned and supplied, these facilities can offer many of the comforts of home and allow staff to satisfy—with a degree of pleasantness—the mission requirements in the local area of operations.

Forward operating bases, fire bases, and PRT sites in Iraq and Afghanistan illustrate the ability of the U.S. military and associated military contractors in taking a barren piece of rock or sand and "instantly" establishing a small city, with adequate food and entertainment and leisure capabilities to enhance morale. At some sites accessible principally by helicopter, there are enough built-in "creature comforts" to allow extended stays. Firebase Anaconda near Tarin Kowt, Oruzgan Province, Afghanistan—the birthplace of Mullah Omar and the Taliban—provides a useful example. In the autumn of 2004, Derrin Smith was on site when the so-called Honolulu Marathon was run around the base perimeter, in honor of its namesake some 8,000 miles to the east. Later, steak and crab legs were served for a holiday meal. The PRT section was then in the process of being upgraded, within the perimeter of the firebase; nightly patrols outside the perimeter swept away attackers. By 2007, long after Smith's departure, this permanent remote facility had become a constant Taliban target. According to a media release by the American Forces Press Service on August 30, 2007:

> Elements of the 1st Brigade, 205th Afghan National Army Corps, along with coalition forces, repelled a direct attack on Firebase Anaconda in Afghanistan's Oruzgan province today, killing 11 of the attackers. Insurgents attacked the base from multiple directions with 72 mm rockets, small arms and heavy machine gun fire, officials said. Coalition close-air support conducted precision air strikes, successfully destroying the enemy fighters. This was the fourth attack on Firebase Anaconda this month. An estimated 74 insurgents were killed in the previous attacks on the base. The recent probing attacks have reinforced credible intelligence gathered by coalition forces of a planned, large-scale attack on Firebase Anaconda, officials said.

During Smith's work in Tarin Kowt in 2004, he had the opportunity to interview the mayor of the city and discuss in detail his plans and desires for both economic development and peace. His supporting infantry group, from the U.S. Army "Bobcats" (based in Hawaii), had recently suffered a loss of four soldiers, killed on patrol. Emotions were running high, and the mayor appealed for help—not for retaliation—but for the support of agriculture and the creation of a foreign market where residents could sell their produce, generating revenues from something other than poppies. "Our guns and our poppies are our only source of revenue," the mayor complained more than once. "If we allow you to take those away, we have nothing. Others will take control of us. That is not acceptable." At the time, the U.S. program for the locals featured disarmament, demobilization, and reintegration (DDR in military parlance) into a civilian economic structure. Tribal chiefs drew their power and influence from their armed supporters, who also were necessary to maintain the local peace, keep other armed groups at bay, and protect the poppy harvest.

The officials at Firebase Anaconda desperately wanted to reduce arms in the district. Given the four recent deaths, as well as the general tension, every insertion into the town, medical exercise, and building project faced the threat of firefights and interdiction. None of the violence could have occurred without the knowledge of or (to some extent) complicity of the mayor himself. It was his turf, his district, his clans. From the perspective of the U.S. team members, it was a tough slog.

Therefore, a permanent remote facility can afford a country team a base for sustained operations—and sustained cross-cultural communications—that include agricultural development, as well as projects benefiting other sectors. Not all will be successful. In Tarin Kowt, scrawled on a piece of container cardboard, was a hand-lettered sign that declared "Mercy Corps," located near a traditional mud structure. The facility was empty.

TEMPORARY REMOTE OPERATIONS

Most remote fixed sites begin as quick response, temporary operations facilities. Refugee camps, medical aid centers, relief distribution points, and disaster assistance encampments represent a few of these types of sites. Note that these sites have a history of becoming more and more permanent. Team members must be aware that every footprint they leave, literal or metaphorical, has the potential of becoming a permanent tent city or shanty town. Something as seemingly simple as a water distribution station can morph over time into a permanent supply distribution center. This can have more negative than positive ramifications. Over the decades Palestinian refugee camps evolved from tent cities to simple stone structures to brick and concrete apartment buildings. In and near Amman, Jordan, "temporary" facilities for Palestinian refugees are actually more permanent, in established metropolitan districts and small towns. This likely was never intended, either by the host governments or by refugees who desperately wish to return to their home territories.

Draining resources away from host government civilian populations and encroaching on tribal lands and locally demarcated territories mean that conflict among external and internal parties is almost inevitable. When addressing urgent human needs at a temporary site, remote from headquarters or the base of operations, use constant vigilance and sensitivities to local customs. The mere presence of a team may generate a permanent population base, often in an area where the added human headcount is not sustainable based on natural resources and local socioeconomic activities.

As Peter Van Arsdale has noted elsewhere (2009), such is the case today in some parts of Darfur, Sudan. Constant harassing attacks by *janjiweed* militia and roaming groups of bandits have placed additional pressures on highly vulnerable refugees and IDPs, making relief operations extremely difficult. Sudanese President Omar al-Bashir's expulsion of such key humanitarian groups as Oxfam early in 2009, in the face of his own indictment by the International Criminal Court for his genocidal crimes, has exacerbated the situation to the highest-level crisis. Most of the food and essential matériel for intra-Darfur IDPs was being transported by trucks and air-mobile operatives. Refugees continued to seek safe harbor at over-taxed camps in Chad and the Central African Republic. Increasingly, truck convoys were being ambushed as high-value targets by bandits and militia forces. In early 2009, MSF personnel fortunately were released unharmed after being held captive by armed militia-men after their vehicles and equipment had been stolen. The truce signed by al-Bashir and representatives of Darfur's Justice and Equality Movement on February 23, 2010, may make little difference. Few ordeals in Darfur have had happy endings since the beginning of this century.

In short, a team must approach temporary remote sites as if they might become permanent. Lesser levels of diligence are unacceptable. Additional considerations include:

- Intelligence and reconnaissance, district and regional, including aerial photography, topographic analysis, meteorological analysis, *in situ*
- Resource survey for site threat assessment, vulnerability, and sustainability
- Needs assessment of client populations, complemented by integrated mission planning and analysis
- Security team insertion to secure and control a small perimeter
- Service team insertion to begin administering to target population
- Buildup of site for security and sustainability enhancements
- Turnover to local population (when coplanned and appropriate)

DISENGAGEMENT

Turnover and disengagement from an area of operations can be a bittersweet moment for country team personnel. By one measure, a fixed site that has been built up and become "home" for foreign aid workers and staff for an extended period can be judged to have become successful when local staff, counterparts, and indigenous personnel are able to take over all operations. In Iraq, where military disengagement theoretically has been planned from the outset, certain upgraded facilities with townlike infrastructures—from water treatment plants to power generation facilities to health clinics—have, in fact, been placed under Iraqi control and ownership. The PIC (Provincial Iraqi Control) process is marked with celebrations and fanfare within some local communities.

At a forward operating base (then named Blue Diamond) near Ramadi, Iraq, which Derrin Smith called home for many months, the PIC event was enthusiastically embraced by the Iraqi people. It created significant goodwill for the coalition forces and aid workers in the area. Immediately thereafter, the Anbar Provincial Council and governor's office unveiled their plans for parks, a tribal sheikh's center, museums, and even a water park on the banks of the Euphrates River. From firefights with dissidents to a ground breaking for entertainment attractions, Blue Diamond had finally achieved success as perceived by both sets of parties. As of early 2009, Saddam's so-called JDAM Palace was being renovated as a museum. It had once served one of his sons as a combination playhouse and torture facility. The museum will not let visitors forget these horrors.

PART III

APPLICATIONS AND IMPLICATIONS

CHAPTER 7

FOREIGN SERVICE, TRIBAL OUTREACH, AND SPECIAL OPERATIONS

Humanitarian initiatives are engaged in a number of ways, some of which are deemed "traditional," "above board," and "diplomatically straight forward." The U.S. Foreign Service exemplifies this approach. Other approaches are deemed "nontraditional," "clandestine," and "diplomatically circuitous." U.S. Special Operations exemplify this. An understanding of country teams and their operations requires a broad understanding of these organizations. Given our special interest in the intersection of civilian and military initiatives, and in certain joint civilian-military programs, we must lay out historical and conceptual developments. We must also delineate precisely where we stand. And insights derived from anthropology are crucial as instances involving tribal outreach.

As civilian and military personnel work together, we can learn how the former influence the latter. How do civilians "push the system"? How are institutions being reshaped as country teams carry out their assignments? How do the ethical "rules of engagement" we have sketched in this text play out? This chapter addresses these questions. Links are explicated between the best practices covered in Chapter 6 (particularly in the case of the Romanian field school) and the lessons learned, as demonstrated by this chapter's case studies from Afghanistan and Iraq.

THE UNITED STATES FOREIGN SERVICE

Images of legionnaires astride camels in the Sahara Desert come to the minds of some who think "foreign service." Although some contemporary U.S. Foreign Service Officers (FSOs) do serve in exotic locations, few ride camels. Most are posted at, or near, any of the over 250 U.S. embassies, consulates, and diplomatic missions worldwide. Others are stationed at various foreign affairs agencies, including the Department of State (DoS), the Department of Commerce, the Department of Agriculture, and USAID.

The DoS serves as the umbrella. It is 220 years old. Early on, the diplomatic service saw the likes of John Adams and Benjamin Franklin in key roles. More recently, such legendary figures as John Foster Dulles, who served as Secretary of State under President Eisenhower, added a spark to international relations. Most recently, the role has witnessed the sharply contrasting styles of Condoleezza Rice and Hillary Clinton.

A merger of the diplomatic and consular services in 1924 led to the creation of the foreign service. Further legislative mandates and policy-driven restructurings occurred in 1927, 1930, 1939, 1946, 1954, and 1980. That of 1946 is of particular interest, because it is tied to the passage of the Foreign Service Act. Among the Act's various provisions was the establishment of the Foreign Service Institute. Charged with training FSOs and other employees, it took as its mantra: "Every successful diplomat has as his [sic] chief duty 'understanding' the people of the nation to which he [sic] has been assigned" (Kennard 1949: 154).

The expertise of cultural anthropologists was tapped early on as seminars in "area studies" were offered. Some were held in university settings. Advanced seminars in the analysis and interpretation of foreign cultures were offered to personnel who already had substantial experience abroad. The expertise of linguists was tapped as seminars in "politically useful" languages were offered: Arabic, Russian, and Chinese (Kennard 1949: 155). Today the Foreign Service Institute remains the federal government's primary training organization for officers and others engaged in the U.S. foreign affairs community. Most courses, including those on area studies, are offered at the George P. Shultz National Foreign Affairs Training Center (NFATC). The institute's five schools cover language studies, applied information technology, leadership and management, professional and area studies, and career transitioning. Speakers regularly include NGO, university, and mission representatives.

Several categories of officers *cum* civil servants are found within the foreign service. As the DoS website states: "Foreign Service Officers (FSOs) are America's advocates, promoting peace and supporting prosperity as they advance our interests and protect American citizens throughout the world." Such officers can choose any one of five career tracks: management, economic, political, public diplomacy, consular. The duties of those on the last-named track can include visa-related work and entrant evaluation at U.S. borders. (Consular Affairs is the bureau that oversees embassies, consulates, and visa issuance.) Foreign Area Officers (FAOs) and Foreign Service Specialists (FSSs) also are integral, with titles such as Regional Security Officer and Information Management Officer. (Derrin Smith is a Political Officer at the U.S. Embassy in Beirut.)

Note that another major category of personnel, that of Foreign Service National, has been revamped. Such personnel are now known as Locally Engaged Staff (LES). This change was made because not all "locals" who work for a given embassy are citizens of that country. In Iraq, for example, many locals are from neighboring countries. The LES service structure also was refined to lend greater credence (and accord greater benefits) to the contributions of such persons. Of the nearly 50,000 people who serve in the DoS/foreign service, some 30,000 are LES.

Originally, the term *ambassador* as used in Europe had referents to individuals representing the royal court. In the contemporary United States, ambassadors (known as ministers until the late nineteenth century) occupy the senior positions in each designated overseas country posting. The senior U.S. representative to the United Nations also is referred to as Ambassador. Persons functioning in other special roles, such as a Middle East peace envoy, are termed Ambassadors-at-Large. About one-third of the ambassadors are political appointees, chosen for reasons as diverse as their philanthropy, political insights, and/or networked connections. About two-thirds are career diplomats, some of these being selected from the ranks of senior USAID, Commerce, or Agriculture FSOs. Most personnel (that is, FAOs, FSOs, and FSSs) compete for their jobs through an examination/interview/selection process. SMEs (Subject Matter Experts) assist in the skills evaluation of candidates. DoS civil service employees at times have the opportunity to bid on jobs overseas, most often in countries with hard-to-fill postings.

An overseas mission is usually centered at the embassy. The Chief of Mission (that is, Ambassador) is assisted by the Deputy Chief of Mission; the latter is the senior office administrator. For example, in our work with the U.S. Embassy in Timor-Leste in 2007 and 2008, Ambassador Hans Klemm was assisted by Deputy Chief of Mission Hank Rector. Both made themselves available to assist us in a number of ways. Various FAOs, FSOs, FSSs, and LES handle the array of economic, cultural, political, logistical, and clerical duties at an embassy. USAID will be represented. Some "reciprocal" staff from other U.S. agencies also may be seconded there. An FSO usually will be a country team's main liaison. (In some parlance, a "mission" also is referred to as a type of "country team.")

Deputy assistant secretaries dominate specific issues and policy battles, as Joel Mowbray (2003) stresses. But desk officers run the show. He notes that there is usually one desk officer for every country, with more important nations having two or three. Between five and ten desk officers usually are assigned to a single office director:

> Each desk officer is considered *the* specialist in Washington on his or her country and also serves as the communication go-between—resulting

in an enormous amount of power in the hands of a typically low-level FSO . . . since all communication from the embassy must go through the filter of the desk officer, what folks in Washington know about the goings-on in a foreign country (particularly those not covered in the American press) largely hinges on what the desk officer chooses to pass on. (Mowbray 2003: 100)

In some cases, a desk officer can come from another venue. For example, in 2009 the desk officer for the Republic of the Congo was a science fellow, trained as a zoologist with a background in East Africa.

Not surprisingly, criticisms of the DoS/foreign service are regularly encountered. The 2001 bipartisan Hart-Rudman Commission termed the department "crippled" (Mowbray 2003: 92). Polarizing issues have included the extent to which the DoS administrative structure or organizational culture needs change; the extent to which diplomacy or security needs greater emphasis; the extent to which foreign interests should be "represented in" or American interests should be "represented out"; and the extent to which recruits to various senior posts should be "insiders" or "outsiders." From the Hart-Rudman report: "We recommend changing the Foreign Service's name to the U.S. Diplomatic Service. This rhetorical change will serve as a needed reminder that this group of people does not serve the interest of foreign states, but is a pillar of U.S. national security" (Mowbray 2003:92).

To the credit of DoS and the foreign service, awards are presented annually to officers and other staffers who offer the most useful constructive dissent. In June of 2008, coincident with the 40th anniversary of the establishment of the first American Foreign Service Association (AFSA) dissent award, named in honor of lawyer, military officer, and ambassador William R. Rivkin, Rachel Schneller was recognized for speaking out about the effects of PTSD on foreign service personnel returning from war zones. The Christian Herter Award for constructive dissent was presented to Jeffrey Feltman, Ambassador to Lebanon, who was recognized for challenging a DoS decision to construct a new compound at a Beirut site that might have put the lives of American and Lebanese personnel at high risk. The third award winner, Luke Zahner, was recognized for effective human rights reporting in Bangladesh under trying circumstances (Dorman 2008).

Virtually all foreign policy agreements and accords go through DoS, and virtually all interactions with the United Nations and other transnational political entities (some in concert with DoD) go through DoS as well. The information flow—policy impact—security development chain, and thus the work of country teams, is influenced accordingly. In our experience, the DoS/foreign service—although highly bureaucratized—works remarkably well.

TRIBAL OUTREACH AND TRANSITION

This section discusses tribal outreach, based on Derrin Smith's experiences in Afghanistan and Iraq in 2004, 2005, and 2007–2008. This sets the stage for the later discussion of possible expansions in special operations capabilities in the Department of State for more remote and independent diplomatic programs, these to include Diplomatic Expeditionary Field Teams (DEFTs), a proposal by Smith advocated via the DoS "Sounding Board." Attention is given to the necessary sustainability of operations in transition periods, from outright conflict to peace transitioning to postconflict operations.

Transition is one of the most dangerous yet potentially creative periods for country teams and their colleagues. As the base of U.S. military support and logistics is drawn down in Iraq (and in the future, in Afghanistan), it will be necessary for DoS diplomatic outreach in remote, semipermissive areas to continue on a much more independent basis. A significant part of this outreach helps NGOs, local PVOs and civilian charities, and new businesses to expand in the so-called tribal areas. Humanitarian work is clearly one of the best mechanisms from a DoS perspective to create a positive image for democracy and free market access. Medical centers, women's resource centers, and community-based economic development offices contribute to the local infrastructure and have the possibility of creating good will, this in turn contributing to stabilization efforts.

At the highest levels of U.S. government, these questions were asked repeatedly after the fall of Saddam Hussein: Should the DoS continue to operate in the more dangerous and remote areas of Iraq, especially as the U.S. military began to withdraw security and combat troops? How could DoS assets continue to function once military logistics and security were withdrawn? Where would country teams (including civilian advisors) fit, as expeditionary diplomacy was being considered?

As of 2009 there were competing opinions at the Department of State about "work at the grassroots" and about remote diplomatic initiatives. For some, the actual practice of diplomacy, as viewed historically, should be limited to major capital cities and should be aimed at facilitating exchanges with the central host government. The use of cement-walled embassy compounds, or fortress-like consulates under embassy control, is then perceived as the norm. First priority is to protect and enhance U.S. interests in the country and region. Second priority is to explain American policy to the host government and to work in cooperative ways that further U.S. interests. Third priority is reflected in the expressed needs filtering through, from local residents.

For others, although not dispensing with diplomatically facilitated exchanges, there is a movement toward greater involvement in remote operations. American presence posts in more removed areas, such as those discussed in Chapter 6, complemented by PRT operations, which by design are temporary, can enhance aid programs. Operations that are closer to the beneficiary populations, especially in rural areas, can be increasingly beneficial. The more face time teams have with their allies and local actors, the better the chances for achieving common goals. Yet, as U.S. military forces draw down, PRT operations are designed to draw down as well. How, then, will the U.S. presence be maintained? Should it be?

PRTs, as noted in Chapter 3, are intended by charter to be a temporary civilian-military presence. Military security and logistics enable such groups to perform a variety of missions to enhance local governance, promote the rule of law, and work toward economic development. Some forward operating base (FOB) equipment, housing units, and logistics structures (such as containerized units, water sanitation and waste treatment structures, power generation plants, and office-type trailers) should be left behind, intact, for the host government to use after withdrawal of U.S. and allied troops. Rather than stripping a site bare and leaving nothing but a desolate patch of land, formally handing over site operations in a "change of command" ceremony—even including ribbon cutting—that includes key equipment is a better approach to sustained operations. The move toward Provincial Iraqi Control (PIC) in various provinces of Iraq recently improved goodwill as local managers moved in to take over reconstruction and development activities. A handover strategy attuned to local citizens' expressed needs will boost the stature of local politicians but, more important, will signal American respect for local interests and capabilities. This approach should be built into mission planning from day one. By contrast, although encumbered somewhat in Afghanistan by NATO and UN restrictions as well as joint military guidelines, the landmark cooperation involving PRTs has been judged by some to be extremely solid.

People wrestling with these questions would say this: There is a delicate balance between foreign coalition military personnel providing the security necessary for humanitarian operations (or conducting peacekeeping missions in otherwise lawless regions or working on reconstruction projects through PRTs) and turning the corner to become oppressors and abusers of the very populations they are charged with protecting. Civilian advisors are pushing the system in directions that better secure informed consent from members of indigenous populations.

THREE CASE STUDIES

One Marine Corps general, in taking over his area of operations, pulled all the tribal leaders together and told them, translated virtually word for word: "I come in peace; I didn't bring artillery. But, if you [mess] with me, so help me God, I will kill you all." The sheikhs were impressed. They understood strength and authority. He got the immediate respect and cooperation of the leaders and was able to lead a successful reconstruction effort in his AO. Guns and money talk. But bullets and ballot boxes remain a bit at odds, and this is something that only a viable civilian presence can adequately address on a sustainable basis. The general had his own style of tribal outreach. By contrast, we need to develop and execute ours using a more diplomatic, peaceful, and interpersonally sensitive model. Approaches long employed by anthropologists in developing rapport with indigenous peoples, such as "tea talk," have substantial merit.

Issues associated with tribal outreach are best addressed by using successful examples. Ours come from missions in Iraq and Afghanistan, each involving Derrin Smith. The first involves Tarin Kowt, Afghanistan, and issues associated with tribal outreach in the Taliban heartland over the issue of opium poppy eradication. The second involves Kandahar, Afghanistan, and issues associated with civilian medical assistance exercises. The third involves Anbar Province, Iraq, and the links of "helicopter diplomacy" with other forms of outreach, as well as the facilitation of political relationships between local Sunni tribesmen and the central ministries in Baghdad. As all three cases demonstrate, whether one is working with quick reaction forces, explosive ordnance disposal (EOD) teams, reconstruction and engineering units, local police training units, refugee or IDP camp residents, or religious clerics, local personal relationships matter. Furthermore, country team members have much greater credibility if tasks are tackled shoulder to shoulder in the field, rather than sitting at headquarters pumping out cables based on second-hand data or hearsay. Getting out of the FOB or outside the wire at the fire base is more than grandstanding or brinksmanship; it is imperative in accomplishing tribal outreach.

Tarin Kowt, Afghanistan

Tribal outreach in Tarin Kowt, Oruzgan Province, Afghanistan is particularly challenging, because it is, literally, the center of Taliban country. It is the birthplace of Mullah Omar, so the Taliban philosophy and ultraconservatism is home grown. Whereas in Iraq much of the insurgent and terrorist influences are imports from Iran and Syria, in Afghanistan local tribes are much more closely aligned with locally attuned Taliban orthodoxy.

By late 2004 the disarmament, demobilization, and reintegration (DDR) program was struggling. Guns and poppies seemingly were the entire economy, yet outsiders were encouraging tribal leaders to hand in their guns, stand down their protective militias, divert from poppy production (Figure 7.1), and become engaged in new forms of training, economic development, and social

FIGURE 7.1   The mayor of Tarin Kowt is interviewed by Derrin Smith. Problems of poppy eradication and economic transformation were the topic of discussion (photo by Derrin Smith).

intercourse. The United States and its allies were pushing against centuries of independent and adaptive tribal existence. Local tribal leaders' respect, livelihood, and security were dependent on their local militia and security teams.

A PRT was being constituted at Tarin Kowt under the Honolulu Bobcats infantry in late 2004 and early 2005. Yet although "the good news" spread, personnel continued to be lost to local firefights in the clearing of roadways, while conducting presence patrols, and while trying to build relationships with local leaders. In turn, insurgents were being killed during multiple attacks against Firebase Anaconda, the local U.S.-run facility. Such assaults cannot occur without some cooperation or complicity by the local tribesmen. Reaching out to provide aid and reconstruction to a local citizenry who continued to act as friends in one instance and launch insurgent attacks in the next was proving a tough challenge for U.S. Army personnel.

Following on Derrin Smith's arrival, and the increased involvement of National Afghan Army troops in joint deployments, more nuanced kinds of outreach were attempted. Heavy reliance was placed on the Tactical Human Intelligence Teams (THTs) and scout/reconnaissance units to prepare the way for meetings in neighboring villages. A Mercy Corps sign scrawled on a chunk of cardboard near a dirt path, but accompanied by no actual Mercy Corps assets, served as a reminder of the difficulties operating in the area. Several NGOs had made bold attempts to use local personnel to set up offices that they could administer remotely from Kabul. However, the initiatives died on the vine, since they did not have additional civilian experts to work closely with the villagers. Perceptions of security problems likely were keeping other NGOs out of the area. Some groups have complained that an increased military presence increases the hazard for their humanitarian operations, by emphasizing foreigners as combatants and invaders. Other aid workers believe the military is a useful enabler, although virtually all civilian groups prefer to maintain a safe distance from military units, convoys, and patrols.

Once the site had been secured and the meeting with the mayor of Tarin Kowt had begun, the mayor talked at length about how his village and adjoining agricultural valleys were before the Soviet invasion. The effects of defoliation and damage to the agrarian infrastructure had never been repaired. Poppies needed to be the economic mainstay, he stressed. They grow readily, with little need for sophisticated agricultural tools or inputs. As long as his local militia remained powerful enough to defend his fields, his export market to Pakistan would be guaranteed.

The mayor was very logical in specifying his requirements for economic development and transformation. He would be happy to have agreements with such U.S. agricultural firms as Monsanto, Cargill, Case Harvester, or John Deere. He was well informed on what the outside world had to offer in terms of technical aid, enhanced seeds, and fertilizers as alternatives to poppies were considered. The mayor emphasized the need for both technical and financial aid to expand agricultural production and return to what had been viable citrus production. He agreed to eradication of poppy plantations in favor of other crops if outsiders could create his export market, assure his income, and guarantee security for his tribe. This was a big "if."

Basically, he told Smith, the Pakistani buyers who visited him had no interest in anything but poppies. They wanted the drug trade to flourish and were being supported by major international players in organized crime. He was even suspicious that perhaps Western governments, secretly, were working at great length with the international drug cartels and organized crime elements to maintain a dependency by Afghan people on the drug trade. He recognized that military engineering units could help dig wells while hiring local labor and project managers. He recognized that irrigation projects could employ large numbers of willing local workers, providing alternatives to "guns and poppy employment." Yet his skepticism was hard to overcome. Smith's outreach team had made a small dent, had established improved communications, but had not facilitated a dramatic economic transformation. As of 2010 the birthplace of Mullah Omar and the Taliban remains hotly contested. The national elections of August, 2009 (later shown to have been rigged), did not eliminate the nay-sayers, despite Hamid Karzai's efforts to minimalize factionalism.

Kandahar, Afghanistan

Civilian military assistance exercises (CMAX) are designed as missions to bring some health care to local populations while concurrently conducting presence patrols, working to develop information resources among village populations, and helping village leaders to identity key problems that can be tackled. Country teams, usually comprising persons from several nations, typically use a PsyOps vehicle with loudspeakers as part of a CMAX convoy. A convoy will roll into position a few kilometers from a village. As soon as a hasty perimeter has been established and mobile medical cases have been set up, the PsyOps team will begin to broadcast its presence to the village. As a general rule, the populace is already aware of what is happening and will stream toward convoy personnel with an array of injuries and illnesses. Radio communications with the nearest tactical operations center (TOC) will be constant. Airmobile assets will be summoned if necessary. A security perimeter will be maintained.

This type of tribal outreach also is sensitive culturally. If too much attention is shown to one tribal leader, or if local hierarchies among various families and tribes are not researched and respected, the balance of power can quickly, inadvertently, and dangerously be altered. The host country national army, law enforcement teams, and local militias are continually realigning themselves and their territories. If a power vacuum is created, the area can rapidly deteriorate into ethnic conflict.

In a 2005 CMAX in Kandahar, Afghanistan (Figure 7.2), Smith and his colleagues prepared the site to receive both male and female patients. The women's "clinic" consisted of a few mud-brick walls, enclosed, where female U.S. Army nurses tended to the women and children who came for examinations, vaccinations, and general health care. For the men, the team selected a site a few hundred meters away, near a brick wall where the clients could be queued with a bit of privacy. The clinic consisted of makeshift folding racks and portable tables. The pharmacy consisted of two footlockers of medications. Romanian doctors and American military medics began seeing clients almost immediately after the loudspeakers had begun broadcasting. Several hundred villagers were assisted on this occasion. In one instance, a very young

FIGURE 7.2 In this 2005 CMAX near Kandahar, a Romanian doctor works with American military medics to assist villagers (photo by Derrin Smith).

girl was diagnosed with possible tuberculosis. Arrangements were made for a helicopter medical evacuation for her, her father, and her mother. They traveled together owing to cultural sensitivities; to send the mother and daughter alone would have been unthinkable.

While villagers were being treated, the THT personnel interviewed various villagers, met with tribal elders, and engaged in conversations about intertribal relations, economic development, security concerns, and especially agriculture. Again, "guns and poppies" were found to best represent the economy. Businessmen/Brokers from as far away as Russia and Italy had been coming to make deals on the drug crops. Infrastructure in terms of water, sewer, electricity, and communications was almost non-existent. One well spout that had been installed by the U.S. military continued to be used regularly, yet decent sanitation was absent.

In addition to the successful CMAX, a successful village *shura* meeting was held. This council-like gathering of over fifty village leaders and tribal elders discussed perceived needs with Smith and his team. Even digital videography was permitted; several leaders were delighted to see their faces as playback in LCD was demonstrated. As each leader was independently interviewed, care was taken to acknowledge rank and tribe in accordance with local custom, to respect seating arrangements, and to courteously assemble an overall "shopping list" of requests and priorities. Wells and irrigation systems were the top priorities for most of the participants. Medical treatment (especially for family or outlying tribal members) was requested; CMAXs were seen as viable options, but the development of medical clinics in each village was a common request. The only comments on disarmament were that it made no sense. The notion of relinquishing the power of security to a national or regional government was met with derision.

Jobs, with an emphasis on prospects for younger people, was a frequent topic of discussion, although hard manual labor was perceived to be the unfortunate duty of the underclass. Norms and mores associated with status, rank, and duty in even the simplest of tasks must be carefully respected. An American team member picking up the backpack of an Afghan colleague to assist him can have negative repercussions. Team leaders also must avoid self-deprecating humor; a slight aura of aloofness is preferred. Not the slightest sign of vulnerability can be shown. "He who loads the camels does not lead the caravan" is an adage that applies throughout the tribal areas.

As this meeting also confirmed, as soon as adequate trust and personal relationships have been established with leading local men, projects to empower and enable women can be pursued. Typically, the outreach of female team members is the only way to engage local women, since cultural taboos prevent any direct contact with male personnel. The mere presence of female team members helps to topple barriers and enhance communications. Micro-entrepreneurial projects aided by microcredit loans proved to be of interest.

Nearby, a UN IDP camp was proving to be a mixed blessing for locals. Although it was providing supplies to address basic needs, it also was creating dependencies. A large population of orphans remained at this site, with tribal members frankly happy that they no longer had responsibility to feed them. With its better housing, sanitation, food, and medical care than that of surrounding villages, the camp also had become a magnet for local scavengers and hangers-on. When local elders were asked about ways to transition IDPs back into society, the most senior leader threaded his worry beads through his worn, wrinkled fingers and replied without mirth: "Stop feeding them. Close up. Go away. They will then return to the tribes where they should be. They are our people and will return to us." Another elder complained that the presence of the IDP camp so close to his territory was a challenge to his honor and authority but that there was no need to attack. "Such things are always temporary," he said. "This is the way for centuries."

Anbar, Iraq

In Iraq in 2007–2008, working closely with MNF-West in Anbar Province, the Marines provided Smith and his teammates with solid helicopter support. Helicopter transport and helicopter diplomacy were taken to high levels. The intent was to take the Governor of Anbar and the Chairman of the Provincial Council to as many city, village, and tribal meetings as possible. (Related convoy problems were noted in Chapter 5.) The overarching goal was to enable effective communications among the Anbar central government in Ramadi, the major tribal councils in Ramadi and Fallujah, and the local tribes and powerbrokers. Working closely with MNF-West to prioritize meetings sites, the special operations teams, military and civilian, reported on their early contacts and assisted in local arrangements. It became possible to facilitate provincial and local government operations through these helicopter diplomacy missions—often several each week—while concurrently facilitating the Anbar Provincial Council meetings in Ramadi at the newly renovated government center.

Best Practices, Lessons Learned #1

Anthropological insights proved valuable in the best practices illustrated in the three case studies in this chapter. Lessons learned benefited from civilian as well as military input. These should be compared with the practices and lessons in Table 6.3.

Cultural Sensitivity and Sociopolitical Awareness

In conflict zones, the stakes are high cross-culturally. Success in tribal outreach in Anbar, at times, hinged on a single handshake and a single spoken word of respect. Even infrastructure was engaged with spiritual appreciation, as mosques and shrines were encountered. "Culturally attuned, facilitated assistance" rather than "Western-oriented programming" increasingly was offered.

Knowledge of Local Authority Structures

Tribal engagement in Iraq and Afghanistan required both knowledge of local authority structures and deferential appreciation of how they work. Tribal dynamics were more complex in the latter. Understanding limitations of democratic electioneering and decision making in Anbar was essential. Negotiation with clerics at the Islamic Center of Anbar was aided by appreciation of the context in which the senior cleric's nephew had been killed. Favorable attention was paid to nonradicalized sermons.

Medical Mission Familiarity

Doctors, nurses, and corpsmen provided the primary medical care. Civilian advisors provided environmental and service support. During one CMAX in

---

(continued)

(continued)

Iraq, the team helped save the eyesight of a boy owing to a medical inter-vention advocated by the DoS, negotiated cross-culturally and supported by a multinational forces med-evac team.

Writing, Reporting, Radioing

Building on daily logs, per normal, status reports were sent up the chain of command. Situation reports, "hot washes," and spot reports were used in urgent situations (complemented by radio reports), with more detailed "reporting cables" sent to higher headquarters. DoS has begun encour-aging "eDiplomacy" and "netCentric Diplomacy" using Wikipedia-type models to create a shared knowledge base, easily accessible to those with management permission and at security levels appropriate to the users' clearances. "The job ain't finished 'til the paperwork's done."

Smuggling and border control became an important agenda item for the provincial council. Smith's team was able to advise on projects to help make the province safer. Anbar went from being one of the most violent provinces in Iraq in 2006 to being one of the safest in 2008. Helicopter diplomacy was aided by on-the-ground coordination between military assets in MNF-West and PRT personnel. Control of airspace proved to be a corollary of success. Aircraft are high-value targets. Air corridors typically require host government cooperation and approval, as well as some formal, technical infrastructure for safety in airlift operations. These were obtained.

Best Practices, Lessons Learned #2

Helo-Diplomacy and Emergency Tactics

Flying to meetings with U.S. diplomats, the Anbar Higher Committee (AHC) and key members of the provincial government, including the Governor, Smith's CH-46 Sea Knight Marine Corps transport helicopter suddenly filled with oily black smoke. The aircraft began to shudder violently, with sounds of metallic screeching coming from the rear rotor area. A precipi-tous descent to the desert floor ensued.

The Marine Corps crew sprang into action, quickly checking seating har-nesses on all passengers, adding a hard cinch on each strap. They took their

(continued)

(continued)

crash-landing positions. Radio headsets squawked with commands regarding the immediate action plan. Gunners and crew chiefs were ready when the CH-46 struck the ground, hard. The rear hatch opened and a ramp dropped as crew and passengers popped their harnesses and began moving rapidly toward the exit. Marine security escorts, first off, already had established a hasty perimeter; other crew members were at the ramp to assist the Anbar VIPs and U.S. diplomats. A second CH-46 had landed nearby, and while the Marines monitored the perimeter, the VIPs were to be moved to this aircraft and quickly made airborne. Desert dust swirled, hammered by the rotor wash. It temporarily choked some of the personnel.

At impact, the diplomatic team leader (who earlier had been suffering from back pains) winced and doubled over. Smith, seated to his left, and an FBI rule-of-law expert, seated to his right, pulled him from his harness, braced him over their shoulders in an assisted carry, grabbed gear bags with their free hands, and hustled him off the damaged aircraft, through the dust and onto the second helicopter. Not a word was spoken. Less than two minutes had elapsed from impact. The teamwork among all the Marines, Anbar officials, and U.S. diplomats was seamless, as if they had practiced such an emergency exercise together. In fact, it was the high overall level of mission experience—military and civilian—that resulted in the safe outcome, in concert with a functional EAP (emergency action plan). The mission was subsequently completed successfully.

Lessons Learned: Complementing the information in Table 6.2 for the 2004 Romanian field school, this incident presents the following best practices with lessons learned:

- *EAP*—An emergency action plan is essential. Those engaging it do not necessarily have to have practiced it together in advance.
- *On-site security*—A team is most vulnerable when moving. Practicing convoy and airmobile procedures and evacuations minimizes injuries and saves lives. The establishing of a hasty security perimeter reduces "soft target" vulnerabilities.
- *Automatic response*—Well-prepared personnel do not have to talk a lot as an emergency response is being engaged. Situational awareness is essential. Triaged (that is, rank-ordered) responses also are essential.
- *Physical fitness*—There often will be incidents when someone has just been injured, is ill, or is in pain. Maintenance of physical

(continued)

(*continued*)

> fitness, complemented by an endurance regimen, by all personnel will improve this person's chance of successful extraction, as well as a teammate's ability to rapidly response in helping. Fatigue and mental pressures will be lessened.
>
> - *24/7 action*—Field operations do not move in office-like, timed precision. Planned and unplanned activities, from the perspectives of friend or enemy, can occur at any time.

THE BATTLE FOR ANBAR PROVINCE

The battle for Anbar Province gripped the world's attention from 2005 through 2007. It began tipping in favor of the United States and its partners in 2007. Public opinion turned against the enemy. The battle occurred at many levels, some involving combat, some involving operations other than war (OOTW). In urban and rural areas, al-Qaeda in Iraq (AQI) was rejected and Coalition Forces (CF) found new support from the citizenry. The role of the mosques in this shift of public opinion remains dimly understood by outsiders, but the mosques were a critical factor in redefining AQI as the enemy and CF as friendly forces. Today, the same influential clerics are preaching moderate theology and are requesting further engagement with Americans. Smith met with two influential and moderate clerics for two hours on April 22, 2008, in Ramadi, at the headquarters of the Sunni Endowment (and later compiled a comprehensive case study of Anbar operations [2008]). The clerics displayed their physical battle scars, and the leader stated that "cooperation in the battle for the minds of Anbar citizens" must be waged through promoting tolerance. The circumstances that preceded the Sunni Endowment meeting, however, could not have been worse from an American perspective.

Based on valid intelligence, U.S. Special Operations forces had taken down a terrorist safe house and explosive factory in Anbar. Unfortunately, one of the insurgents killed in the raid was a member of the influential al-Faraj tribe. He was a relative of one of the most influential and powerful of the religious leaders at the Sunni Endowment, the center for Islamic thought in Anbar Province.

This situation led to complaints by many sheikhs and tribal leaders that the military raid had been wrong, with claims on the street that the victims were mere innocents and victims of unnecessary violence by infidel occupiers. Sensitive reporting indicated otherwise, but it still was a major public relations scandal for the U.S. presence in Anbar. Relations with al-Faraj became strained as a result, and the influence of the Sunni Endowment through weekly sermons from the major mosques needed to be taken into account. Therefore, a goodwill visit to the heart of the Sunni religious leadership in Anbar was deemed essential.

The intention was for a civilian visit by Smith with leaders of the Sunni religious center and al-Faraj tribal leaders. To maintain progress toward peace and reconstruction in Anbar, the ongoing support of the religious leaders was paramount. Uniformed military personnel could not take on this mission in light of the recent killing by the special operations team. In addition, the clerics did not allow uniformed military inside the religious center or military convoys on the streets outside. The presence of uniformed military, even at a distance, can promote street riots. The mission had two components: first, to visit the top leadership of the Sunni Endowment and dispel any myths or doubts about the tactical raid; second, to set new plans for future collaboration and establish a basis for follow-on projects. The lack of personal security at the Islamic center, owing to religious concerns, presented a challenge. The physical layout of the street in front, access to the neighborhood, and clerical mandates forced deviation from the standard protocol of a three-vehicle military movement team (MMT) with eight shooters. It would be a meeting at a static site, with no perimeter, in an unsecured, unsearched, and exposed building. Essentially, the safety of the visit would be dependent on the goodwill of the religious leaders and al-Faraj family members on site.

Sunni Endowment leader Sheikh Abdullah Jalal al-Faraj, a powerful relative of the deceased terrorist, was the first person engaged. His leadership during earlier battles against AQI had earned him deep respect from the populace. He had created the Sunni Endowment (*al-Waqf al-Sunni*) and a fledgling center to combat radical ideologies (*al-Markez al-Wiqaii li muajihad al-Afkhar al-Dakheela*). Then and now, the Sunni Endowment maintains responsibility for the operations and teachings of all mosques in Anbar. He stated that "500,000 citizens hear our message of peace and tolerance every Friday. If you find a mosque that is preaching radicalism, please tell us. We will visit and using the teachings, we will change their messages to moderation and tolerance." During this meeting (Figure 7.3), Dr. Thamir al-Assafi presented himself as the senior theological leader for the Sunni Endowment and a claimant to the leadership of all Muslim scholars in Anbar.

Turning the Tide through Fatwa

A brief history of the battle in Anbar Province against AQI helps to illustrate the importance of these powerful Sunni clerics to the overall efforts toward peace and stability. Tribal outreach to appropriately include religious specialists has become a central component in the U.S. engagement philosophy.

Figure 7.3   Leaders of the Sunni Endowment gather for a meeting with American civilian liaisons (photo by Derrin Smith).

In late 2006 Sheikh Sattar abu Risha, as leader of the Anbar Awakening Council, proclaimed his determination to battle AQI with the assistance and will of the people. However, his penchant for alcohol and other vices had reduced his spiritual authority to mobilize the people. The Sunni Endowment provided the necessary Fatwa to legitimize the aims of the Anbar Awakening Council against AQI. This religious ruling, issued throughout the province, explicitly gave the people permission to join with the Sheikh. Not only did the Fatwa advocate resistance to AQI, it also authoritatively stated that AQI did not follow true Islam and that it engaged in un-Islamic practices. The Fatwa did not suggest moral absolutes, but a more utilitarian/situational ethics approach. It also suggested "bridges" to non-Islamic colleagues. As a further sign of their authority and as an example to the citizens, several religious leaders themselves engaged in direct combat against AQI in Anbar and endorsed direct cooperation with CF as friendly forces (the first time that terminology had been used). In the words of Abdullah Jalal, it was the combination of Sheikh Sattar's vision for the Anbar Awakening Council and the support of the Sunni Endowment that turned the tide against AQI from 2006 through 2007.

As the battle raged for Anbar, AQI influence and penetration of some mosques led to continued radicalization in some locations. Early in 2007, Abdullah Jalal contacted CF with a request for a personal security detail (PSD) in order to move around the province to major mosques to help moderate the messages. Visiting the ten most radical mosques, he fired some speakers and "re-inserted" more moderate teachings to sway other preachers and their followers. He directly enforced the religious authority of the Sunni Endowment, *al-Waqf al-Sunni.* Ground that had been lost was regained. The Sheikh told Smith's team that the messages had changed in the major mosques, that concepts of moderation, tolerance, and the welcoming of CF were reaching an audience of over a half million worshippers each Friday. His concern as of 2008 was that some citizens are "untouchables," being very poor and uneducated, and that AQI therefore can corral them. He is especially fond of using the quote in Haddith that "moderation is the essence of goodness." Dr. Thamir added that "if America wants to weaken the appeal of al-Qaeda and increase its cultural dialog with Iraqis and Muslims in Anbar, then building a U.S. Consulate, establishing an American Cultural Center," and other initiatives were vital. The mosques must provide the guidance, and certain aspects of American culture must become accessible to everyday citizens in the province. NGO outreach and medical outreach are seen as central to this goal.

A Center to Confront Extremism

Sheikh Abdullah Jalal, as the senior leader of the Sunni Endowment, has developed a fledgling center to confront extremism. The two central messages are that "extremism works to divide the people" and "moderate thinking will help build a bridge between the citizens for a better Iraq." The center's first teachings are distributed throughout Anbar Province. Short-letter publications (each about 20 pages long) are being distributed weekly, covering topics such as Muslim sanctity; the damages of extrimist ideology; who has the rights and authority to judge; multitude and masses in Islamic thinking; and a Muslim's rights and responsibilities.

The clerics are planning 22 books and studies (each approximately 100 pages long) that teach modernism and fairness. Distributed monthly, these books will include topics such as extremism and how to survive it; who is the Guardian of Islam; public freedom in Islam; the balance between interests and corruption; the international relations of Islam; and moderate criteria of the Fatwa.

In addition to monitoring and moderating the weekly speeches in the Anbar mosques, leaders are preparing 20 speeches to be used as Friday sermons when needed. These are posted on the internet, including these topics: mercy in Islam; Muslim behavior; curing extremism; moderate understanding; kindness in Muslim life; loving your country; respecting people's rights; and the Muslim role in reform. On February 1, 2008, the prestigious Humayim Mosque in the al-Mulaimeen District of Ramadi broadcast a sermon supporting the new center's ideals.

Evolving Roles for PRTs

As of 2008 the Anbar PRT was in the early stages of sophisticated engagement with the moderate clerics. As members of the city council of Ramadi, both clerics were well known, and conversations with Derrin Smith revealed commonality on many key issues. For example, their interest in further dialog with Christians, Jews, and other Muslims led to the PRT exploring with the Anbari clerics an International Visitor Leadership Program during which the U.S. visit could be used to open new dialogs that captured the lessons learned from the Anbari experience with AQI and radicalized ideologies. The PRT therefore actively explored ways to assist and support the Al-Markez al-Wiqaii limua Jihad al-Afkhar al-Dakheela Center for Resisting Extremist Ideology to help expand the audience for their messages and formal publications.

The civilian members of the Anbar PRT planned to find help to support both American and local NGOs to increase their presence within Iraqi society. The Sunni Endowment itself has now formed an NGO focusing on humanitarian assistance, medical care, widows, orphans, and IDPs. The clerics concurred that a more well-rounded, visible American civilian presence—complemented by fewer uniforms—would help break down barriers, diminish enmity, and put a human face on American friendship and support. A proposed English-language center would break down the communication barrier and further facilitate understanding between Iraqis and Americans; the availability of American literature and textbooks in Arabic was deemed a priority. Sheikh Abdullah Jalal and Dr. Thamir began preparing materials for the next set of meetings with American civilians, a strategy mirrored coincidentally by members of the Iraq Civil Society Initiative, who met with Peter Van Arsdale and his colleagues in the United States at about the same time.

The PRT's communication/liaison role proved key. Its members were able to solicit requests for more culturally attuned types of American engagement. Issues involving interdenominational religious dialogue, literary exchange, humanitarian assistance, NGO partnering, and election education all were covered. Workshops were sponsored by the Independent Higher Electoral Commission (IHEC), which encouraged women to vote.

Best Practices, Lessons Learned #3 (where civilian input also was key)

These best practices, viewed in concert with lessons learned from the Battle for Anbar Province, are illustrative for field training purposes, especially when compared with the information in Table 6.1.

Establish Entrée and Rapport

Connections with local councils and elected officials were necessary but not all-encompassing. Differential power relations played out as U.S. civilians engaged Iraqi civilians, less so than when engaging Iraqi military personnel.

Promote Personal Relationships

These were three-fold:

1. between civilian and military members of country teams;
2. between country teams and Iraqi military personnel;
3. between country teams and Iraqi civilian personnel, particularly tribal leaders. The latter were the most difficult to manage.

Work Shoulder to Shoulder with Others

Every-day field operations, such as those involving Iraqi clerics, were essential to moving discussions about socioeconomic development forward. An act as simple as helping build a mud wall can pay huge dividends.

Perform Careful Reconnaissance

In protecting AHC members, civilian and military intelligence reporting was used. Country team members compared various intelligence inputs to uncover inconsistencies and "unusual activities" around a proposed meeting site in the run-up to the AHC-Ministry meetings in Baghdad.

Perform Careful Route Assessment

"Low-pro" (low-profile) route assessment in Baghdad was a standard procedure. U.S. military and civilian contractors regularly patrolled and swept

(continued)

(continued)

common routes, and reconnaissance units maintained near-constant surveillance over primary routes. Low pro vehicles scouted routes in Baghdad in advance of the arrival of Anbar VIPs for meetings.

Perform Careful Site Assessment

Perimeter assessment at the Finance Ministry during a threat/vulnerability survey led to discovery of a gate being opened between the Red and Green Zones for the first time since 2003, inferring possible presence of unsearched vehicles, defective security devices, and unsecured entry (for example, by caterers).

Maintain Situational Awareness

Aided by civilian advisors, the country team gained essential knowledge of animosity between Shi'a ministers and Sunni Anbar tribal and provincial leaders. Threat assessment input was received from High Threat Protection Office and was treated seriously as plans for meetings were established.

Respond to Mission Based on Assessment

The "mission" (that is, meetings among AHC personnel from Anbar, Finance Ministry officials, and Baghdad central government officials) had to be cancelled, but in a way that would not antagonize any of the VIPs. Flights were scrubbed and then the meetings quietly rescheduled with an unannounced appearance in Baghdad.

Reconciliation between Tribal Leaders and Elected Officials

Another of the significant battles in Anbar again did not take place on the battlefield. During 2007 and 2008 the challenge was to develop a viable cooperative arrangement between the politically elected officials and the tribal leaders in the province. When an ad hoc reconciliation committee consisting of politicians and tribal leaders was formed, American and Iraqi counterparts were aware of the potential for success but also of the risks involved. This group of men soon became one of the highest value targets of the terrorists and insurgents, in part exacerbated by the fact that Anbar Awakening Council members and other tribal leaders in Anbar were, for the first time, working shoulder to shoulder with elected officials. A number of attacks and close calls did, in fact, later ensue.

This effort grew out of a debate triggered by the Iraqi elections. Many tribal leaders, sheikhs, and elders believed the elections to be illegitimate. In fact, so many Sunni leaders had boycotted the original elections, they were not inclined to cooperate—or even have a dialog with—the Governor of Anbar, the Chairman of the Provincial Council, or the Anbar council members. The situation had devolved to a stalemate, with the result that tribal leaders were not attending the Provincial Council meetings. With so much at stake regarding the improving peace and security of Anbar, a temporary arrangement to jumpstart the dialog between elected and tribal officials was needed. With the aid of Derrin Smith, a "reconciliation committee" was recommended, to comprise an equal number of top elected officials and tribal leaders. It was entitled the Anbar Higher Committee (AHC), to give the sheikhs and tribal leaders a sense of greater importance. It was suggested that Governor Ma'moun, Council Chairman Dr. Abdul-salaam, and Engineer Othman (a trusted vice governor of Ma'moun and well-educated businessman) represent the elected parties. On the tribal side, Sheikh Ahmad abu Risha of the Anbar Awakening Council, Sheikh al Turqie heading the Anbar Tribal Council (although feuding with the Anbar Awakening Council over tribal influence), and Sheikh Tariq (residing for security reasons in Amman, Jordan) agreed to carry the torch on the AHC.

Press releases, widely publicized meetings, and sessions with dignitaries in Baghdad, including U.S. Ambassador Ryan Crocker, helped provide immediate traction for this new committee. In spite of incessant jockeying for position by the AHC members, negotiations commenced among them on the best future for Anbar Province. In spite of attacks targeting the AHC, including a deadly bombing at the checkpoint leading to a sheikh's compound, the committee succeeded as the first official cooperation between the tribal leaders and the elected officials (including the Iraqi Islamic Party). As a civilian country team member, Smith was able to assist with advance arrangements, intelligence, and security precautions for a major meeting in Baghdad. The last task included a route and site reconnaissance to check timelines, route security, meeting site security, and logistics. The meeting originally was to be held in a building just inside the Green Zone, near the Finance Ministry.

In fact, this security analysis revealed a number of potential problems. For example, information surfaced that two trucks were to be brought in by the Finance Ministry under security of local Iraqi personnel. The trucks were not to be intercepted or screened by the team's security personnel and would be parked next to the office building where the meeting would be held. Given the animosity that had developed between the Finance Ministry and the Sunnis representing the AHC, a concern arose that the trucks might contain bombs. This concern, along with two other problematic pieces of intelligence, led the planning team to "summon" a "freak dust storm" that closed the Anbar helipad on the day of departure for Baghdad. Given the high visibility of the meeting, and a concern that security paranoia might stop a very important discussion between Sunni and Shi'ite leaders from happening, cancellation of this event posed a real diplomatic problem. However, it was essential to err on the side of caution. Never revealing its real concerns, the team cancelled the meeting at the last second with great regrets, then brought the AHC members quietly to Baghdad on an entirely different schedule. The meeting was then held at the residence of the Deputy Prime Minister.

In making the determination to cancel the original meeting, Smith and his team used a threat/vulnerability assessment calculus akin to that presented in Chapter 3. (Despite efforts to maintain its viability as a key transnational meeting place, the Finance Ministry building was heavily damaged in a targeted blast in August of 2009. In December of 2009, 127 people were killed and more than 500 wounded in yet another series of blasts near the same location.)

Solidifying Political Relations

Subsequent to the ultimately successful Baghdad meeting, the Anbar Higher Committee for Reconciliation prompted all key sheikhs and tribal leaders to begin attending the meetings of the provincial council in Anbar. The Awakening Council, after several more face to face tribal-outreach meetings with DoS representatives at the Council's tribal compound, went so far as to order members who had been appointed to the Anbar Provincial Council to attend 100 percent of the meetings or be removed by Sheikh abu Risha. Within just a few months, the AHC as an ad hoc reconciliation body had served its purpose and was officially set aside as formalized communications between the tribes and elected officials began to occur every two weeks in the council chambers of the Ramadi government center. The tribal leaders began to embrace the elective process with more enthusiasm, creating computer databases, member registrations, and supportive office operations—trappings of a more democratic electoral process.

Since that time, several more insurgent and terrorist attacks have occurred against Anbar provincial officials and tribal leaders. In particular, members of the Anbar Awakening Council have been targeted. After one large car bomb attack blew a small car into a second-story balcony wall of a building used as a residence by political officials, Governor Ma'moun quipped: "It's no problem. It just makes all the real estate here cheaper now!" As a politician with no small enthusiasm for business opportunities, the Governor knew what he was talking about.

The ongoing draw-down of U.S. troop levels in Iraq under the Obama administration must be viewed in light of what has been accomplished in Anbar Province. In many ways the successes there have precipitated elements of the broader military planning process for the country. Tribal outreach will continue to be a key component of what unfolds.

Special Operations

Special operations can be defined in both the connotative and denotative senses. In the first sense, special operations can involve one-of-a-kind projects or unusual assignments, many of which incorporate the services of country teams of various types. The special joint training operation we mounted in Romania in 2004, described in the preceding chapter, serves as an example. Several of the activities covered in the preceding section for Afghanistan and Iraq also serve as examples. In the second sense, from the perspective of the U.S. military, special operations are those behind-the-scenes, behind-the-lines operations involved in counterterrorism and related activities, such as hostage rescue. They are mounted by professionally trained members of the military. Special operations also must be understood in the context of special forces.

A Brief History of Special Operations

The U.S. Special Operations Command (USSOC) includes the Navy SEALS, the Army Green Berets and Rangers, and the Air Force Special Operations Wing. In concert with this aggregate of units, reference is often made to the Joint Special Operations Command.

U.S. special forces, as Harvey Kushner notes, are military units dedicated to "small-scale, clandestine, unorthodox, and high-risk operations, often behind enemy lines" (2003: 105). A well-known example is Delta Force, the special forces unit dedicated to counterterrorism and hostage rescue. It was created in 1977, aided by the diligent efforts of "Chargin' Charlie" Beckwith, a Green Beret with experience in Vietnam and Laos, who went on to lead Delta's first overseas mission, to Iran in 1980. Operation Eagle Claw was intended to rescue U.S. Embassy staff being held hostage in Tehran (a crisis whose consistent and persistent nightly reporting by Ted Koppel, incidentally, led to the creation of the long-running ABC news program *Nightline.*) The rescue failed. A later re-evaluation of the approach led, in 1987, to all special forces being placed under a single command (USSOC), which is under the purview of the Assistant Secretary of Defense for Special Operations and Low Intensity Conflict. Delta Force is based at Ft. Bragg, North Carolina, and is composed of about 2,000 volunteers from various branches of the armed services. Although increasingly coming to maintain a low profile, it has recently been engaged in the search for al-Qaeda members in Afghanistan.

Several Navy SEAL operations also have gained the attention of the public over the past three decades. SEAL Team Six (ST6) is the original name of the Navy's top-level special operations commando group, responsible for counterterrorism operations worldwide. It was established in 1980, in part in response to the failure of Operation Eagle Claw and in part to consolidate the operations of several earlier teams. It is now referred to as the Naval Special Warfare Development Group (DEVGRU) and employs about 2,000 operators.

DEVGRU is part of the Joint Special Operations Command (Kushner 2003: 325–326).

The U.S. Air Force's Special Operations Wing is responsible for the air power involved in the military's counterterrorism operations. It works in concert with other special forces, such as the SEALs, usually behind enemy lines. However, in 1989 it spearheaded the invasion of Panama, an intervention that led to the downfall of General Manuel Noriega. The overarching Air Force Special Operations Command (AFSOC) was established in 1980 also.

The Green Berets are the Army's most well-known special forces. Originally raised in 1942 for sabotage operations in German-occupied Norway, they were revived in 1952 but were not supported heartily until they received the enthusiastic backing of President John Kennedy in 1961. Their efforts in Vietnam from 1961 to 1971 confirmed the president's support from the perspective of the military establishment (Beckett 1999: 85).

The failed 1980 raid in Tehran (under President Jimmy Carter's watch) was a first threshold in the evolution of contemporary special operations; a second threshold (under President Ronald Reagan's watch) was linked to developments in Central America and the Middle East, as reflections of the Soviet Union's influence. Reagan's Defense Guidance Statement of 1982 stressed that special operations "must be revitalized to address a number of issues, including the Soviet challenge" (Kushner 2003: 341). With a few twists and turns, this enhanced emphasis has carried to the present. Overall, special operations have seen a growth in field operations, a consolidation of leadership at the highest military levels, a more effective interservice collaboration, and a greater interest in what social scientists have to say.

The Hunt for Pablo

Country teams can find themselves in precarious positions when it comes to special operations. Any that are attached to the U.S. Embassy in a foreign country must be sensitive to the political pressures that the ambassador is facing. This situation can be compounded by the fact that other U.S. agencies likely are in theatre and active as well. This can be further compounded by the fact that the local government likely has numerous actors at play. Nowhere was this fact more evident than in Colombia during the 1980s and early 1990s. It was then that the hunt for the man described by Mark Bowden (2001) as "the world's greatest outlaw"—Pablo Escobar—was unfolding. As will become clear, this operation is illustrative in that it falls short of the ethical rules of engagement we laid out in Chapter 1.

Colombia had undergone multiple upheavals during the period since *La Violencia* had erupted in 1948. The murder of popular politician Jorge Gaitán in April of that year had fed what became riots and civil disruption. The dictatorship established in the 1950s quashed some of the simmering dissent, but a pattern had been established. By the 1960s the nation had settled into what Bowden (2001: 13) describes as a "forced stasis," with Marxist guerrillas ensconced in the jungles and the ruling elite ensconced in the larger cities. It was during this period that terror began to take on new and more ominous forms. It was also during this period that the U.S. government began to take a stronger interest in things Colombian, in large part because of the copious amounts of potent—and highly desirable—marijuana that were being shipped north. By the mid-1970s the "pot routes" began to be transformed into "coke routes," as vast numbers of *norteamericanos* with money discovered cocaine. From his base in Medellín, Escobar was positioned to build on his earlier successes as a crime boss and gangster and become one of the route's bosses. By 1980 he was of one the world's wealthiest people. By 1985 he was one of the world's most notorious killers.

The hunt for Escobar (as well as other cocaine kingpins) took many twists and turns, as Bowden masterfully recounts. Of relevance here is the role that the United States came to play. We believe that the effort eventually took on a life of its own, becoming reified, as the hunt became "THE hunt." As time went on, ethical considerations seemingly diminished in inverse proportion to the efforts and resources being expended.

The Colombian government, through several administrations during the 1970s, 1980s, and early 1990s, was variously co-opted, compromised, and compelled by the exploding drug trade. It variously sought, and yet kept at arm's length, U.S. help with intelligence and the training of police and military professionals who could serve as trackers. Police and judges were being killed in extraordinary numbers; they also were being paid off and corrupted in extraordinary numbers. To some of Colombia's poorest citizens, Escobar was seen as a kind of Robin Hood, to others a kind of Pancho Villa, further complicating efforts to capture or kill him. He invested heavily in projects benefiting the poor of Medellín. He also sponsored paramilitary organizations—in concert with the Colombian military—bent on destroying the guerrilla movement.

This situation was occurring within a broader one of severe societal disruption and sustained political violence that Whittaker and his colleagues (2003) link directly to terrorism. Such groups as FARC (Revolutionary Armed Forces of Colombia) and M-19 had established footholds. Further complicating the situation was the fact that landlords were battling sharecroppers, squatters, and peasant farmers; police (many of them corrupt) were battling criminal gangs; and *narco* kingpins representing the emergent Medellín and Cali cartels were battling administrative officials.

Vice President George H. W. Bush was appointed to lead a forceful U.S. crackdown on drug trafficking in 1982. By the time he assumed the presidency in 1989, he had shifted the effort from stopping drugs as they crossed the U.S. border to stopping *narco* kingpins at their home bases (Bowden 2001: 41). U.S. intelligence officers and country teams operating under embassy auspices already had been in place in Colombia, the former supplying "HumInt" (human intelligence) of mixed usefulness, the latter operating at the fringes of the nasty business at hand—primarily on traditional development projects. Since 1983 the drug/cartel issue had been rated as the number-one priority by the U.S. Department of State and therefore by the U.S. Embassy in Bogotá. It was not until a decade later, in December of 1993, that Pablo Escobar finally was killed.

During that decade the embassy-linked country teams working on (primarily rural) development projects had had to skirt United States' DEA, CIA, Centra Spike intelligence, and Delta Force military—if the traditional country team members even knew of them. By our more expansive definition, the U.S. drug enforcement, intelligence, and counterinsurgency operatives also constituted a kind of country team. As various documents covering the era suggest (for example, Bowden 2001; Randall 1992), the U.S. Embassy served as a kind of filter, keeping various agents and agencies "in play" and "out of play" while also brokering diplomatic communications with the Colombian government. So-called civilian militia, which were very brutal, had joined the hunt and were in touch with U.S. and Colombian agents; brokering also was required here. "Soft measures" became less of an option.

Today, with President Barack Obama and President Álvaro Uribe attempting to promote the Colombia Free Trade Agreement, in unfortunate lockstep with the violence targeting the country's trade unionists, things remain tenuous. Working as private contractors, DynCorp International and Northrup Grumman are largely carrying out the antinarcotics campaign in the country. In December of 2009 the Council on Hemispheric Affairs noted that, despite what it terms Colombia's "bleak human rights performance," the country was recertified by the DoS owing to its government and armed forces "meeting statutory criteria related to [their] enforcement." Key ethical criteria regarding accountability and transparent operations, as specified in this book, had not been met. Country teams, whether traditionally or nontraditionally defined, that are working in this type of conflictive zone indeed are in precarious positions.

The Advent of Human Terrain Teams

The roles that anthropologists should play in U.S. government overseas activities—including special operations—have long been debated. In the period between World War I and World War II, several served as advisors or consultants. As early as 1951 it was suggested that a social scientist be attached to each of the country's foreign aid missions. Although little came of this (Langley 2000: 52), many social scientists did receive assignments as consultants to, and evaluators of, community development programs. But a dichotomy unfolded. Those who performed analyses of the "classic" ethnographic sort had little influence on policy; those who moved into administrative jobs that could influence policy had little time to spend on integrating ethnographic insights. In 1961 the Foreign Assistance Act was signed into law, and

USAID was created by executive order. The 1973 congressional mandate that USAID work more effectively on behalf of the poor facilitated anthropological involvement. Foci became redirected less toward top-down and more toward bottom-up programs affecting (for instance) land tenure, credit schemes, food distribution networks, water resources, and agriculture inputs. Social scientists gained employment opportunities that were more in tune with their training and skills (Langley 2000: 54). Peter Van Arsdale built on such an opportunity in his work as Chief-of-Party for USAID in El Salvador in 1984.

During the 1980s and 1990s social scientists and social science advocates played modest roles in terms of military operations. Some, such as the late Fred Cuny, worked best as they cajoled military specialists into action on humanitarian projects, as occurred in Sarajevo during the Bosnian civil war. Others, such as John Prendergast, worked best as they reported on site in the most problematic of regions (especially Africa), in both ethnographic and journalistic modes.

Human terrain refers to the sociocultural, socioeconomic, and sociopolitical environment that is engaged and unfolds around a military force. It is reflective of the human population and society in the AO (area of operations). As Roberto González (2009: 25–26) notes, human terrain can be contrasted with *geophysical terrain*, a term favored by forces trained for conventional warfare. Human terrain indicates a newer form of battlefield engagement and fighting, played out on a sociocultural plane. It is conceptually represented by the military in the human terrain system (HTS).

Human Terrain Teams (HTTs) have been developed and deployed in Iraq and Afghanistan during the last several years. The developmental phase spanned 2005 and 2006. These teams consist of military and civilian personnel trained in ethnographic and related qualitative methods. A number of the civilians have been anthropologists. Although the current format and application of the term is new, González (2009: 28–29) traces its origins and early usages back at least four decades, to a report by the U.S. House Un-American Activities Committee as it dealt with perceived threats by the Black Panthers within the United States. Traditional guerrilla and urban warfare was being linked to seizure and control of human terrain. Authorities believed that insurgency needed to be met by counterinsurgency; population control was at issue.

HTTs also grew from military experiences with other types of teams, other types of foreign assistance, and other types of intervention. To the extent that they grew from a desire to better grasp the nuances of local culture, they are partially traceable to earlier courses in social science offered at such institutions as the National Defense University and the various service academies. To the extent that they grew from theoretical underpinnings, these are traceable to the counterinsurgency premise "where the critical point is to make links with local populations" (Brown 2008: 449). The latest military perspectives on effective counterinsurgency (COIN) are outlined in *The U.S. Army/Marine Corps Counterinsurgency Field Manual*, published in 2007. General David Petraeus's imprint therein is large; he co-authored the original foreword and advised on the remaining text. Having previously led the multinational force in Iraq, he assumed the top post at CENTCOM in October, 2008. Among field manual strategies that are intended to benefit from HTT insights: attacking the enemy's strategy, rather than the enemy per se; separating insurgents from the local populace; getting ready for handover (from one unit to the next) from day one; working regionally, attuning operations locally; knowing the AO culturally.

A contrasting perspective, built on a critical assessment of counterinsurgency, is that the human terrain system is structured such that new forms of intelligence can be collected that prop up the failing U.S. occupations of Iraq and Afghanistan, and (even if unintentional) subvert the local populations and co-opt the social scientists involved (González 2009: 2–3). The work is dangerous. That as many as three anthropologists have been killed while performing their duties as HTT members has added fuel to the fire. González states that HTS is seemingly "seductive." He asks rhetorically, given the central role of anthropology: "Who could be against such an initiative?" (2009: 19). A related concern of his, in fact, is that the program is "designed to provide brigade commanders with intelligence for achieving short-term combat goals in a theatre of war—not for improving the well-being of people living under military occupation. . . . Cultural awareness per se may indeed be a good thing, but not when placed in the context of counterinsurgency warfare" (2009: 19).

Ethical issues of data use and potential abuse are key to understanding the arguments against deploying human terrain teams. The memories of ill-fated and potentially data-abusive efforts such as Project Camelot, in 1964, still ring powerfully in the ears of social scientists.

Robert Albro, chair of the AAA Commission on the Engagement of Anthropology with the U.S. Security and Intelligence Communities (first referenced in Chapter 1), believes it best not to be simply "for" or "against" HTS, as he noted in a 2008 interview with Peter Van Arsdale. An evaluation of HTS was produced by the commission and published in 2009. Multiple perspectives were considered; appropriate forms of engagement between military personnel and anthropologists were noted. However, with a move toward HTS-type programs becoming greater fixtures within the U.S. military, grave concerns were expressed about possible harm in the treatment of human subjects, that is, indigenous respondents/residents. Potentially irreconcilable goals include pursuit of "a research function, as a data source, as a source of intelligence, and as performing a tactical function in counterinsurgency warfare" (2009: 3). Although HTS personnel recently have taken steps to systematically address ethical concerns, the commission notes "the lack of a well-defined ethical framework of conduct for the program and inability of HTT researchers to maintain reliable control over data once collected" (González 2009: 3).

Cpl. Greg Farrell, a PsyOps specialist in the Army Reserves, also shared important insights in a 2008 interview with Van Arsdale. He had recently returned from Anbar Province, where he served with the 324th Psychological Operations Company, based at Camp Haminiyah. In a discussion of HTTs in the broader context of other special operations, he noted by way of background that some PRTs, long the byword in on-site assistance, are morphing into embedded Provincial Reconstruction Teams (ePRTs), with even greater civilian involvement. (This development also was noted in Chapter 3.) This change occurred in Ar Ramadi and Fallujah, where they came to be operating at strategic "umbrella levels"; their Marine counterparts came to be working more at tactical levels. Civil Affairs Groups (CAGs), some with as many as twenty persons each, continued their work with the civilian side of reconstruction and also were charged with securing funding for certain projects. Human Exploitation Teams (HETs), with approximately six persons per unit (attached to a battalion), continued to serve in more traditional intelligence gathering operations; their HumInt specialists operated tactically, usually under the supervision of a warrant officer. SigInt (signals intelligence) was of less concern to them. PsyOps teams also continued traditional operations, but with somewhat less intelligence gathering than before. Farrell's unit covered a broad spectrum of duties, from making public announcements to dealing with shopkeepers to leafleting. For example, in Anbar Province one activity involved a combined medical engagement wherein both Iraqi and American doctors were helping villagers. He gathered "atmospherics" on the landscape, while also assisting in teaching on topics related to health care.

Each type of team mentioned above—akin to country teams in some respects—would intersect, on occasion or regularly, with HTTs. The large International Recovery and Development Group (IRDG) would have an HTT attached to it. Although some of the HTTs were temporarily reduced in size, even these would recruit fifty or more local nationals (LNs) as part of their support networks. Farrell saw their roles as important, but no more so than other of the myriad teams on site. Civil affairs officers remain essential to maintaining an effective military-civilian interface and to securing useful sociological information. The training/expertise of other personnel in this regard varies widely in his opinion.

Farrell believes that, should HTTs continue as a viable concept, ideal traits for their (at times younger) members should include an outgoing personality, skills in public speaking, an openness to different cultures and ethnicities, and curiosity. He believes that at least one member of each team should have formal social science training (this is particularly useful as kin structure, patronage systems, and subtle political customs are broached); team-building skills; computer/data entry skills; mechanical skills; and administrative skills. He believes these skill sets also are needed on other types of PsyOps, CAG, HET, PRT, and ePRT units as well. He stresses the immense value of using "engaged local interpreters" methodologically. He saw competent Sudanese interpreters, for example, who were not treated well by Iraqis.

Much of the concern expressed by anthropologists about HTS in both concept and practice has been about the potential for abuse (by those engaged) and misuse (of the data collected). Caution indeed is warranted, especially regarding the criteria of obtaining informed consent. Yet, as Lucas (using the lens of the AAA Committee on Ethics) notes, "neither [HTS] practitioners nor its critics have yet come forward with specific case studies of moral conflicts or questionable practices whose analysis might provide sound moral and professional guidance to others" (2009: 15). Marietta Baba stresses the need to look at the HTS issue through both professional and personal lens: "Whether such engagement is ethical, feasible, or warranted should be based upon a carefully considered assessment of the activities and actions of such systems and teams, in conjunction with ethical principles that are relevant to contexts of knowledge production and utilization" (2009: 388). In our parlance, one's discipline provides the ethical guidelines; one's personal "moral toolkit" provides the grist. The former is necessary but not sufficient. Ethical rules of engagement require personal introspection and assessment on site, before actions are undertaken.

In summary, HTTs are a recent development in the field of international affairs. They have become both bellwethers and lightning rods for pioneering fieldwork taking place at the civilian-military interface. They have been referenced in relatively favorable news articles (for example, Goldstein 2007), balanced analytic treatises (for example, AAA Commission 2007; Baba 2009; Lucas 2009), and scathing attacks (for instance, González 2009). As representatives of the Office of Naval Research (in contact with Peter Van Arsdale) have noted, these teams are in no way regarded as the be-all and end-all. Other options engaging cultural sensitivities and sensibilities are being pursued by both military and civilian specialists. Both Van Arsdale and Smith are helping in this pursuit.

The Roles and Methods of HTTs

Human Terrain Teams, per the Human Terrain System's handbook, are intended to be five- to nine-person teams deployed to support field commanders "by filling their cultural knowledge gaps" (Finney et al. 2008: 2).

(continued)

(continued)

They provide cultural interpretations of events within an AO. Teams include both military and civilian personnel, the latter contracted through the Army and trained (in many cases) at Fort Leavenworth, Kansas. The team includes personnel with both operational and social science backgrounds. It is the intent to bring knowledge about local populations into a systematic analytic framework, to build relations with local power brokers, and to provide advice of use to troops.

"Civil considerations" were codified as key to this type of operation by the Army in 2007. The handbook states: "The human dimension is the very essence of irregular warfare environments" (Finney et al. 2008: 3). Human terrain information is gathered to benefit planning, preparation, execution, and assessment of operations in the most difficult of nontraditional combat environments. Indeed, concerns about asymmetrical and irregular warfare have driven this initiative, with the focus being on establishing teams in Iraq and Afghanistan.

HTTs are regionally focused; the knowledge of the team members is intended to span cultural, religious, economic, political, and (to a lesser extent) ecological domains. Members rely on unclassified, open-source documents and field research, as well as their own expertise; they are supported by U.S.-based researchers. One such HTS researcher and anthropologist whom we interviewed works entirely within the library and archival system, never setting foot overseas. Another we interviewed advises from a corporate base within the United States and rarely travels overseas. Both work diligently and take pride in what they are contributing anthropologically.

Those HTTs that work with the Marine Corps attach to Regimental Combat Teams. Those that work with the Army attach to Brigade Combat Teams, which usually contain between 1,500 and 4,000 personnel. Others attach to certain Division-, Corps-, and JTF-level headquarters. All team members are considered to be "embedded."

A review of the methods section of the training manual used by Human Terrain Teams yields few surprises. It builds on the well-respected work of such anthropologists as Russell Bernard and James Spradley. It includes recommendations from anthropologists who have worked with the HTS program on site, such as Marcus Griffin. In brief, it touts CPE (cultural preparation of the environment), such that troops can better interact with the civilian population, better anticipate adversarial actions, and better identify potential hot spots. Geopolitical features, infrastructure, and social networks all are of significance. Human rights are addressed. Stated differently, HTT members attempt to be attuned to roles, events, processes, and resources.

(continued)

(*continued*)

> Power, as locally defined and managed, is key. Six questions are asked: What type of power does the group have? What does it use its power for? How is it acquired and maintained? Which leaders have power within particular groups? What type of power do they have? How is their power acquired and maintained? A subset of questions involves grievances, the thought being that an understanding of both insurgents' grievances and the local population's grievances can lead to better, nonfatal interventions.
>
> A review of the manual, other documents, and interviews with HTT personnel make it clear that—despite some critics' assertions to the contrary—all information collection is performed in nonclandestine fashion, remains open-source and open-access, and attempts to follow sound ethnographic principles.

SUSTAINING OPERATIONS THROUGH DEFTs

Sustaining reconstruction and development activities during the sometimes-dangerous transition period from military presence to civilian-run programs will require additional capabilities in special operations. One such concept involves possible Diplomatic Expeditionary Field Teams (DEFTs). DEFTs can act as enablers for NGOs and other humanitarian organizations, can serve innovative functions as suggested below, and can be the successors to PRTs (whose basic structure and function were covered in Chapter 3). Some of their protocols can build on what has been learned through HTTs. They will be able to complement and contrast with Quick Reaction Forces (QRFs), which will continue to be deployed near hot spots and likely continue to be fielded in Iraq and Afghanistan by representatives of several allied nations, such as the United States, Ukraine, and Romania.

As troop draw-downs occur in the primary overseas theaters, the Department of State will need to continue to evaluate its procedures. As activities gear up through AFRICOM (United States Africa Command) and continue through other of the military COCOMs (United States Combatant Commands), alterations will be needed. New thinking will be required about how to sustain remote diplomatic operations in semipermissive areas of operation. Unlike

HTTs, DEFTs would have an official diplomatic status and could engage in what we have referred to as expeditionary diplomacy. Although this status likely would make DEFT members targets for kidnapping and interdiction by hostile forces, it also would provide an added measure of official credibility to projects requested by local populations and regional authorities.

DEFTs could be further established in the DoS to alter and enhance the United States' special operations capabilities for tribal outreach and remote activities in dangerous areas of operation. Field data would be collected. They could work in concert with smaller, quasi-independent civilian teams, carrying out election guidance, poll observation, and public administration training. Our research in such diverse locales as Timor-Leste and Afghanistan reaffirms the need for improved public administration in the context of building a civil society.

Regarding air insertions, sea operations, and other special field teams' practices on land, DEFTs would have to serve in secondary auxiliary roles. They should offer finesse, not muscle. DEFTs could draw heavily on special forces, Tactical Human Intelligence Teams, and enhanced Provincial Reconstruction Teams to create an adjusted curriculum better tailored to the emergent needs of State Department and foreign service officers. Members of Civil Affairs Groups also would benefit. Innovative ideas should be incorporated from academic, civilian/NGO, and military sources, exemplified by the Humanitarianism and War Project, InterAction, and CALL (Center for Army Lessons Learned), respectively. Former Peace Corps volunteers, as well as current regional administrators, should be consulted. Agencies on contract with the Office of Naval Research and engaged in social science work, including computational modeling, also should be consulted. Specialists in overseas psychological adjustment, as well as adjustments facing returning humanitarian personnel, should be tapped through the so-called Helpers Fire network.

Innovatively structured DEFTs could facilitate information sharing among the representatives of different cultural theaters. Greater inclusion of the views of professionals from other agencies, as well as other countries, would serve to enhance the creative mix. The role that applied social scientists and other civilians can play as interlocutors cannot be overemphasized; leaders of the

Sunni Endowment (for example) made this clear. In general, there now are more inter-agency committees and working groups than ever, even so-called fusion teams to break down the stovepipes of specialized information and cross-germinate the knowledge base. Such groups are beginning to accomplish their missions, as the work of InterAction exemplifies. We believe that more government funding is needed for this type of endeavor.

This strategy would take grassroots diplomacy to the next level, evolving U.S. capabilities as the diplomatic landscape is changing. From Beirut to Dili, diplomats can just hunker down in hardened mission posts and engage clients there, or they can reach out and engage the populace in innovative ways, some of which extend into the most remote, semipermissive environments. Increasingly, those diplomats we are working with prefer the latter strategy.

CHAPTER 8

CONCLUSION:
BACK TO THE FUTURE

A NON-IDEOLOGICAL STANCE

The following position statement is drawn not only from our academic experiences but also from decades of fieldwork and humanitarian activity in both remote and proximate areas. It also is drawn "from the gut." We believe in a pragmatic humanitarianism that is carried out on site, when necessary in the toughest of conditions outside the Green Zone. Civilian personnel, including social scientists, often are required to work alongside military personnel. In the examples we feature, this activity takes place through country teams. As sociopolitical difficulties are encountered, these teams must emphasize soft measures whenever possible. A respect for ethical rules of engagement is paramount.

We do not believe that American country team operations are driven by any kind of need to install democracies worldwide. We do not believe that the United States is an imperial giant whose world mission is undeniable. We do not believe that there is a simple, polarizing "right" and "wrong" that underpins transnational activities, including those of a humanitarian nature, such that one course of action will solve the problem. We do not believe that might makes right but do believe that the modern military offers certain options, opportunities, and openings that can be "right." We are not apologists for the U.S. military, the Department of State, or USAID, but we do believe that their programs can be beneficial. As the previous chapters have indicated, we offer compliments and critiques as needed, all aimed at more constructive country team operations and humanitarian outreach. Rights-based development is the ultimate goal.

Like Doctors Without Borders, we do not believe in a simple pre-emptive interventionism but do believe in a kind of liberal interventionism, aimed collectively and proactively at helping the powerless in other countries who are faced with oppressive circumstances. Much of this plays out as we work with country teams, those comprising primarily or exclusively civilian personnel, those comprising primarily military personnel, and those comprising both, in a balanced fashion.

We do not believe that ideology should drive this work. Although recognizing that, on the global front, the United States broadly propounds a loosely interlocking set of propositions that involve democratization, development, and defense and although recognizing that American country teams represent government interests, we do not believe that team members who are not Chief of Mission should be "ideological ambassadors." The president serves as the senior spokesman. In a major international speech delivered in Cairo, Egypt, on June 4, 2009, President Barack Obama stressed that the colonialism that the United States has sometimes supported works against the American ideals of liberty. He spoke forcefully of the need for cross-cultural tolerance and equally forcefully against violent extremism. While noting the suffering of

Palestinians, he also noted the need for Hamas to recognize the state of Israel. He decried the slaughters of innocent people in Bosnia and Darfur (locales where Peter Van Arsdale has worked). He said: "It's easier to start wars than to end them. . . Blessed are the peacemakers" (Obama 2009). Although analyst David Bromwich contends that Obama broke no new ground (2009: 6), none-theless by addressing the Arab world without condescension he "placed the United States on a different footing. . . . The Cairo speech played for higher stakes than any strategist in an earlier mold could have advised or foreseen" (Bromwich 2009: 4). Even if only indirectly, this speech will drive what country teams are able to accomplish in places such as Lebanon, where Derrin Smith now is working.

Although it is being refined by President Obama, the longer-term U.S. global mandate remains focused on the central issues of terrorism reduction, trade balance improvement, nuclear weapons reduction, and foreign relations reframing with such countries as Iran and North Korea. The speech he made on receipt of the Nobel Peace Prize makes it clear that he understands "just war" theory. Policies based on "gap reduction" and better "connectedness," including those propounded by Pentagon experts during the previous admin-istration, remain prominent (cf. Barnett 2005).

Effective Partnerships or Dangerous Liaisons?

We believe that effective partnerships can be developed between mili-tary and civilian personnel and that military operations can thus be made more humane and vulnerable populations can be better assisted. We believe that the so-called humanitarian space in high-risk zones can better be defined. Effective country teams, complemented by DEFTs (Diplomatic Expeditionary Field Teams), are one way of accomplishing this. Partnerships can be arranged where anthropologists, economists, and other social scientists are not co-opted, do not "sell out," and do not oper-ate unethically; these can and must be effected. They can contribute sub-stantively to understandings of the human terrain, human landscape, and human dynamics.

As of 2009 certain relatively liberal military strategists were beginning to refer to processes of "command-and-collaboration" rather than "command-and-control." In simple terms, here is what country teams of the twenty-first century must do: be attentive to the felt needs of local populations, be accountable, be ethical, be multidisciplinary, be interactive with other teams and units in place in the field, develop effective training-based partnerships, and seek "ground truth."

A recent report authored by members of the Defense Science Board's Task Force on Understanding Human Dynamics presents a number of suggestions of direct relevance to ideas discussed in this book. Regarding training, it recommends that the Secretary of Defense instruct his staff to:

> Initiate inter-departmental action to establish, with congressional support, an Institute for Public Administration Training with a faculty of military experts, skilled engineers, public safety advisors, medics, social scientists, and NGO representatives, tasked (1) to assist the [Armed] Services and civil participants with readiness for catastrophic relief and stability operations, and (2) to form and train multi-disciplinary teams for augmentation of any U.S. country teams. (Defense Science Board 2009: xiii)

This is complemented by recommendations inviting participation of inter-agency and NGO representatives in mission readiness exercises—to enhance collaborative services that facilitate cultural awareness efforts of the armed services and to modify the standard curriculum at U.S. military academies (as well as service-specific curricula) to incorporate basic training in human dynamics.

Foreign Area Officers (FAOs) might be expected to provide much of this expertise, but as the task force's report notes, the majority are currently spread too thin to provide adequate coverage. Expert cultural consultants have been used, but they have not been systematically integrated into the network. DoS recognizes that academia, NGOs, and certain commercial operations/corporations have a great deal to offer; steps are being taken to build a whole-of-government solution.

CIVIL SOCIETY AND PRAGMATIC HUMANITARIANISM

Country team operations can contribute to the development of civil society. A civil society is one that functions via rule of law. It is one that encourages an effective judiciary, allows debate and disagreement (including during the election cycle), affords human rights and civil rights protections to its citizens (including the most vulnerable), enjoys an active press, and innovates "at the edges." It is expressive but not oppressive. The ideal civil society does not have a constraining military or overly constrained diplomatic corps.

There is no unified transnational humanitarian regime. There is no single theory of humanitarianism. By contrast, the paradigm of critical theory and the theory of structural violence provide a useful frame as abuse and oppression are considered in institutional contexts. As reported elsewhere (Van Arsdale 2006: 189), we believe in a pragmatic humanitarianism that builds on the principles of civil society and that respects these principles:

- *Moral imperative*: Changes and peaceful interventions that address the felt needs of beneficiaries are the right things to do. This requires sensitivity to the beliefs and values held by others.
- *Benign intervention*: Intervention conducted in concert with beneficiaries can be both effective and nondamaging, even if enacted in a conflictive or postconflictive environment.
- *Liberal tradition*: The individual, usually working with a team, has the power to effect meaningful change. Concerted efforts with NGOs, PVOs, and IGOs are essential. (This is to be distinguished from "liberalism.")
- *Integrated solutions*: Multiple agents should work in concert to cause effective change. These persons usually represent different disciplines and always consider multiple tactics and strategies before acting.
- *Incremental change*: Successful change occurs bit by bit, step by step. It is not so much revolutionary as evolutionary. It is rarely dramatic, usually cumulative. Critical incidents do play important roles, however.
- *Learning environment*: Interventions that work are regularly used as learning devices by the change agents involved. Lessons learned are

diffused to other actors; best practices are recognized, discussed, and routinized.

- *Facilitative empowerment*: Change agents, in this text represented by country teams, must work to create environments wherein beneficiaries not only survive but also thrive as they assume positions of leadership. They become the leaders.

This form of humanitarianism is built on an understanding of rights-based development and an appreciation of social justice. It also is predicated on the premise that institutions can be changed, that instrumentality is essential, and that sensible transnational rules and norms exist that can serve as guideposts.

THE CO-EVOLUTION OF WARFARE AND HUMANITARIANISM

The contemporary battlefield during war, the theater as a battle winds down, and the war zone during the postconflict phase are confusing and, at times, hectic places. There is an array of military, quasimilitary, and nonmilitary actors. State actors (from the perspective of the West) include soldiers, support personnel, logisticians, agents, advisors, and contractors. They are complemented by friendly non-state actors, predominantly representing NGOs and IGOs. Often in opposition (again from the perspective of the West) is a similar array of state actors but, increasingly, a dissimilar array of armed non-state actors: insurgents, guerrillas, militants, operatives.

Country operations, and the work of country teams, must take the evolving nature of warfare into account. As indicated in Chapter 2, warfare has evolved in remarkable ways over the past several centuries. Simple polarities (between "good guys" and "bad guys," between "warmongers" and "peacekeepers," between "interventionists" and "bystanders") rarely capture what is happening. Rather than a polarized landscape, an asymmetrical landscape has evolved, with military and civilian personnel interacting in unusual ways. Derrin Smith has worked alongside troops in Iraq and Afghanistan, providing advice on such issues as unexploded ordnance (UXO) and tribal outreach.

Peter Van Arsdale has worked alongside field personnel in El Salvador and Bosnia, providing advice on such issues as personal safety and land mines. As detailed in Chapter 6, we both participated in university co-training activities in Transylvania with staff and cadets representing the Romanian Land Forces Academy and Air Force. Some of these troops recently have been deployed with NATO forces.

We now live and work in an era of post-Pollyannaish humanitarianism. The simplistic notion of the good guy Westerner has been replaced by more nuanced notions of indigenously inspired humanitarianism, intricately crafted aid programs, and (still imperfect) military-inspired interventions. Military operations have long shaped certain humanitarian operations. However, during the post-World War II era—and especially since the end of the Cold War—humanitarian operations have come to shape certain military operations. War and humanitarianism, as Hoffman and Weiss (2006) emphasize, traditionally were understood as encompassing discrete spheres of activity; warriors and humanitarians were seen to have little in common. This is not the case now. And, as we have indicated, lessons of warfare can benefit the "learnings" of humanitarianism. Warfare—when viewed both tactically and strategically—offers important lessons for humanitarian programming (for example, as personnel are deployed in the field). In addition, the military's ability to adapt rapidly to ever-changing environments offers lessons for humanitarians (for instance, as supplies are transported and emplaced). And the military's propensity to analyze and re-analyze an action/event offers a lesson in analytic persistence that humanitarians can afford to heed.

The normative conditions and assumptions underlying the use of force obviously are very different from those underlying the implementation of humanitarian measures and relief. Force aims at damage; relief aims at repair. A postmodernist might quip that warriors focus on deconstruction, humanitarians on reconstruction. Often, force is proactive and relief is reactive. Troops are trained to deal with the enemy and humanitarians to deal with the victims. Yet a bridge is being built between troops and humanitarians. Asymmetrical warfare is paradoxically affording a greater opportunity for this bridging to succeed.

However, the normative assumptions blur as the threat of force is considered. The threat can be more important than its actual use. The peaceful use of military power can be intimidating, as Robert Art (1999) stresses, and often serves as a deterrent to aggressors. Indeed, most states use their military might more often in peaceful than in forceful modes. Humanitarians can help shape this usage, as is occurring (with limited success) in Darfur.

Concomitant to military force used peacefully are recent instances of military force used distantly. That is, there has been an increased recognition—as political and humanitarian realities are considered—that technologically sophisticated equipment can supplant on-site troop deployments. Military and civilian losses are reduced. B-2 bombers, each costing nearly $1.2 billion, were the primary means of attack in the 1999 war in Kosovo. These aircraft permitted President Bill Clinton, who had little appetite for incurring casualties in a humanitarian intervention, to launch effective strikes with minimal risk to pilots and support personnel (Kaplan 2007: 92). Ground troops were not deployed by the United States or its allies, yet—from their perspective—it was a resounding victory.

This victory may well have been the precursor to the strategy of effects-based warfare espoused by the Bush administration. Effects-based warfare was championed by the neo-cons in general and former Secretary of Defense Donald Rumsfeld in particular, in both Afghanistan and Iraq. Limits of technology and limited engagement opportunities revealed weaknesses in the strategy. More recently it has fallen to an expanded combination of special forces and special operations groups, traditional military actors, and dramatically expanded civilian country teams to try to turn the tide toward improved civil societies in both countries. As of early 2010 progress in Iraq remained steady but uncertain, and activities in Afghanistan were absorbing civilian country team resources like a dry sponge.

Humanitarian-Military Cooperation

Humanitarianism and warfare have evolved while interlinked; the two are reciprocal and interactive. Among the most significant recent developments regarding linkages derived from a conference held in March of 2005 under the auspices of the United States Institute of Peace (InterAction 2007b). For the first time, specific nonbinding guidelines for facilitating cooperation between U.S. armed forces and nongovernmental humanitarian organizations (NGHOs) were promulgated. The Department of Defense played a key role, while noting that forces under its ultimate control will observe the guidelines as they deal with the broader humanitarian assistance community. They are "premised on a *de facto* recognition that U.S. Armed Forces and NGHOs have often occupied the same operational space in the past and will undoubtedly do so in the future" (2007b: 1). Both sides will make best efforts to observe the guidelines; if deviations occur, transparent explanations will be provided.

Some of the guidelines, while essential, are obvious. For example, military personnel should wear distinctive clothing to avoid being mistaken for NGHO representatives. NGHOs should use their own logos (such as the Red Cross) on clothing. Several of the recommendations focus on ways to maximize coordination in order to minimize risk of confusion between military and NGHO roles in hostile environments and to maximize inter-agency communication. For example, NGHO liaison officers should participate in unclassified security briefings conducted by armed forces personnel. Unclassified information regarding security conditions, operational sites, locations of land mines and UXO, humanitarian activities, and population movements should be shared, to the extent this facilitates humanitarian operations. Military personnel should provide assistance to NGHO personnel for humanitarian relief activities *in extremis*, when civilian providers cannot and when it does not interfere with higher priority military activities.

A brief referent is provided that suggests procedures for NGHOs and the military to access assessments of humanitarian needs. Websites, including that of the DoD, are a valuable source for such procedures. (Our own independent research has identified fourteen major websites where humanitarian information of this type can be readily accessed.) The guidelines propose interagency collaborations of a complementary sort, as well. They state that if USAID or the Department of State's Office of the Coordinator for Reconstruction and

Stabilization agrees to serve a liaison function, it should be prepared to work with the NGHO community as well as the U.S. government's implementing partners. They also indicate that the UN's Humanitarian Coordinator could be a solid candidate to serve as liaison.

Within the American military, the Joint Task Force (JTF) is the most common kind of organizational structure used for foreign humanitarian assistance (FHA). Various special configurations can be employed within this structure, such as joint civil-military operations task forces. Personnel are recruited from a variety of agencies and deployed as needed. For each emergency, these efforts are coordinated by a Civil-Military Operations Center (CMOC), which also serves as a central clearing house for event-specific information and coordination. In larger FHA operations, such as the 2006 CHE in Lebanon (discussed in Chapter 2), a Humanitarian Operations Center (HOC) is engaged. This is a senior-level international and interagency coordinating body. It usually is established under the auspices of the government of the affected country or the United Nations. Careful attention is paid to the interactive roles and responsibilities of NGOs and IGOs; when necessary, a local humanitarian assistance coordination center also is set up under advisement of the combatant commander (U.S. Joint Chiefs of Staff 2009).

Civilian-run "drivers of change" include the informal grouping known as the Friends of Human Security. Founded in 2006 as an advisory body for the UN, it recently has advised on the effects of the economic crisis on human security, the progress being made toward achievement of the UN's Millennium Development Goals, peace-building processes, and the protection of at-risk civilians. Its meetings are chaired by various ambassadors, one of the most recent being hosted by Claude Heller of Mexico and Yukio Takasu of Japan (ReformtheUN.org 2009). The UN Office for the Coordination of Humanitarian Affairs (OCHA), and its Undersecretary General for Humanitarian Affairs and Emergency Relief usually plays an important coordinative role—and, indeed, civilian input is pre-eminent.

Other forms of innovative efforts involving humanitarian/civilian and military personnel are being promoted by the DoD. In 2008 it established a new research and development program aimed at developing a science basis and associated technologies for modeling human, social, and cultural behavior. The HSCB (Human, Social, Culture, Behavior) Modeling Program is directed by Dylan Schmorrow, Assistant Director for Human Systems in the Office of the Deputy Undersecretary of Defense for Science and Technology. It is vertically integrated across domains encompassing applied research, advanced technology, and advanced component development (HSCB 2009). In late 2009 an open-access interactive electronic e-group of professionals representing these three domains was established. It is informally known as the DIME/PMESII LinkedIn Group. At the broadest levels, the HSCB effort is being driven by the recognition that social scientists have much to offer the military, that accurate on-site cultural assessments in conflictive and postconflictive areas are beneficial, and that computational models that complement field work can be very useful, once they are sufficiently developed. Needs stem from those associated with modeling for irregular warfare, asymmetrical warfare, and SSTR. Among the several corporations and universities involved is eCrossCulture Corporation, which includes Peter Van Arsdale as advisor/senior researcher. It is engaged in ways to improve on-site military assessments, using methods such as those tested in Tigray Province, Ethiopia, as described in Chapter 3.

ANTHROPOLOGY AND THE MILITARY

Anthropologists continue to be among the social scientists most strongly positioned to work with country teams and the military in challenging twenty-first-century field settings. Yet strong disagreements exist between many anthropologists and many military specialists who have analyzed the U.S. military and its emergent role in world affairs. A number of synthetic articles have been written since World War II by representatives of both camps, one of the most recent in anthropology being that of Brown (2008) and one of the most recent in military affairs being that of Chilton and Weaver (2009). Before World War II, as a review of thirty-nine seminal papers from the pages of the *American Anthropologist* (edited by George Stocking, Jr., 1976) indicates, little attention was being shown this topic by anthropologists. Only one in this volume, a short essay by John Embree published in 1945, discussed the role of anthropology in this context. He noted that "it would save anthropology some future embarrassment if its representatives in government would not insist on calling all of their present activities true anthropology (e.g., work in military intelligence, 'psychological' warfare, administration). . . . The present [World War II] has brought greatly increased demands on anthropology to provide personnel in various fields of applied anthropology" (1976: 468–470). He saw a tension that needed to be resolved between "pure" and "applied" research, and he voiced concerns with "national character studies" of the Japanese aimed at gaining some greater insight into "the enemy."

In the 1940s, 1950s, and 1960s a few of the nation's Cultural Relations Officers and Cultural Attachés were chosen from the ranks of anthropologists and other social scientists. That they were posted in what the U.S. government termed "exotic locations" may have helped with cultural sensitivity and cross-cultural communication, but there is little evidence that they were able to influence perceptions of and by U.S. military personnel. During this same span, as Baba and Hill (2006: 189) note, American anthropologists became involved in a wider range of projects involving social change and intervention. They came to appreciate that their work was not values-free. They also came to realize that this type of work can be fraught with moral contradictions, a point that Baba returned to in a more recent essay covering Human Terrain Teams (2009: 389). Some of those who were employed by governments and aid agencies came to be criticized by postmodern academic anthropologists as unethical. "Such criticisms had the tendency to reinforce earlier disciplinary biases against anthropological employment by powerful sponsors, lest the anthropologist become the target of attacks leveled against these employers" (Baba and Hill 2006: 190).

In the decades following World War II anthropological research involving the U.S. military, other U.S. institutions engaged overseas, and modern warfare continued on both "pure" and "applied" tracks. Identifiable threads include the roles of applied anthropologists working with U.S. development agencies, such as USAID (for example, Langley 2000), the understanding of Western warfare in the context of studies of power and traditional warfare (for instance, Ferguson 1989), the ethnographic interpretation of violence and killing (for example, Scheper-Hughes 2004), and, most recently, the health and mental health of military personnel—including those returning from deployments in Iraq and Afghanistan—viewed ethnographically (for instance, Hautzinger, Cunningham, and Scandlyn 2009). Civil wars and proxy wars in such places as Bosnia, Timor-Leste, Sierra Leone, and Sri Lanka have been analyzed ethnographically in the context of human rights abuse (for example, Van Arsdale 2006). Issues associated with genocide have been studied extensively (for instance, Hinton 1998). Put differently, pure research continued to focus on the nature of warfare, with an emphasis on understanding what "tribal and traditional" societies can teach us; applied research increasingly came to focus on the nature of contemporary battlefield engagements and their effects on indigenous populations, tribal and others. A better understanding of the modern military community also began to emerge. Topically, much of the writing can be divided into studies of resources, identity, nationhood, organizational capacity, and war-peace linkages.

Anthropology from the 1960s on has "embodied a strong sentiment against war and militarism" (Gusterson 2007: 157). Anthropologists from this era have come to view engagements with military and intelligence as "significant ethical issues" even though some of those in other disciplines have found this stance "strange and incomprehensible" (Doughty 2009: 2). The American Anthropological Association appropriately has taken a firm stance against covert research activities that might be associated with interests of the national security state. Yet, as asymmetrical warfare has developed, primarily since 1990, anthropologists have had more difficulty keeping pace, carving space, or finding place. This situation is in part due to the problems associated with accessing fighters variously described as "insurgents," "terrorists," and "counterinsurgents" ethnographically, but it also is due to the relatively stronger position that some scholars (especially political scientists) have when based in departments of international relations. Political anthropologists have made fewer contributions than might have been expected, for example, as differential power relations between tribal leaders and military personnel in such places as Iraq and Afghanistan are considered.

Where We Stand

The key assumptions that underpin our analyses are these: (1) U.S. military institutions dictate much of what transpires in international affairs worldwide; (2) the United States is an efficiently militarized state where civilians have a good deal of say in what transpires; (3) the U.S. government retains the capacity to command the economy, with the military "not only giv[ing] rise to but continuing to serve as a broad social welfare safety net" (Simons 1999: 91); (4) openings exist in the U.S. institutional structure such that innovations benefiting humanitarian outreach and peacekeeping can be made within—or in concert with—the military; (5) in postconflictive environments, the uniformed military presence must be drawn down as the civilian presence assumes center stage; (6) critiques of operational mistakes and military problems are important, and indeed, the critical process must be supported—yet this must not stop us from being engaged, both conceptually and pragmatically.

Given normal security concerns and the pressures being exerted by al-Qaeda and other insurgent groups, we do not believe that any decreases in military strength or dismantling of military organizations will occur in the near future. We agree with those whose work has been summarized by Simons (1999: 91) and who state that, for better or worse, there is a "specifically American military history" and an "American Way of War." Nonetheless, we believe that civilians (including academics) and prospective country team members with expertise in SSTR will continue to find roles where their work can make a difference.

Again, our position is not ideological but pragmatic. The American military establishment is not going away but in fact is growing. According to the OMB, as a percentage of discretionary budget authority by agency, the defense/military component was estimated at 55.1 percent in 2009. The next largest, at a mere 6.6 percent, was health and human services. As a percentage of GDP, defense/military was estimated at 3.1 percent. The aggregate discretionary expenditure was estimated to be more than $670 billion for 2009, the largest figure in half a century (when calculated in constant FY2000 dollars). An additional $83 billion was to be spent on defense-related research and development (Office of Management and Budget 2008: 118, 126, 155, 190).

These calculations do not include certain military facilities, procurement, and housing figures; they also do not include certain additional appropriations passed by Congress on an annual basis to support the wars in Iraq and Afghanistan.

Our position reflects our belief that representatives of civil society, including anthropologists and economists, regularly can influence U.S. foreign policy. Human rights specialists, including those with ties to past and present administrative and federal offices, are increasingly doing so. As Julie Mertus notes, "human rights organizations now reach deeper into the U.S. foreign policy establishment and make new demands on the behavior of the U.S. government and military" (2004: 150). The Clinton administration was a watershed in facilitating these possibilities, the subsequent Bush administration less so. That human rights organizations' members have become more professionalized has aided their ability to achieve results. But Mertus also warns that, when a person becomes part of the dominant discourse, that person also can be "spun" or otherwise used for an administration's ends.

Rather than polarizing, our approach is integrative. Rather than pitting academics against the military, we are looking for ways to better integrate what each has to offer in the context of humanitarian service. Rather than ideologically contrasting conservatives and liberals, we are attempting to take a non-ideological approach that focuses on in-situ improvements in the human condition. Rather than suggesting that war be abolished (a desirable but entirely unrealistic vision), we are suggesting that country teams work in ways that diminish war's negative impacts. Rather than harping on American exceptionalism (which we believe is severe), we are seeking ways to work in transnational partnerships at local levels that are "less exceptional."

Both of us have served in academic posts. Both of us have served as proponents of, and participants in, humanitarian outreach programs. Both of us have worked for government organizations. Our position parallels that suggested by Noah Feldman, a professor of law at Harvard University who also has advised the Coalition Provisional Authority in Iraq. "Are academics so much purer than anybody else that we can't ever be in situations where we are confronting tough ethical choices?" (Goldstein 2007: 2).

Tension

Some of the tension among social scientists and military specialists revolves around the structures and functions that modern Western militaries exhibit. Those of the United States in some key areas are unique, representing "an American Way," but they also fit a broader template. As Catherine Lutz summarizes, mass industrial warfare emerged in concert with industrial capitalism and the nation-state. "World Wars I and II were fought in this mass industrial mode and helped shape the labor geographies and gender/race/class structures of the societies that waged them" (2002: 727). Nuclearism and the Cold War built on this substructure in polarizing fashion; secret programs proliferated, and increasingly complex intelligence operations evolved. Proxy wars raged in such places as Ethiopia and El Salvador. Overt forms of violence were accompanied by structural forms of violence, at times less obvious but at least as ominous (Van Arsdale 2006: 6–7, 47, 90). During the 1990s the U.S. military did restructure, downsizing the number of full-time troops and upping the number of reserves, outsourcing more of its work both at home and abroad, and privatizing certain security operations. New doctrines were developed, as Lutz goes on to report, that broadened those missions that could be tackled (2002: 729): Evacuation operations, support to domestic civil authorities, and disaster relief serve as examples. Yet she shades her perspective with misgivings.

Tension incorporates the debate among those who think that the United States represents a militarized state that—despite cosmetic changes—is compromising the possibility for non-aggressive intervention and assistance for at-risk people in developing nations and those who think that the United States is a militarized state—with continuing humanitarian potential—that is not compromised in its ability to assist those civilians at risk in conflictive and postconflictive environments. Better strategies are needed. "Humanitarian war" can take on a euphemistic meaning for those in the former camp, as pretext for other national purposes (Lutz 2002: 729). For those in the latter camp, it can take on a pragmatic meaning, one that also engages the notion of the post-1990 "new humanitarianisms."

Militarism and *militarization* are important terms. Both suggest avenues of needed analysis by anthropologists and other social scientists; both are undertheorized (Gusterson 2007; Lutz 2002). We believe that both would benefit from more thorough understandings of culture *writ large*: (1) "local culture," as this is seen to represent the essence of a community (read: society) that a military brigade would be encountering in conflictive or postconflictive circumstances overseas; (2) "strategic culture," as this is seen to represent the (in fact, multidimensional) institutionalized perspective of the U.S. military; (3) "preferred culture," as this is seen to reflect the stance of a liberal academe/liberal citizenry who perceive the U.S. military to be ever dangerous and who perceive that social scientists must avoid involvements that could readily become "mercenary," "co-opted," or "militarized." The intersection of these "three cultures" needs to be better delineated. This is not to diminish—but in fact to enhance—the valued insights to be obtained from a critical ethnography of the military and of security operations. Reflexive self-questioning by anthropologists, economists, and other social scientists, as well as by military personnel, remains essential.

Some of the tension therefore revolves around the perceived roles that anthropologists, economists, and other social scientists should play in military affairs. Should they work with military personnel in field operations (including humanitarian relief)? Should they advise military personnel, including those associated with the various COCOMs, on ways to better incorporate ethnographic and socioeconomic information into their analyses of at-risk populations? Should they serve as advisor-analysts on the battlefield?

Since 2007 a number of articles, commentaries, and briefs have appeared regarding the intersection of the anthropology/ethnography and military/intelligence communities. Summative, balanced, and highly comprehensive was the report of the AAA Commission on the Engagement of Anthropology with the U.S. Security and Intelligence Communities (2007). Roberto González's book *American Counterinsurgency: Human Science and the Human Terrain* (2009) also was published; providing a longer historical perspective, it is primarily critical. Another brief was published in *Anthropology News* in February of 2009. In this, Lucian Gomoll recapitulates some of the sessions held on the topic at two recent annual meetings of the American Anthropological Association. Also primarily critical, the sessions nonetheless presented a wide array of perspectives.

Peter Van Arsdale interviewed several senior anthropologists and military specialists to obtain their perspectives. Particularly useful were the comments of anthropologist Robert Albro, chair of the AAA Commission on the Engagement of Anthropology with the U.S. Security and Intelligence Communities (CEAUSSIC), as noted in Chapter 7. As the debate about the engagement of social scientists with military personnel in conflictive and post-conflictive environments continues to unfold, he believes it particularly helpful not to reify either "anthropology" or "the military." These are not monoliths but highly diversified and complex enterprises. Engagement with the issues, especially in the context of public anthropology, is preferable. (James Peacock, former commission chair and former AAA president, told Van Arsdale that "engaged discussion" is essential on these issues. Bill Roberts, not interviewed personally, stressed the need for "informed dialogue" in this regard [2007: 24].) Albro believes the ethics discussion—which has a number of dimensions, ranging from the obtaining of informed consent from potential beneficiaries in the field to the sharing of the information obtained with U.S. personnel—is best engaged programmatically, cross-referencing specific cases, as opposed to assuming an *a priori* "thou shalt not" stance. He has written that "CEAUSSIC's dialogue has sought to explore the diversity of institutional settings and accompanying activities composing this broad arena, to better contextualize the circumstances of ethical decision making they engender" (2009: 21). Indeed, the commission's twelve members are developing an Ethics Casebook that will include approximately two dozen cases for which anthropologists have negotiated complex commitments of this type (McNamara 2009). An online discussion community also is being initiated.

Kerry Fosher, a commission member and security anthropologist, reminds us that anthropologists have diverse engagements with the security sector, and these are complemented by diverse ethical challenges. Protecting informant communities is still central, but responsibilities toward deployed U.S. personnel also are important (Nuti 2007).

The issues being raised by discussions occurring at the anthropology-military interface are being broadly engaged at three levels, as Albro reiterated: (1) policy, (2) program, and (3) implementation. The U.S. Department of Defense is particularly concerned with policy; the AAA Commission with program; and groups like country teams with implementation. Choice of method, as well as evaluation of outreach effectiveness, fits within the last category.

Opportunities

The points just raised can, in part, be dealt with by providing specific examples. In the context of expeditionary diplomacy and humanitarian intervention, we need to maximize three kinds of resources to accomplish our objectives: human, network, and fiscal. Operations outside the Green Zone must not cause residual harm (for example, create a vacuum of local leadership) or unintended consequences (for instance, increase dependency in a refugee camp). Insights gained from anthropology can be exceedingly useful, as demonstrated below.

By expanding the information on Anbar covered in Chapter 7, we present two analytic opportunities. In the first, emergent democracy was at issue. The head of the Islamic Center in Ramadi decided to take his wife with him to register to vote. They intended to set an example for universal suffrage and to establish the precept that voting is a duty of women as well as men. Little was said, no flowery speeches were delivered. Yet, the tribal sheikhs of Anbar did not feel threatened by this deviation from gender partitioning. Both the Sahwa under Sheikh abu Risha and the Anbar Tribal Council under Sheikh al Turqie remained actively engaged in the politics and election processes within Anbar; their teams canvassed voters, registered tribal members (including women), and promoted visible campaigns. The result was an unusual blend of democratic electioneering and tribal leadership/customary practice, advised by American civilians, which worked relatively well.

In the second example, on-site tensions and military bravado were at issue. Despite some personnel trying to create their own oversized desert legends, useful interlocution can be generated by joint civilian-military teams and the steadying hand of civilian diplomats, applied social science consultants, and their local counterparts. A tempered, culturally attuned advocacy and counseling can be offered. During the course of 2008 activities in Anbar, the Marines rotated in a cadre of battle-hardened infantry to secure the Ramadi provincial buildings and Civil-Military Center. In addition to remote reconnaissance and sweep-clear-hold operations, these units had been responsible for security at a prison facility that was holding terrorism and insurgent suspects. Used to the toughest of conditions and the most unruly of persons, the units also were focused on rotating home in a few months. They had no intention of incurring further loss of life.

Observing these new security personnel in action at the perimeter, the Marines' mannerisms—and manners—struck the diplomatic corps as being unnecessarily harsh and disrespectful. Many Iraqi civilians needed to access the government buildings each day to process a variety of legal documents and permits; in the process, lengthy queues of hard-pressing people formed at the perimeter. As the gates to the complex were being opened each day, the Marines were pushing back, even shoving women and children, while yelling obscenities at the surging crowds. (It struck Derrin Smith as being reminiscent of the 1975 evacuation of Saigon.) The seeming deadliness of their warnings and aggressive crowd control technique led the diplomats to believe that any small miscalculation would trigger a major incident.

The military deputy of the Anbar PRT and his civilian team leader made a rapid assessment, determining that the daily situation on the perimeter needed to be cooled off. They advocated for a plan that involved counseling Marines and modifying perimeter controls. The Marines were reminded of the difference between the kinds of terrorism suspects they had been guarding and the every-day citizens they now were confronting, about ways to remain alert for suicide bombers while not disrespecting crowds, and about Iraqi customs involving crowd behavior. Iraqi security interpreters then were placed along the queues to prescreen Anbari citizens, aided by a handful of well-counseled Marines. On the first day of implementation, the transformations in both citizen behavior and Marine behavior were dramatic. A tinderbox had been cooled. A cross-referenced understanding of local culture and strategic culture, as defined earlier, had played out well.

SCENARIOS AND SIMULATIONS

We believe that one of the best ways to bridge the efforts of civilians and military personnel is to codevelop and cotrain with realistic scenarios and simulations. These already are being used by American personnel training for country operations and related overseas humanitarian, military, or development activities. The scenarios are case-based, providing realistic situations (with future implications and options) to be analyzed "in the classroom" along one or more dimensions: cultural, political, economic, military. The simulations, exemplified in Chapter 6, engage those being trained "in the field" in on-site or online/interactive activities, where skills are tested.

In June 2009 Peter Van Arsdale engaged in the analysis of a scenario covering the Democratic Republic of Congo (DRC). It was proposed and presented by military and civilian personnel associated with the COCOM/HSCB (Human, Social, Culture, Behavior) Modeling Conference hosted by Michael Baranick of the National Defense University. Although of particular interest to representatives of AFRICOM, it was of importance to the applied anthropologists in attendance as well. Options for humanitarian intervention, in the broader context of a conflictive political milieu, were considered.

In this scenario, the U.S. (through AFRICOM) provides targeted and delimited assistance to the DRC in a time frame ending in 2014. Extrapolating from the situation as it existed in 2009, the DRC was presented as further devolving into a near-failed state with a government corrupt at all levels, a weak economy, poor infrastructure throughout its rural areas, widespread crime, and unchecked diseases. Warlords and foreign militias continue to destabilize the east region; some are linked to Uganda's LRA (Lord's Resistance Army). Over 400,000 IDPs remain in camps run, with difficulty, by UN and affiliated NGO partners. These agencies are considering withdrawal. A UN peace keeping force is operational but able to provide security only to a portion of the country. At the request of the DRC's further-weakened central government, the United States intervenes to improve security and prevent total governmental collapse.

The scenario contains a number of assumptions. Understanding them is essential to the situational analysis and the evaluation of military and country team options. They include:

- DRC instability will increase without external assistance.
- DRC will allow a limited U.S. presence.
- Any U.S. intervention will receive DRC, UN, EU, and AU approval. Only Belgium provides direct troop support, on a limited basis.
- There will be no large-scale conflict involving neighboring states. FARDC (DRC government) troops will assist the United States.
- The United States has sufficient funding for its operations.
- The UN mandate continues, through MONUC (its current initiative there).
- The United States has overflight authorization from DRC and neighboring East African nations. Its air base in Djibouti remains operational.
- The People's Republic of China provides a small training/advisory mission for the Republican Guard, as well as matériel.
- NGOs and PVOs intend to resume full operations when security improves.
- DRC leadership expresses its clear dedication to reducing corruption and promoting more effective governance.

A well-written and comprehensive scenario of this type will include appended data covering what we term *terrain* (which is more geographic and physiographic) and *landscape* (which is more historical, cultural, economic, and political). The scenario presented for the DRC included tribal/ethnic, religious, and socioeconomic information, up to date as of 2009. Key to determining options for intervention(s)—by type, intensity, number, and duration—were data about four kinds of forces (extant as of 2014):

- "Red," that is, a large number of domestic and foreign ethnic-based militias, criminal gangs, and insurgent groups. Some ex-FARDC soldiers have joined the last group;
- "Brown," that is, Rwandan armed forces and UN peacekeepers, deployed within DRC;
- "Green," that is, Government of the DRC and its security forces (FARDC, National Police). The Republican Guard, armed with Chinese equipment, is included;
- "Blue," that is, U.S. civilian and military assets, under AFRICOM JTF (Joint Task Force), in coordination with the U.S. Department of State.

Mission statements are associated with each of the four force options listed above. The fourth category, "Blue," is of particular interest. JTF will:

- Train, equip, and advise FARDC to a standard such that near-term SSTR operations can be carried out without foreign assistance;
- Be prepared to assist both U.S. Department of State and Department of Justice in training and advising DRC National Police and other paramilitary security forces;
- Assist DRC in achieving east-region stability;
- Assist the U.S. "whole of government" operations to strengthen DRC's civil society and form of governance.

In his options analysis, which differed from that of most of the military personnel attending the conference where the scenario was presented, Peter Van Arsdale determined that U.S. intervention would be of limited effectiveness. A multilateral approach more broadly involving E.U. forces and affiliated NGOs (these to include specialists in humanitarian assistance) was preferred.

In different settings, our university students have been afforded (in addition to air mobile training) more rigorous training simulations than usually are provided through the DoS as officers and contractors are prepared for deployment in Afghanistan and Iraq. Although PRT personnel headed

to Afghanistan now engage a core curriculum at Fort Bragg that better pre-
pares them to be embedded in military-led PRTs at firebases, there is more
that the Department of State could provide Foreign Service Officers, Foreign
Area Officers, and Foreign Service Specialists regarding state-of-the-art training in remote, small-scale field-team special operations. In the rigorous ten-
week field training program in Romania discussed in Chapter 6, University
of Denver graduate students experienced realistic simulations that included
ambushes, kidnapping and hostage taking, interrogation and resistance techniques, and remote survival skills. They also learned basic emergency first aid
and field communications techniques.

COMING FULL CIRCLE

Rights-based development is the ultimate goal, as stressed earlier. However,
such development does not equal human rights. Development does not
equal diplomacy. Development does not equal political assistance. These
are complementary and interactive process, not to be conflated one with
another.

The bridge between civilian and military affairs remains imperfect. In
conflictive and postconflictive zones, difficulties remain between the DoS
and DoD regarding chain of command and ultimate authority in-country.
Those projects and personnel that can be better placed under Chief-of-
Mission authority, and those that can be better placed under operational
military command, need further "boundary delineation." NGOs operating
separately, or in tandem with agencies based in other (especially European)
countries, occupy still another portion of the "humanitarian space." U.S.
Ambassador Ryan Crocker and General David Petraeus are respected
for their abilities to install a cohesive management team in Iraq in 2007,
improving boundary delineation. That Crocker years earlier had helped pull
employees to safety from the rubble of the bombed U.S. Embassy in Beirut,
and that Petraeus years earlier had earned a Ph.D. in international relations
from Princeton, is indicative of their abilities to cross disciplinary lines and
see the "big picture."

There is an obligation to assist and also a responsibility to protect. Injured, impaired, and otherwise at-risk people must be assisted by those with the resources, capabilities, and opportunities to help them. A liberal interventionism is required. We lean toward a neo-Kantian approach, one that stresses the need for informed consent as interventions are considered and that sees value in the evolution of liberal democracies. These options should be facilitated, not imposed. New types of expeditionary diplomacy, aided by country teams, can be useful. Expeditionary diplomacy benefits the new humanitarianisms.

We have come full circle. In a sense, we have come back to the future. The 2006 crisis between Lebanon and Israel was analyzed in depth in Chapter 2. While the fighting still raged, the Archbishop of Akka, Haifa, Nazareth and Galilee, Abuna Elias Chacour, wrote: "Both [sides] use the languages of hate and revenge and uncontrolled threats. They use the language of total destruction of the enemy. . . . It is billions of dollars that have been wasted on the altar of war, pride, and arrogance . . . [O]ur children and grandchildren . . . need life whether they are Jewish, Palestinians, or Lebanese." As a complex humanitarian emergency, the war engaged a number of actors—including country teams—on a large scale. We hope that the cries reported by Sabrina Tavernise (2006a) of Ahmed Daibis, a blind man caught in the fighting in the town of Bint Jbail, will not be forgotten. More than anything, he was afraid of losing his shoes.

APPENDIX

Note: This is the training handbook used by the University of Denver's Josef Korbel School of International Studies for M.A. candidates training for possible field deployments. A majority of the candidates also are members of the school's training program in humanitarian assistance, cofounded by Peter Van Arsdale in 2007 and building on concepts earlier developed by Derrin Smith. Students are deployed to a "remote fixed site" located near Colorado's Lost Creek Wilderness, where a camp is constructed and a four-day series of training sessions and simulations are engaged.

HANDBOOK FOR RAPIER TEAM DEPLOYMENT IN COLORADO MOUNTAINS: THREAT ASSESSMENT, SECURITY, AND COMMUNICATIONS PLAN

Country Team Operations

You are being deployed to the Colorado mountains to establish a remote, fixed site in a (simulated) potentially hostile, semipermissive environment. All mission time data and transmissions will utilize MST. Additional details and operational orders will be provided after arrival of the Rapid Emergency Response (RAPIER) team.

Mission Overview

Primary Mission: Establishment of relief camp for six teams of workers. Search & Rescue (SAR) for debris and personal effects from two aircraft accidents; emergency response. Primary mission also encompasses IDP (internally displaced person) campsite identification for expected surge of IDPs; search for missing IDPs; assistance and transport of wounded IDPs.

Secondary Mission: Observation and reporting of local conditions affecting relief team and IDPs, including terrain reconnaissance and mapping.

Primary and secondary mission details and orientation to be provided on site. Area of Operations (AO) is remote and mountainous; spring weather conditions.

Area Awareness

Terrain: Mountainous, activities engaged up to 9,500 feet elevation.
Weather: Spring conditions (snow, rain, wind possible)
    20 to 30 degrees F during the night
    50 to 70 degrees F during the day
Wildlife: Confirmed bear and mountain lion activity
Fire Danger: Moderate

Threats and Incidents

Threats include the possibility that some individual or group might harm or target RAPIER personnel and materials, possibly through secretive, subversive, or violent means—anything that could adversely affect RAPIER operations.

There are significant threats that RAPIER operations will face:

- Accidental involvement in civil conflict—death or injury possible
- Vandalism to RAPIER property/matériel
- Local militia incursions
- Road or air accidents
- Weather—rock slides during the spring and the potential for hypothermia
- Wildlife attacks
- Illness

Recent security incidents:

- There has been ongoing tension between local separatist militia and relief personnel. There is a minimal civil authority in the AO.
- Catholic Relief Services reported theft of cargo from a relief convoy, perpetrators unknown.
- Mercy Corps confirmed that its remote medical aid site was attacked at night and razed by local militia.
- "Safe passage SAR activity agreements" outside camp have been negotiated with local militia.
- Relief organizations have reported some IDPs on foot in the AO.
- The two lost aircraft were responding to perform needs assessments when they dropped from radar. Crews were located on foot, 5 miles distant, successfully rescued.

Operational Security Phases

Because of the incidents reported above, the RAPIER team will be operating in a *Security Phase One, Precautionary* mode, with the option of increasing the security phase if additional incidents warrant.

PHASE ONE, PRECAUTIONARY   This phase is designed to warn staff members that the security situation is such that caution should be exercised.

PHASE TWO, RESTRICTED MOVEMENT   This phase signifies a much higher level of alert and imposes major restrictions on the movements of staff members.

PHASE THREE, RELOCATION   This phase indicates a substantial deterioration in the security situation, which may result in the relocation of some or all staff members.

PHASE FOUR, PROGRAM SUSPENSION   Declaration of this phase enables the operations director or camp commander to recommend relocation of all remaining staff members.

PHASE FIVE, EVACUATION   The decision to initiate Phase Five signifies that the situation has deteriorated to a point where all remaining staff members are required to leave the AO immediately.

Site Management for Moderate Risk Level

- Familiarize all staff with evacuation procedures and rendezvous points.
- Establish a good communications link with at least two other fixed locations.
- Prominently display all emergency phone numbers.
- Ensure the compound is self-contained (with supplies of fuel, food, water, and electricity/batteries).
- Erect perimeter markers around camp and all facilities, noting alternative entrances/exits.

- Never rely on a single means of exit or communication.
- Access to the premises should be controlled 24/7. Any visitors must be accompanied while on the premises.
- All movement by foot, outside the camp perimeter, must be done in pairs (with a walkie-talkie). All movement to the pit latrine also must be done in pairs.
- A "bug-out bag" must be maintained by personnel and kept handy at all times.

Vehicles and Convoy Operations

Overall convoy operations, to and from the site, are the responsibility of the camp commander and assistant camp commander, in liaison with the six team leaders.

Convoy predeparture checklist (using standard form):

- Vehicles have full gas tanks; fluids are topped off; necessary repair tools are available; spare tires have been checked.
- Staff have been briefed on SOPs for communication and possible route changes.
- Chain of command and personnel assignments have been confirmed.
- Cargo has been checked, loaded, and verified.

Convoy must communicate inter-vehicle at time of departure, at predetermined intervals en route, and at arrival. Drivers and passengers must always wear seatbelts.

En route, always check to see if you are being followed or paralleled by unknown vehicles. Should a roadblock be encountered, all personnel should remain together.

After arrival at site, one communications chief should be designated to ensure that all vehicles are maintained on a regular basis—ready for use at a moment's notice.

Vehicles should have radios/walkie-talkies available at all times. Make it a habit to check in regularly by radio, and if anything suspicious arises, make immediate contact, giving location.

No RAPIER personnel are to travel without proper communication equipment; this includes while transporting water. Always travel, even informally, with at least one other person.

Minimize Risk of Kidnapping and Hostage-Taking

To be kidnapped, victims have to be accessible to potential captors. Often, potential captors will watch and follow a potential victim. The easier you are to follow, the more likely you are to become a viable target.

Don't be predictable. Vary routes and daily times of travel.

About half of all kidnapping victims are taken from their cars; this normally happens close to home or their place of work/deployment. The morning is more common for kidnapping attempts, because one is more vulnerable, owing to a focus on the start of daily activities.

Captivity

A kidnapping or hostage-taking situation comes in four stages: capture, transport, holding, and termination. If captured:

- Explain your status as a humanitarian worker.
- Fully cooperate with the captors. Do not argue.
- Keep calm and obey captors' orders.
- Remember that the two most dangerous times of a hostage situation are the time of abduction and time of release, especially if a rescue is involved.
- Do not whisper to colleagues, make any sudden moves, or try to be humorous.

- Try not to give up detailed identification.
- Try not to allow covering of your head. This is dehumanizing.
- Be polite to your captors and treat them with respect.
- Try to rest, when possible.
- Try to be physically active, when possible.
- Do not reject food or water.
- Keep track of time and days.
- Converse with your captors as often as possible.
- Talk about your family.
- Do not beg or plead.
- Do not give away personal belongings.
- Always face your captors, when they are armed or unarmed.
- Physically distance yourself from armed captors; avoid eye contact.
- Listen for names and events being discussed, trying to commit them to memory.
- Be aware of "Stockholm Syndrome."
- Keep up a daily routine.
- Attempt to stay together with other hostages.
- Remember that no item or piece of property is worth a life.
- Think positively.

Land Mines (FYI—not found in this AO)

Antipersonnel Mines are designed to maim and kill. This type of mine takes 3–5 kg of pressure to activate, contains normally 50 g or more of high explosive (depending on the type of device), and can be set off by small children or medium-sized animals.

Antitank Mines are designed to destroy vehicles. This type of mine can have a devastating effect on the vehicle and its occupants. It takes 150–200 kg of pressure to activate and contains 5–20 kg of high explosive. An antitank mine is sometimes set up with an antipersonnel mine (a "squash") as a trigger. In this case, a person also can set off the mine.

Areas most likely to be mined:

- Military bases and compounds
- Battlefield areas
- Civil and military infrastructure/installations (radio masts, power pylons, and so on)
- Less-used dirt tracks and roads
- Shoulders and verges of roads, especially near bridges and culverts

Attacks (FYI—not occurring in this AO)

Gunfire/Crossfire

- Take immediate cover on the ground. Lay flat, face down.
- Stay calm. Do not panic or run.
- Determine the direction of firing. Are you the target?
- If possible, improve your protection by crawling to a ditch or hole, behind a wall, or inside a building.
- Observe the reaction of the local population. Get additional information about the situation if conditions permit.
- Leave the scene only after firing has ceased.

WHILE IN A VEHICLE   Precautions and tactics to be taken if traveling in a vehicle include: reverse/back up slowly to show peaceful intentions; switch on headlights; drive to a safe area when conditions permit.

AMBUSH   Get down. Communicate with team leader.
Send a call for help on your radio/walkie-talkie.
If safely able, take your radio/walkie-talkie and "bug-out bag" and head for cover. Stay there until advised by team leader.

Natural Disasters

Forest Fire: Obtain information on location of fire, decide on safe exit route, and immediately evacuate AO in vehicle if possible.

Flood: Move to higher ground immediately and plan for the water level to rise.

Communications

Radio Transmission Guide, Call Signs

- Use as means to identify the caller; should be unique to each user.
- Use an alphanumeric combination allocated by communications chiefs. Always use this while talking by radio/walkie-talkie.
- Frame/confirm a key question that can be used to verify your identification to colleagues.

Speaking on the Radio

- Brevity
- Clarity
- Need
- Do not pass on security information
- Start on channel 1 or a prearranged channel

Prowords (to be used in all radio/walkie-talkie communications)

- Loud and clear = good reception
- Readable = poor reception but workable
- Difficult = very poor reception
- Say again = last transmission should be repeated
- I spell = use when radio communications are difficult
- Figures = say before sending numerals
- Affirmative = yes
- Negative = no
- Over = you have finished but expect a response
- Roger = your message is understood
- Out = conversation finished

Phonetic Alphabet

Alpha	Juliet	Sierra
Bravo	Kilo	Tango
Charlie	Lima	Uncle
Delta	Mama	Victor
Echo	November	Whiskey
Foxtrot	Oscar	X-ray
Golf	Papa	Yankee
Hotel	Quebec	Zulu
	Romeo	

Emergency First Aid

A healthy person should have:

- Pulse rate of 70 to 80 per minute
- Breathing rate of 12 to 16 times per minute
- Body temperature of 36.8°C/98.6°F

Immediate action (remember "ABC")

- Airway—clear it if blocked
- Breathing—begin rescue breathing if there is none
- Circulation—cardiac compression if no pulse

Mouth-to-mouth ventilation

- Put patient on back.
- Bend head back to open airway.
- Clear airway if obstructed.
- Pinch nose and blow into mouth.
- Check to see that chest rises.
- Do this 12 times a minute until breathing starts/normalizes.
- Check pulse regularly.

Bleeding

- Raise limb and apply direct pressure to wound, using a dressing and bandage.
- Use pressure points if dressings do not stop the bleeding.
- Do not try to pull any foreign objects out; apply dressing around the object.
- Check pulse regularly and treat for shock.

Breaks

- Symptoms—pain, unable to move limb, swelling, and deformity.
- Stop any bleeding and dress wound.
- Move as little as possible.
- For any pain and obvious fracture, keep the body/limb in the most comfortable position.
- Immobilize a fracture by splinting (leg) or using a sling (arm) if patient is to be moved.
- Check pulse regularly and treat for shock.

Burns and Scalds

- Try to cool burn/scald area as quickly as possible with water, ice, and so on; this minimizes tissue damage. Do not worry if water is not clean—any subsequent infection can readily be treated.
- Apply light, nonstick dressing.
- Do not remove any burnt clothing.
- Do not remove any burnt skin or blisters.
- Check pulse regularly and treat for shock.

Shock

Expect anyone who requires first aid to be suffering from some degree of shock.

Symptoms:

- Pale, cold, and clammy skin
- Fast and weak pulse
- Rapid and shallow breathing
- Blurred vision and giddiness
- Apprehensive, thirsty, and restless
- Could be semiconscious or incoherent

Treatment:

- Stop bleeding and relieve pain if possible.
- Try to identify cause, if not obvious.
- Keep airway clear.
- Loosen tight clothing, belts, and so on.
- Provide warmth and shelter.
- Provide fluids (but not with chest or abdominal injuries).
- If conscious, lie flat and raise feet slightly.
- If unconscious, put in recovery position and check pulse regularly.
- Reassure the patient.

Cross-reference should also be made to the Colorado Division of Wildlife's *Survival Manual* regarding the preceding guidelines.

Outline of Security Plan (general, for all types of fixed-site operations)

I.   Mission Statement as Representatives of Humanitarian Agency/Relief Operation
       Reviewed, communicated, understood by all team members

II.   Standard Operations Procedures (SOP)

     A. Site/compound security

     B. Mobile security (foot, vehicle, convoy, boat, railway, and so on)

     C. Cash security

     D. Communications

E. Incident reporting

F. Security assessments, "hot washes"

G. Security training

III. Contingency Plans

A. Attacks (bombings, missiles, gunfire/crossfire, ambushes, grenades)

B. Robbery/armed assault

C. Car hijacking

D. Kidnapping and hostage-taking

E. Landmines

F. Natural disasters—fire, earthquake, flood, hurricane, and so forth

G. Civil disturbances

H. Evacuation/relocation

I. Medical evacuation of staff or victims

IV. Supporting Documents

A. List of staff, addresses, telephone numbers, passport details, blood group, family contacts

B. List of international organizations, contact persons, contact details including radio frequencies

C. Resource people (medical, UN security, NGO security, immigration, travel agencies)

D. Maps indicating terrain and landscape features, assembly points, evacuation routes, and preferred primary route

RAPIER TEAM DEPLOYMENT

Incident and Field Exercise Report

Date and Time:

Location:

Project Area:

Incident Type:

Situation (describe in detail):

Staff Involved:

Response to Incident (describe in detail):

Threat Assessment:

___ *no potential threat*

___ *potential threat*

___ *increasing threat*

___ *unable to determine*

Date of Report:

Name of Compiler(s):

Title/Role(s):

Signature(s):

RAPIER TEAM DEPLOYMENT

"Hot Wash" Report

Team Name(s):

Date:

Timeline:

Description:

Analysis:

Lessons Learned:

Action Plan Template for Developing, Implementing, and Aligning
Standards/Procedures

Date: _____   *Team:* _____

Phase/activity: _____

Describe goal: _____

Action Step	Action Step	Resources Available	Person(s) Responsible	Timeline

Convoy Itinerary

University of Denver to Lost Creek Wilderness
(include below name of driver, passengers, type of vehicle, license plate
number)

Predeparture tasks and assignments:

En route check points:

Immediate tasks on arrival:

REFERENCES

AAA Commission/CEAUSSIC. 2007. *Final Report: AAA Commission on the Engagement of Anthropology with the U.S. Security and Intelligence Communities.* Arlington, VA: American Anthropological Association.

——. 2009. *Final Report on The Army's Human Terrain System Proof of Concept Program.* Arlington, VA: American Anthropological Association.

Albro, Robert. 2008. Personal interview by Peter Van Arsdale, November 20. San Francisco.

——. 2009. CEAUSSIC online: Fostering public dialogue on the state of the field, *Anthropology News* 50(4) (April), 21.

Alter, Jonathan. 2007. Foreword, in Dina Rasor and Robert Bauman, *Betraying Our Troops: The Destructive Results of Privatizing War*. New York: Palgrave Macmillan.

American Forces Press Service. 2007. *Troops Kill 11 Insurgents: Firebase Anaconda Report*. Accessed online March 1, 2009, www.defenselink.mil/news/.aspx?id=47241.

Anderson, Mary B., and Peter J. Woodrow. 1998. *Rising from the Ashes: Development Strategies in Times of Disaster*. Boulder, CO: Lynne Rienner.

Annan, Kofi. 2006. Five lessons. Address presented at Truman Presidential Museum and Library, Independence, Missouri, December 11.

Applied Social Science and Health Consultants. 1984. *Evaluación del Proyecto No. 519-0184, USAID/El Salvador, Oficina de Pequeñas Obras de Riego*. San Salvador: USAID.

Archer, Robert. 2009. Linking rights and development: Some critical challenges, in Sam Hickey and Diana Mitlin (Eds.), *Rights-Based Approaches to Development: Exploring the Potential and Pitfalls*, pp. 21–30. Sterling, VA: Kumarian Press.

Art, Robert J. 1999. The fungibility of force, in Robert J. Art and Kenneth N. Waltz (Eds.), *The Use of Force: Military Power and International Politics* (5th ed.), pp. 3–22. Lanham, MD: Rowman & Littlefield.

Baba, Marietta L. 2009. Disciplinary-professional relations in an era of anthropological engagement, *Human Organization* 68(4) (Winter), 380–391.

Baba, Marietta L., and Carole E. Hill. 2006. What's in the name "applied anthropology"? An encounter with global practice, in Marietta L. Baba and Carole E. Hill (Eds.), *The Globalization of Anthropology*. NAPA Bulletin #25, pp. 176–207. Arlington, VA: American Anthropological Association.

Baker, James A., III, and Lee H. Hamilton. 2006. *The Iraq Study Group Report: The Way Forward—A New Approach*. New York: Vintage.

Baker, Mike. 2009. Blackwater changes tarnished name to Xe, *Rocky Mountain News*, February 14, 27.

Banisar, David. 2002 [1993]. Battle for control of encryption technology, *IEEE Software* 10 (4) (July 1993, revised August 2002), 95–97.

Baranick, Michael, and colleagues. 2009. Democratic Republic of Congo, Analytic Scenario. Presented at the COCOM/HSCB Modeling Conference, Washington, D.C., June 9.

Barnett, Thomas P. M. 2005. *Blueprint for Action: A Future Worth Creating.* New York: G. P. Putnam's Sons.

Beckett, Ian F. W. 1999. *Encyclopedia of Guerrilla Warfare.* Santa Barbara, CA: ABC-CLIO.

Bell, Trudy E. 2006. Prisoners of war, *American Archaeology* 10(4) (Winter), 12–18.

Binnendijk, Hans, and Richard L. Kruger. 2006. *Seeing the Elephant: The U.S. Role in Global Security.* Washington, D.C.: National Defense University Press/Potomac Books.

Blanford, Nicholas, and Scott MacLeod. 2006. The war for hearts and minds, *Time,* September 4, 22–27.

Boas, Adrian. 2006. The rugged beauty of Crusader Castles: Holy wars in a holy land, *Biblical Archaeology Review* 32(1) (January/February), 50–61, 71.

Bogdanos, Matthew. 2005. Tracking down the looted treasures of Iraq, *Biblical Archaeology Review* 31(6) (November/December), 26–39.

Boot, Max. 2006. *War Made New: Technology, Warfare, and the Course of History, 1500 to Today.* New York: Gotham Books.

Bourge, Christian. 2003. Mercenary as future peacekeeper? *Common Dreams NewsCenter,* UPI, August 26. Accessed online April 11, 2007: www.commondreams.org/headlines03/0826-06.htm.

Bowden, Mark. 2001. *Killing Pablo: The Hunt for the World's Greatest Outlaw.* New York: Penguin.

Broder, John M. 2007. Report says firm sought to cover up Iraq shootings, *The New York Times,* October 2. Accessed online October 2, 2007: www.nytimes.com/2007/10/02/washington/02blackwater.html.

Bromwich, David. 2009. Advice to the prince, *New York Review of Books* 56(12) (July 16), 4, 6.

Brown, Keith. 2008. "All they understand is force": Debating culture in Operation Iraqi Freedom, *American Anthropologist* 110(4), 443–453.

Burnside, Craig, and David Dollar. 2004. Aid, policies, and growth: Revisiting the evidence, *Policy Research Working Paper Series*, No. 3251. Washington, D.C.: The World Bank. Accessed online December 24, 2009: http://ideas.repec.org/p/wbk/wbrwps/3251.html.

Butler, Mary Odell, and Jacqueline Copeland-Carson (Eds.). 2005. *Creating Evaluation Anthropology: Introducing an Emerging Subfield.* NAPA Bulletin #24. Arlington, VA: American Anthropological Association.

Cahill, Kevin M. (Ed.). 2003. *Basics of International Humanitarian Missions.* New York: Fordham University Press/Center for International Health and Cooperation.

CALL. 2007. *Provincial Reconstruction Teams: Tactics, Techniques, and Procedures.* PRT Playbook No. 07-34. Ft. Leavenworth, KS: Center for Army Lessons Learned.

Chacour, Abuna Elias. 2006. Letter from Lebanon. Personal collection of Peter Van Arsdale, dated August 5.

Chandrasekaran, Rajiv. 2006. *Imperial Life in the Emerald City: Inside Iraq's Green Zone.* New York: Alfred A. Knopf.

Chilton, Kevin, and Greg Weaver. 2009. Waging deterrence in the 21st century, *Strategic Studies Quarterly* 3(1), 31–42.

Clarysse, Willy, and Dorothy J. Thompson. 2006. *Counting the People in Hellenistic Egypt*, Vol. 2: *Historical Studies.* Cambridge: Cambridge University Press.

Cochrane, Glynn. 1971. *Development Anthropology.* New York: Oxford University Press.

Colorado Division of Wildlife n.d. *Survival Manual.* Denver: Colorado Department of Natural Resources.

Cooper, Helene. 2006. Bush calls need for robust Lebanon force "Urgent," as Europeans continue to seek specifics, *The New York Times*, August 22. Accessed online August 22, 2006: www.nytimes.com/2006/08/22/Washington/22prexy.html.

———. (2007). "Donors Pledge $7.6 Billion for Lebanon." *The New York Times*, January 25. Retrieved online January 27, 2007: www.nytimes.com/2007/01/25/world/middleeast/25cnd-diplo.html?ex=1327381200&en=31f7d0c6d72928df&ei=5090&partner=rssuserland&emc=rss.

Corrêa d'Almeida, André. 2009. *Poverty Alleviation in Mozambique: The Differentiated Value of Mediating Institutions, Government Intervention, and Highly Skilled Returnees' Personal Satisfaction.* Unpublished manuscript, School of Public Affairs, University of Colorado-Denver.

Council for Court Excellence. n.d. *Personal Affairs Record Book.* Washington, D.C.: Probate Council for Court Excellence. Available online at www.courtexcellence.org.

Council on Hemispheric Affairs. 2009. *The Ill-Advised US Certification of Colombia on Human Rights.* COHA Research Memorandum, December 3. Distributed via COHA@coha.org.

Cuny, Frederick C., with Richard B. Hill. 1999. *Famine, Conflict and Response: A Basic Guide.* West Hartford, CN: Kumarian Press.

Cuzzort, Raymond P., and Edith W. King. 1989. *Twentieth-Century Social Thought* (4th ed.). Ft. Worth, TX: Holt, Rinehart and Winston.

Dallas, Gregor. 2006. *1945: The War That Never Ended.* New Haven, CT: Yale University Press.

Dalton, George. 1961. Economic theory and primitive society, *American Anthropologist* 63(1), 1–29.

Davison, Gary Marvin. 2003. *A Short History of Taiwan: The Case for Independence.* Westport, CT: Praeger.

Deeb, Lara. 2006. "Hizbullah strongholds" and civilian life, *Anthropology News* 47(7) (October), 10–11.

Defense Science Board. 2009. *Report of the Task Force on Understanding Human Dynamics: Executive Summary.* Washington, D.C.: Office of the Under Secretary of Defense for Acquisition, Technology, and Logistics.

DoC (Department of Commerce). 2004. *Spectrum Policy for the 21st Century— The President's Spectrum Policy Initiative: Report 2.* Washington, D.C.: Department of Commerce.

DoD (Department of Defense). 2003. *Country Handbook: A Field-Ready Reference Publication.* Publication 2630-IRQ-005-04 (Iraq Transitional Handbook). Washington, D.C.: Department of Defense.

Dorman, Shawn. 2008. Honoring dissent and performance in the Foreign Service, *Foreign Service Journal* 85(9) (September), 69, 74.

Doughty, Paul. 2009. Growing pains and anthropological challenges: Lessons from an earlier era, *Society for Applied Anthropology Newsletter* 20(2) (May), 2–5.

Douthat, Ross. 2006. They made America, *The Atlantic* 298(5) (December), 59–65, 72–78.

Dyson, Freeman. 2005. The bitter end, *New York Review of Books* 52(7) (April 28), 4–6.

Easterly, William, Ross Levine, and David Roodman. 2003. *New Data, New Doubts: A Comment on Burnside and Dollar's "Aids, Policies and Growth (2000)"*. Development Research Institute Working Paper Series, No. 4, July. New York: Development Research Institute.

(The) Economist (Eds.). 2006. The accidental war, *The Economist* 380(8487) (July 22–28), 13–14.

El Sayed, Carol, Arafat Jamal, Arjun Jain, Astrid van Genderen Stort, Michael Bavly, Annette Rehrl, and Lisa Quarshie. 2007. Lebanon diaries, *Refugees* 145(1), 20–31.

Eliasson, Jan. 1999. The challenges of humanitarian action: Protecting people and supporting peace, in Kevin M. Cahill (Ed.), *A Framework for Survival: Health, Human Rights and Humanitarian Assistance in Conflicts and Disasters*, pp. 189–199. New York: Routledge.

Embree, John F. 1976 [1945]. Applied anthropology and its relationship to anthropology, in George W. Stocking, Jr. (Ed.), *Selected Papers from the American Anthropologist, 1921–1945*. Washington, D.C.: American Anthropological Association.

Erasmus, Charles J. 1961. *Man Takes Control: Cultural Development and American Aid*. Indianapolis: Bobbs-Merrill.

Ervin, Alexander M. 2005. *Applied Anthropology: Tools and Perspectives for Contemporary Practice* (2nd ed.) Boston: Pearson Education.

Evans, Gareth. 2006. The responsibility to protect: Unfinished business, *International Crisis Group Report on G8 Summit, Issues and Instruments*, July 15–17. Accessed online July 21, 2006:
www.crisisgroup.org/home/index.cfm?id=4269.

Farmer, Paul. 2003. *Pathologies of Power: Health, Human Rights, and the New War on the Poor.* Berkeley and Los Angeles: University of California Press.

———. 2009. Mother Courage and the future of war, in Alisse Waterston (Ed.), *An Anthropology of War: Views from the Frontline,* pp. 165–184. New York: Berghahn.

Farrell, Greg. 2008. Personal interview by Peter Van Arsdale, December 4. Parker, CO.

FCC (Federal Communications Commission). 2005. *Connected on the Go: Broadband Goes Wireless.* Report by the Wireless Broadband Access Taskforce. GN Docket No. 04-163. Washington, D.C.: Federal Communications Commission.

FEMA (Federal Emergency Management Agency). 2004. *Are You Ready? An In-Depth Guide to Citizen Preparedness.* Washington, D.C.: Federal Emergency Management Agency/Department of Homeland Security.

Ferguson, R. Brian. 1989. Anthropology and war: Theory, politics, ethics, in Paul R. Turner and David Pitt (Eds.), *The Anthropology of War and Peace: Perspectives on the Nuclear Age,* pp. 141–159. Grandy, MA: Bergin & Garvey.

Finney, Nathan, and colleagues. 2008. *Human Terrain Team Handbook.* Human Terrain System. Fort Leavenworth, KS: United States Army.

Fischer, David Hackett. 2004. *Washington's Crossing.* Oxford: Oxford University Press.

Fontaine, Laura (Ed.). 2004. *Creede Convoy Manual and After-Action Report.* Unpublished manuscript, Graduate School of International Studies, University of Denver.

Friedman, Joshua. 2003. Humanitarians and the press, in Kevin M. Cahill (Ed.), *Basics of International Humanitarian Missions.* New York: Fordham University Press/Center for International Health and Cooperation.

Friedman, Thomas L. 2005. Syria's "Hama Rules," *The Denver Post,* February 18, 7B.

Gamel, Kim. 2009. Briton in Iraqi custody after contractor killings, *The (Albany) Daily Gazette,* August 10, A2.

Gannon, Kathy. 2006. Push for peace widens, *The Denver Post*, July 24, 1A, 8A.

Gardner, Nikolas. 2009. Resurrecting the "Icon": The enduring relevance of Clausewitz's *On War, Strategic Studies Quarterly* 3(1) (Spring), 119–133.

Geddes, John. 2008. *Highway to Hell: Dispatches from a Mercenary in Iraq.* New York: Broadway Books.

Giunta, Ray, with Lynda Rutledge Stephenson. 2002. *God @ Ground Zero.* Nashville, TN: Integrity Publishers.

Godoy, Ricardo, Victoria Reyes-García, Elizabeth Byron, William R. Leonard, and Vincent Vadez. 2005. The effect of market economies on the well-being of indigenous peoples and on their use of renewable natural resources, *Annual Review of Anthropology* 34, 121–138.

Goldstein, Evan R. 2007. Professors on the battlefield, *The Wall Street Journal On-Line*, August 17. Accessed online November 8, 2007: http://online.wsj.com/article/ SB118732042794000715.html.

Gomoll, Lucian. 2009. Anthropology and war: An ongoing debate, *Anthropology News* 50(2) (February), 26.

González, Roberto J. 2009. *American Counterinsurgency: Human Science and the Human Terrain.* Chicago: Prickly Paradigm Press.

Goodenough, Ward H. 1963. *Cooperation in Change: An Anthropological Approach to Community Development.* New York: Russell Sage Foundation.

———. 1981. *On the Role of Theory in Applied Anthropology.* Paper presented at Annual Meeting of the Society for Applied Anthropology, Edinburgh, Scotland, April 20.

Gordon, Michael R. 2007. In Baghdad, justice behind the barricades, *The New York Times*, July 30. Accessed online July 30, 2007: www.nytimes.com/2007/07/30/ world/middleeast/30military.html.

Green, Joshua. 2006. Company, left, *The Atlantic* 297(1) (January/February), 40, 42.

Gusterson, Hugh. 2007. Anthropology and militarism, *Annual Review of Anthropology* 36, 155–175.

Hastings, Max. 2005. *Warriors: Portraits from the Battlefield.* New York: Vintage.

Hautzinger, Sarah, Marilyn Cunningham, and Jean Scandlyn. 2009. *Soldier-Family Wellness: Getting PTSD/TBI Resources to Those Who Need Them*. Paper presented at Annual Meeting of the Society for Applied Anthropology, Santa Fe, NM, March 20.

Haynes, Donald W. 2006. Methodism must speak out against rapture theology, *United Methodist Reporter*, February 17, 17a.

Hedges, Chris, and Laila al-Arian. 2008. *Collateral Damage: America's War against Iraqi Civilians*. New York: Nation/Perseus.

Hentea, Călin. 2007. *Brief Romanian Military History*. Lanham, MD: Scarecrow Press.

Herspring, Dale R. 2001. *Soldiers, Commissars, and Chaplains: Civil-Military Relations since Cromwell*. Lanham, MD: Rowman & Littlefield.

Hinton, Alexander Laban. 1998. Why did you kill? The Cambodian genocide and the dark side of face and honor, *Journal of Asian Studies* 57(1), 93–122.

Hoben, Allan. 1982. Anthropologists and development, *Annual Review of Anthropology* 11, 349–375.

Hoffman, Peter J., and Thomas G. Weiss. 2006. *Sword & Salve: Confronting New Wars and Humanitarian Crises*. Lanham, MD: Rowman & Littlefield.

Hoge, Warren. 2006. U.S. shift kicked off frantic diplomacy at UN, *The New York Times*, August 14. Accessed online August 17, 2006: www.nytimes.com/2006/08/14/world/middleeast/14reconstruct.html.

HSCB (Human, Social, Culture, Behavior Modeling Program). 2009. Introduction to the HSCB Program, *HSCB/Human Social Culture Behavior Modeling Program Newsletter* 1 (Spring), 1, 6.

Human Security Report Project. 2006. *The Human Security Brief 2006*. Human Security Centre, Liu Institute for Global Issues, University of British Columbia, Vancouver; available online at www.humansecuritybrief.info.

Hutchinson, Julie. 2009. 3 return to comforts of home, *Rocky Mountain News*, February 21, 2.

ICG (International Crisis Group). 2006. The Arab-Israeli conflict: To reach a lasting peace, *International Crisis Group: New Report*. Distributed via notification@crisisgroup.org on October 5.

ICRC (International Committee of the Red Cross). 2009. *Report on the Treatment of Fourteen "High-Value Detainees" in CIA Custody.* Washington, D.C.: International Committee of the Red Cross/Regional Delegation for United States and Canada, February 14.

InterAction. 2007a. *Annual Report, 2007.* Accessed online July 18, 2009: www.interaction.org/files.cgi/6311_Annual_Report_2007.pdf.

———. 2007b. *Guidelines for Relations between U.S. Armed Forces and Non-Governmental Humanitarian Organizations in Hostile or Potentially Hostile Environments.* Washington, D.C.: InterAction/United States Institute of Peace Press.

Iris, Madelyn. 2004. What is a cultural anthropology field school and what is it good for? in Madelyn Iris (Ed.), *Passages: The Ethnographic Field School and First Fieldwork Experiences.* NAPA Bulletin #22, pp. 8–13. Arlington, VA: American Anthropological Association.

Kaplan, Robert D. 2007. The plane that would bomb Iran, *The Atlantic* 300(2) (September), 90–95.

Keath, Lee. 2006. Lebanese flee shelling, *The Denver Post*, July 21, 1A, 6A.

Kedia, Satish. 2008. Recent changes and trends in the practice of applied anthropology, in Carla Guerrón-Montero (Ed.), *Careers in Applied Anthropology in the 21st Century: Perspectives from Academics and Practitioners.* NAPA Bulletin #29, pp. 14–28. Arlington, VA: American Anthropological Association.

Kedia, Satish, and John van Willigen. 2005. Applied anthropology: Context for domains of application, in Satish Kedia and John van Willigen, *Applied Anthropology: Domains of Application*, pp. 1–32. Westport, CT: Praeger.

Kennard, Edward A. 1949. Anthropology in the Foreign Service Institute, *American Anthropologist* 51(1), 154–155.

Kindleberger, Charles P. 1965. *Economic Development* (2nd rev. ed.). New York: McGraw-Hill.

King, Laura. 2006. Death and diplomacy, *The Denver Post*, July 18, 1A, 8A.

Kohn, George Childs. 1999. *Dictionary of Wars* (rev. ed.). New York: Facts on File.

Kristof, Nicholas. 2006. Aid: Can it work? *The New York Review of Books* 53(15) (October 5), 41–44.

Kushner, Harvey W. 2003. *Encyclopedia of Terrorism.* Thousand Oaks, CA: Sage Publications.

Langley, Grace. 2000 [1980/1981]. The use of social scientists in the United States Foreign Aid Program: A retrospective, in Patricia J. Higgins and J. Anthony Paredes (Eds.), *Classics of Practicing Anthropology 1978–1998,* pp. 51–55. Oklahoma City: Society for Applied Anthropology.

Lardner, Richard. 2009. War contracts take flak, *The Denver Post,* February 2, 6A.

Lenz, Ryan. 2006. Iraq civilian toll 6,000 in 2 months, *The Denver Post,* July 19, 2A.

Little, Peter. 2005. Anthropology and development, in Satish Kedia and John van Willigen (Eds.), *Applied Anthropology: Domains of Application,* pp. 33–59. Westport, CT: Praeger.

Lucas, George R., Jr. 2009. *Anthropologists in Arms: The Ethics of Military Anthropology.* Lanham, MD: Rowman & Littlefield.

Lucena, Juan. 2006. Personal interview by Peter Van Arsdale, December 12. Golden, CO.

Lucena, Juan, Jon Leydens, Carl Mitcham, Junko Munakata-Marr, David Muñoz, Marcelo Simoes, and Jay Straker. 2006. *Enhancing Engineering Responsibility with Humanitarian Ethics: Theory and Practice of Humanitarian Ethics in Graduate Engineering Education.* Unpublished manuscript, Colorado School of Mines, Golden.

Lutz, Catherine. 2002. Making war at home in the United States: Militarization and the current crisis, *American Anthropologist* 104(3), 723–735.

Marsella, Anthony J., Thomas Bornemann, Solvig Ekblad, and John Orley (Eds.) 1994. *Amidst Peril and Pain: The Mental Health and Well-Being of the World's Refugees.* Washington, D.C.: American Psychological Association.

Masaki, Katsuhiko. 2009. Recognition or misrecognition? Pitfalls of indigenous peoples' free, prior, and informed consent (FPIC), in Sam Hickey and Diana Mitlin (Eds.), *Rights-Based Approaches to Development: Exploring the Potential and Pitfalls,* pp. 69–84. Sterling, VA: Kumarian Press.

Massing, Michael. 2007. Iraq: The hidden human costs, *The New York Review of Books* 54(20) (December 20), 82–87.

McCullough, David. 2006. A man worth knowing, *Imprimis* 35(5) (May), 1–7.

McNamara, Laura A. 2009. CEAUSSIC dispatch: Information gathering and casebook continue, *Anthropology News* 50(5) (May), 22.

McNeill, William. 2006. Conspicuous proliferation, *The New York Review of Books* 53(20) (December 21), 16–20.

Mertus, Julie A. 2004. *Bait and Switch: Human Rights and U.S. Foreign Policy.* New York: Routledge.

Metzler, Barbara R. 2006. *Passionaries: Turning Compassion into Action.* Philadelphia: Templeton Foundation Press.

Meyer, Josh. 2008. Probe: Blackwater defied orders, *The Denver Post,* December 9, 2A.

Minear, Larry. 2002. *The Humanitarian Enterprise: Dilemmas and Discoveries.* Bloomfield, CT: Kumarian Press.

Moore, Lorna G., Peter W. Van Arsdale, JoAnn E. Glittenberg, and Robert A. Aldrich. 1980. *The Biocultural Basis of Health: Expanding Views of Medical Anthropology.* St. Louis, MO: C.V. Mosby.

Moran, Mary Catherine (Ed.). 2005. *Essays on the Principles of Morality and Natural Religion, by Henry Home, Lord Kames.* Indianapolis: Liberty Fund.

Mowbray, Joel. 2003. *Dangerous Diplomacy: How the State Department Threatens America's Security.* Washington, D.C.: Regnery.

Nguyen, Vinh-Kim, and Karine Peschard. 2003. Anthropology, inequality, and disease: A review, *Annual Review of Anthropology* 32, 447–474.

Nockerts, Regina A., and Peter W. Van Arsdale. 2008. A theory of obligation, *Journal of Humanitarian Assistance,* May. Available online at www.jha.ac.

Nordstrom, Carolyn. 2009. Prelude: An accountability, written in the year 2109, in Alisse Waterston (Ed.), *An Anthropology of War: Views from the Frontline,* pp. 1–11. New York: Berghahn.

Nuti, Paul. 2007. Kerry Fosher: Reflecting back on a year of debate with the Ad Hoc Commission, *Anthropology News* 48(7) (October), 3–4.

Obama, Barack. 2009. *Remarks by the President on a New Beginning.* Speech delivered in Cairo, Egypt, June 4. Accessed online July 17, 2009: www.whitehouse.gov/the_press_office/remarks-by-the-president-at-Cairo-University-6-04-09.

Office of Management and Budget. 2008. *Historical Tables: Budget of the United States Government, Fiscal Year 2009*. Washington, D.C.: U.S. Government Printing Office.

Peacock, James. 2008. Personal interview by Peter Van Arsdale, November 20. San Francisco, CA.

Perito, Robert M. (Ed.). 2007. *Guide for Participants in Peace, Stability, and Relief Operations*. Washington, D.C.: United States Institute of Peace Press.

Posen, Barry R. 1999. Explaining military doctrine, in Robert J. Art and Kenneth N. Waltz (Eds.), *The Use of Force: Military Power and International Politics* (5th ed.), pp. 23–43. Lanham, MD: Rowman & Littlefield.

Prendergast, John. 1996. *Frontline Diplomacy: Humanitarian Aid and Conflict in Africa*. Boulder, CO: Lynne Rienner.

Randall, Stephen J. 1992. *Colombia and the United States: Hegemony and Interdependence*. Athens: University of Georgia Press.

Rasor, Dina, and Robert Bauman. 2007. *Betraying Our Troops: The Destructive Results of Privatizing War*. New York: Palgrave Macmillan.

Redfield, Peter. 2005. Doctors, borders, and life in crisis, *Cultural Anthropology* 20(3) (Fall), 328–361.

———. 2006. A less modest witness: Collective advocacy and motivated truth in a medical humanitarian movement, *American Ethnologist* 33(1) (February), 3–26.

Redlener, Irwin. 2006. *Americans at Risk: Why We Are Not Prepared for Megadisasters and What We Can Do about It*. New York: Alfred A. Knopf.

ReformtheUN.org. 2009. "Friends of human security" call for GA debate, *ReformtheUN.org Latest Developments*. Accessed online December 22, 2009: www.reformtheUN.org/index.php/eupdate/5345.

Refugees International. 2006. Lebanon: Living in a parking garage, *Refugees International On-Line Newsletter*. Distributed via www.refugeesinternational.org on August 10.

Roberts, Bill. 2007. Practicing anthropology, *Society for Applied Anthropology Newsletter* 18(3) (August), 23–24.

Rodenbeck, Max. 2006. War within war, *The New York Review of Books* 53(14) (September 21), 6–12.

Rodenbeck, Max. 2007. Lebanon's agony, *The New York Review of Books* 54(11) (June 28), 10–14.

Rothenberg, Daniel M. 2009. *Testimony, Truth, Politics, and Atrocity.* Paper presented at the Annual Meeting of the American Anthropological Association, Philadelphia, December 4.

Ryan, Alan. 2003. The way to reason, *The New York Review of Books* 50(19) (December 4), 43–45.

———. 2008. What happened to the American empire? *The New York Review of Books* 55(16) (October 23), 59–62.

Salween Watch Coalition. 2006. Damming Burma's war zone: Proposed Salween dams cement military control over ethnic peoples, *World Rivers Review* 21(5) (October), 6–7, 15.

Scahill, Jeremy. 2007. *Blackwater: The Rise of the World's Most Powerful Mercenary Army.* New York: Nation Books.

Scheper-Hughes, Nancy. 2004. Violence foretold: Reflections on 9/11, in Nancy Scheper-Hughes and Philippe Bourgois (Eds.), *Violence in War and Peace: An Anthology*, pp. 224–226. Malden, MA: Blackwell.

Schultz, Jack, Peter Van Arsdale, Ed Knop, and Morgen Warner. 2009. *Rapid Ethnographic Assessment: Final Report.* ONR Award No. N00014-08-M-0389, eCrossCulture Corporation, Boulder, CO.

Schwartz, Norman B., J. J. Molnar, and L. L. Lovshin. 1988. Cooperatively managed projects and rapid assessment: Suggestions from a Panamanian case, *Human Organization* 47(1), 1–14.

Selmeski, Brian R. 2007. *The Empire Speaks Back: Anthropology and the Military.* Paper presented at the Annual Meeting of the American Anthropological Association, Washington, D.C., November 29.

Sen, Amartya. 1999. *Development as Freedom.* New York: Random House.

Shin, Dennis, Charles Uphaus, Todd Shelton, and Evan Elliott. 2008. Why the "F" process deserves that grade, *Foreign Service Journal* 85(9) (September), 51–55.

Shorto, Russell. 2004. *The Island at the Center of the World: The Epic Story of Dutch Manhattan and the Forgotten Colony That Shaped America.* New York: Doubleday.

Sides, Hampton. 2001. *Ghost Soldiers: The Epic Account of World War II's Greatest Rescue Mission.* New York: Anchor Books.

Simons, Anna. 1999. War: Back to the future, *Annual Review of Anthropology* 28, 73–108.

Singer, Peter W. 2008. *Corporate Warriors: The Rise of the Privatized Military Industry* (updated ed.). Ithaca, NY: Cornell University Press.

Slackman, Michael. 2006. Lebanon official critical of Syria is assassinated, *The New York Times,* November 22. Accessed online November 24, 2006: www.nytimes.com/2006/11/22/world/middleeast/22lebanon.html.

Small, Meredith. 2006. Chimps, bonobos, and humans: Discovering the moral template, *The Common Review* 4(3) (Winter), 38–41.

Smillie, Ian, and Larry Minear. 2004. *The Charity of Nations: Humanitarian Action in a Calculating World.* Bloomfield, CT: Kumarian Press.

Smith, Craig G. 2006. Freeing prisoners key goal in fight against Israel, *The New York Times,* August 4. Retrieved online August 4, 2006: www.nytimes.com/ 2006/08/04/world/middleeast/04prisoners.html.

Smith, Derrin R. 2008. *Anbar Case Study,* documented from in-situ participation and synthesis of unclassified/draft cable notes, Ramadi, Iraq.

Smith, Derrin R., and Adrian Bejan. 2009 [2006]. *Implementing Transformational Diplomacy based on Constructal Global Design Theory.* Unpublished white paper for international studies, Venice, FL.

Stocking, George W., Jr. (Ed.). 1976. *Selected Papers from the American Anthropologist, 1921–1945.* Washington, D.C.: American Anthropological Association.

Tavernise, Sabrina. 2006a. For Lebanese, calm moment to flee ruins, *The New York Times,* July 31. Accessed online August 2, 2006: www.nytimes.com/2006/08/01/world/middleeast/01scene.html.

———. 2006b. Sects' strife takes a toll on Baghdad's daily bread, *The New York Times,* July 21. Accessed online July 21, 2006: www.nytimes.com/2006/07/21/world/middleeast/21bakers.html.

Thomas-Slayter, Barbara P. 2003. *Southern Exposure: International Development and the Global South in the Twenty-First Century.* Bloomfield, CT: Kumarian Press.

Toffler, Alvin. 1980. *The Third Wave*. New York, Bantam.

Torchia, Christopher. 2006. Gunmen kidnap aid workers in Baghdad, *The Denver Post*, December 18, 8A.

U.S. Army. 2007. *The U.S. Army/Marine Corps Counterinsurgency Field Manual*. (U.S. Army Field Manual No. 3-24, Marine Corps Warfighting Publication No. 3-33.5). Chicago: University of Chicago Press.

U.S. Department of State. n.d. *Department of State Careers*. Accessed June 28, 2009: http://careers.state.gov/officer/index.html.

U.S. Joint Chiefs of Staff. 2009. *Foreign Humanitarian Assistance*. Joint Publication 3-29, Washington, D.C. Accessed online September 30, 2009: www.reliefweb.int/rw/lib.nsf/db900sid/EGUA-7R7PVJ/$file/usmil-foreign-hum-assistance-mar09.pdf.

UNIRIN News. 2006. *Egeland Asks for $3.9 Billion for World Crises in 2007*, United Nations Integrated Regional Information Networks web posting, December 1. Accessed online December 5, 2006: www.allafrica.com/stories/printable/ 200612010012.html.

Van Arsdale, Peter W. 1993. A brief history of development, *High Plains Applied Anthropologist* 13(2) (Fall), 47–51.

———. 2001. Darkness in anthropology, *Human Rights & Human Welfare* 1(4), 13–20. Available online at www.hrhw.org.

———. 2004. Rehabilitation, resistance, and return: Service learning and the quest for civil society in Bosnia, in Madelyn Iris (Ed.), *Passages: The Ethnographic Field School and First Field Work Experiences*. NAPA Bulletin #22, pp. 72–86. Arlington, VA: American Anthropological Association.

———. 2005a. Ground truth, *The Applied Anthropologist* 25(2) (Fall), 183–184.

———. 2005b (Ed.). *Applied Field Methods: A Manual of Practice* (3rd ed.) Centennial, CO: Center for Cultural Dynamics.

———. 2006. *Forced to Flee: Human Rights and Human Wrongs in Refugee Homelands*. Lanham, MD: Lexington.

———. 2008. Learning applied anthropology in field schools: Lessons from Bosnia and Romania, in Carla Guerrón-Montero (Ed.), *Careers in*

Applied Anthropology in the 21st Century: Perspectives from Academics and Practitioners. NAPA Bulletin #29, pp. 99–109. Arlington, VA: American Anthropological Association.

Van Arsdale, Peter W. 2009. *The Tragedy of Darfur.* Invited lecture presented at Mesa State College, Grand Junction, CO, April 18.

Van Arsdale, Peter W., and Connie J. Holland. 1986. Responses to disaster: A comparative study of indigenous coping mechanisms in two marginal third world communities, *International Journal of Mass Emergencies and Disasters* 4(3) (November), 51–70.

Van Arsdale, Peter W., and M. Wray Witten. 2006. Effective collection action: A consultative approach to enhancing ecologically responsible development in Tigray, Ethiopia, *The Applied Anthropologist* 26(1) (Spring), 65–80.

Vasquez, Jose N. 2009. Seeing green: Visual technology, virtual reality, and the experience of war, in Alisse Waterston (Ed.), *An Anthropology of War: Views from the Frontline,* pp. 87–105. New York: Berghahn.

Von Drehle, David. 2007. Briefing: Courage under fire, *Time,* July 2, 15.

Von Zielbauer, Paul. 2007. Civilian claims on U.S. suggest the toll of war, *The New York Times,* April 12. Accessed online April 12, 2007: www.nytimes.com/2007/04/12/world/middleeast/12abuse.html.

Wadhams, Nick. 2006. Mideast truce on table, *The Denver Post,* August 6, 1A, 10A.

Watson, Ivan. 2008. Iraq forces agreement ends contractor immunity, *National Public Radio On-Line,* December 9. Accessed online March 13, 2009: www.npr.org/templates/story/story.php?storyId=98045131.

Weiss, Thomas G. 2005. *Military-Civilian Interactions: Humanitarian Crises and the Responsibility to Protect* (2nd ed.). Lanham, MD: Rowman & Littlefield.

Welch, Alyson L. 2009. *The Need for Family Liaison Services in the Humanitarian Field.* Unpublished manuscript, Graduate School of Professional Psychology, University of Denver.

Whittaker, David J. (Ed.). 2003. *The Terrorism Reader* (2nd ed.). London: Routledge.

Williams, Holly Ann. 2001. Caring for those in crisis, in Holly Ann Williams (Ed.), *Caring for Those in Crisis: Integrating Anthropology and Public Health in Complex Humanitarian Emergencies*, NAPA Bulletin #21, pp. 1–16. Arlington, VA: American Anthropological Association.

Womeldorff, Javier. 2009. *Operation Jaque: Colombia's Rescue of Fifteen Hostages from FARC.* Unpublished manuscript, Josef Korbel School of International Studies, University of Denver.

Wyllie, Robert E. 1919. The romance of military insignia, *National Geographic* 36 (6) (December), 463–501.

INDEX

Page numbers in *italics* refer to illustrations.

abduction, 20, 90, 104, 162
Aborigines' Protection Society, 39, 61
Adams, John, 29–30, 42
Addams, Jane, 38–39, 66
Afghanistan, 57, 223, 226–227, 241–247
African Development Bank, 74, 118
AFRICOM (U.S. Africa Command), 273,
    297, 299
agency (human), 33, 62
aid (foreign), 49–51
    critiques of, 21, 50–52
    Israel-Lebanon conflict and, 84
al-Arian, Laila, 163
al-Assafi, Thamir, 253, 255, 256
Albro, Robert, 269, 294, 295
al-Faisal, Saud, 85
al-Faraj, Abdullah Jalal, 252–253,
    254–255, 256
al-Qaeda, 80, 251, 252–255, 262

al-Qaeda in Iraq (AQI). *See* al-Qaeda
al-Sadr, Muqtada, 94, 96
ambassadors, 236
Anbar Awakening Council, 254, 258, 259
Anbar Higher Committee (AHC), 259, 260
Anbar Province (Iraq)
    tribal outreach in, 247–248, 253–256,
        258–261
    voting in, 295
Anderson, Mary, 122
Andersonville (prisoner-of-war camp),
    195–196
Angola, 199
Annan, Kofi, 42, 82, 87, 130–131
anonymity, 38
anthropology, 61–63, 287–289, 293–295
    development, 47, 62
    foreign aid and, 50
    foreign service and, 235

military and, 287–289
political, 41
tribal outreach and, 241
U.S. government and, 266–267
See also ethnography; Human
    Terrain Teams (HTTs)
architecture, 192–193
area studies, 235
Arian, Laila al-, 163
Armor-Group North America, 101
army. *See* military; U.S. Army
Art, Robert, 284
Assafi, Thamir al-, 253, 255, 256
assessment, 105–107
    country, 73, 117–120
    in Darfur, 121
    in Ethiopia, 107–108
    in Iraq, 257–258
    threat, 121–123, 171–174, 175, 258
    See also rapid ethnographic
        assessment (REA)
Australia and New Zealand Army Corps
    (ANZAC), 76
authority, 246, 248, 251–253, 273
autonomy, 31, 33–34
Avars, 197

Baghdad Museum, 75–76
Baker-Hamilton report (2006), 131
banks, 49, 73–74
Bataan death march, 41
Beckwith, "Chargin' Charlie," 262
benevolence, 30, 31
Bengtson, Angela, 112
Bernard, Russell, 272
Berreman, Gerald, 33
best practices, 51, 204, 207–212,
    248–251, 257
    for country teams, 175
    risk and, 172
    NGOs and, 190
    in transit operations, 170
Betancourt, Ingrid, 149
Black Panthers, 267
Blackwater Worldwide (Xe Services), 95,
    97, 99–101

Blake, Robert, 178
Bodo, Dawn, 38
Boot, Max, 77
Bosnia
    humanitarianism and, 36
    mines in, 165
    post-war reconstruction, 199
    prisoner-of-war camps in, 195
    warfare in, 36, 80, 289
Boulding, Kenneth, 59
Bowden, Mark, 264
Bremer, L. Paul, 100, 101
Bromwich, David, 279
Brzezinski, Zbigniew, 79–80
bug-out bag, 136, 141, 146, 147–148, 222
Bulgaria, 197
Burma (Myanmar), 45, 53
Burnside, Craig, 51
Bush, George H.W., 265
Bush, George W., 173, 178, 182
    administration of, 72, 291

Cabanatuán (Philippines), 195
Cahill, Kevin, 68
CALL (Center for Army Lessons Learned),
    274
camps (prisoner-of-war), 195–196
    See also sites (fixed)
Canada, 76
capacity, 125–126, 127
casualties
    aid workers as, 19–20, 103–104
    civilian, 40, 163
    Iraqi, 163
    in Israel-Lebanon conflict, 82–83,
        84, 86
    during transit, 161–162
Ceauşescu, Nicolae, 198
CEAUSSIC (Commission on the
    Engagement of Anthropology with
    the U.S. Security and Intelligence
    Communities), 34, 293, 294
cellphones, 185–186
CENTCOM (U.S. Central Command), 268
Center for Army Lessons Learned (CALL),
    274

Chacour, Abuna Elias, 301
chaplains (military), 55–56
Chávez, Hugo, 149
Cheney, Dick, 99
China, 194, 215, 298
Chevron Australia, 74
Christianity, 30
Chu, Jonathan, 112
Civil Affairs Group (CAG), 116, 269, 274
civilians, 36
civilian medical assistance exercises
    (CMAX), 212–213, 244–246, 245,
    248
civilian-military cooperation, 55–58, 66,
    80–82, 115, 233–234
    guidelines for, 285–286
    in Iraq, 257, 295–297
    in Israel-Lebanon crisis, 82–83
    potential of, 279–280
    in Romania, 203–204
    training for, 200, 204
Civil-Military Operations Center
    (CMOC), 286
Civil War (U.S.), 40, 56, 195–196
Clausewitz, Carl von, 77–78
clerics (Muslim), 248, 252–253, 255, 256
Clinton, Bill, 284
    administration of, 291
Clinton, Hillary, 234
clothing, 148–150
cocaine, 264
Cochrane, Glynn, 60
Cold War, 36, 49, 60, 292
Colombia, 149, 263–266
    army of, 75
Colorado School of Mines, 64–65
Commission on the Engagement of
    Anthropology with the U.S. Security
    and Intelligence Communities
    (CEAUSSIC), 34, 293, 294
communications, 178–187
    outreach and, 249
    team members and, 155–156
    training in, 206
communism, 49, 198
complex humanitarian emergency, 91

confidentiality, 115
    See also informed consent
Congo, Democratic Republic of (DRC), 19,
    93, 95, 297–299
consent (informed), 33, 34, 113, 114,
    115, 271
conservation, 60
contractors (military), 97–99
    See also Blackwater Worldwide (Xe
    Services)
convoys, 162–164, 164, 165–168, 170, 205
cooperation, 48
    See also civilian-military cooperation
counterinsurgency, 267–268
country assessment. See under assessment
country operations, 73, 74–76
    plans, 117–120
    training for, 204–207
country teams, 18–19, 22, 42, 73–74, 257
    in Colombia, 265, 266
    NSAs and, 94–96
    role of, 278, 279–280, 291
    See also civilian-military cooperation;
        Provincial Reconstruction Teams
        (PRTs); teams (humanitarian)
        and team members
cover and concealment, 216–217
CPR, 205
Crader, Mike, 57
critical theory, 43, 44, 281
Crocker, Ryan, 259, 300
Crosiers, 55
culture, 109, 293
    See also anthropology
Cunaeus (Piet van der Cun), 31
Cuny, Fred, 58, 122, 267

Dacians, 197
Dalton, George, 60
dams, 53
Darfur, 103, 120–121, 228–229
data, 268–269, 271
debt forgiveness, 59
Deeb, Lara, 92
Defense, U.S. Department of, 285,
    286–287, 300

Defense Science Board, 280
DEFTs (Diplomatic Expeditionary Field
    Teams), 238, 273–274, 279
de Groot, Hugo (Hugo Grotius), 31
Delta Force, 262
Dependency School, 46
deployment, 135–145, 145–151
desk officers, 236–237
development, 45–46, 67–68
    in Afghanistan, 243–244, 246, 247
    agricultural, 59, 62, 63
    rights-based, 47, 300
    security and, 130–131
    theories of, 46–47, 52–53
de Waal, Frans, 30–31
DIME/PMESII LinkedIn Group, 287
diplomacy, 188, 235–237, 275
    expeditionary, 238–239, 274, 295, 301
    helicopter, 247–248, 249
    presence posts and, 224–225, 239
Diplomatic Expeditionary Field Teams
    (DEFTs), 238, 273–274, 279
disasters (natural), 62, 95–96, 120, 122, 175
    relief and, 292
    training and, 209, 212, 214, 216, 222
disease, 64, 120, 175
disengagement. See withdrawal
Doctors Without Borders (MSF), 37, 159
documents, 160
Dollar, David, 51
driving, 156
drug trade
    in Afghanistan, 241, 243–244, 246
    in Colombia, 264–265
Dulles, John Foster, 234
Dunant, Henri, 38, 39
Dutch, 42, 178, 194
DynCorp International, 97, 266
Dyson, Freeman, 76

Easterly, William, 51
East Timor. See Timor-Leste
economics, 46–47, 50, 59–61
economy (political), 46–47
eCrossCulture Corporation, 108–110, 112,
    113, 287

education. See training
Egeland, Jan, 84
Egypt, 49, 84, 192
elections, 256, 258–259
El Salvador, 127, 128, 292
    foreign aid to, 50, 118
    human rights and, 65
emergency action plan (EAP), 209, 250
emergency (complex humanitarian), 91
encryption, 187
engineering, 56–58, 64–65
England, 22, 40, 55, 178
equipment, 145–151
Erasmus, Charles, 50, 60, 62, 129–130
Ervin, Alexander, 106
escape, 216–217
Escobar, Pablo, 263–265
ethics, 54, 64, 67, 288–289, 294
    assessment and, 114–115
    of field research, 43–44
    human terrain and, 268–269, 271
    praxis and, 23, 44
    rules of engagement and, 32–34
Ethiopia, 107–108, 110–115, 165,
    219, 292
ethnography, 61, 113, 266–267,
    288–289, 293
    See also anthropology
evacuation, 83–84
evaluation (program), 129–130
Evans, Gareth, 78–79
event calendars, 114
explosives, 163, 165, 176
    See also IEDs (improvised explosive
        devices)
extremism, 254–255, 256

factionalism, 94
    in Afghanistan, 244
    Islamic, 88, 92, 94
    study of, 110, 112
    See also non-state actors (NSAs)
Faisal, Saud al-, 85
famine, 120, 124, 125
Faraj, Abdullah Jalal al-, 252–253,
    254–255, 256

FARC (Revolutionary Armed Forces of
   Colombia),75, 149, 265
FARDC (DRC government troops),
   298, 299
Farrell, Greg, 269–270
Fatah, 90
Fatwa, 253–254, 255
Feldman, Noah, 291
Feltman, Jeffrey, 237
felt needs, 48–49, 52, 62, 105
field protocol and survival (handbook),
   303–320
field schools, 200–207
Finley, Bruce, 189
Firebase Anaconda (Afghanistan),
   226–227, 242
first aid, 157–159
fitness (physical), 142–143, 209, 250–251
fixed sites. *See* sites (fixed)
Fluer-Lobban, Carolyn, 33
focus groups, *111*, 114, 115
Fontanetta, Anthony, 57
footwear, 142–143
foreign aid. *See* aid (foreign)
Foreign Area Officers (FAOs), 235, 236, 280
Foreign Assistance Act (1961), 49, 51, 266
Foreign Service (U.S.), 234–237
Foreign Service Act, 234
Foreign Service Institute, 234, 235
Foreign Service National, 235
Foreign Service Officers (FSOs), 234,
   235, 236
   PRTs and, 115–116, 299–300
Foreign Service Specialists (FSSs), 235
fortresses, 191–193, 236
Fosher, Kerry, 115, 294
Fowler, Robert, 220
France, 40, 76, 86, 87
Friedman, Joshua, 189
Friends of Human Security, 286
Fukuyama, Francis, 80

Gamayal, Pierre, 88
Gardner, Nikolas, 77
Gates, Bill and Melinda, 294
gear. *See* bug-out bag; equipment; footwear

Geddes, John, 163
gender, 53, 121, 295
Geneva Conventions, 38, 65
genocide, 65
Giunta, Ray, 56
González, Roberto, 267, 293
Goodenough, Ward, 48
GPS (global positioning system), 154, 180
Great Britain. *See* England
Green Berets, 262, 263
Green Zone, 71–72, 258
   beyond, 185, 277, 295
Griffin, Marcus, 272
Grotius, Hugo (Hugo de Groot), 31
Group of Eight Forum (G8), 118

Haiti, 80
Halliburton, 97
Hamilton, Alexander, 30
handbook (field protocol and survival),
   303–320
Hariri, Rafik, 90
Hart-Rudman Commission, 237
health, 64, 136–141
Hedges, Chris, 163
Heller, Claude, 286
Hentea, Călin, 196, 199–200
Hezbollah, 83, 85, 86–87, 88–89, 90–92
Hobbes, Thomas, 79
   neo-Hobbesian approach, 79–80
Hoffman, Peter, 36
Home, Henry (Lord Kames), 30
Hospitallers, 55
housing, 218–219, 222–224
HSCB Modeling Program, 287, 297
Human Exploitation Teams (HETs), 270
HumInt, 265, 270
humanitarianism, 20–21, 35, 37–41,
   67–68, 283
   Israel-Lebanon conflict and, 84,
      85–86, 91
   military in Darfur, 121
   "new," 36–37, 292, 293, 301
   pragmatic, 68, 211–212, 277, 281–282
   responsibility to protect and, 78–80
   Romanian military and, 198–200

world wars and, 40–41
    See also benevolence; civilian-
        military cooperation
Humanitarianism and War Project, 93,
    119, 274
Human Relations Area Files (HRAF), 110
human rights, 65, 281, 291
human terrain system (HTS), 267, 268, 269
Human Terrain Teams (HTTs), 108,
    267–273
Hurricane Katrina, 37
hygiene, 140–141, 217–218

IDPs (internally displaced persons),
    205, 247
    Israel-Lebanon conflict and, 84, 86,
        87–88
    See also refugees
IEDs (improvised explosive devices), 163,
    165, 176–177
immunizations, 137
individuals, 38–39
Indonesia, 95, 96
    development in, 53, 119
    human rights and, 65
inequalities, 44–45
informants, 111, 113
informed consent, 33, 34, 113, 114,
    115, 271
insignia, 149, 285
Institutional Review Board, 115
institutions (role of), 39
    See also military; NGOs; United
        Nations; non-state actors (NSAs)
intelligence, 265, 270
    See also Human Terrain Teams
        (HTTs)
InterAction (NGO coalition), 190, 274
internally displaced persons (IDPs),
    205, 247
    Israel-Lebanon conflict and, 84, 86,
        87–88
    See also refugees
International Committee of the Red Cross
    (ICRC), 41, 83, 96–97, 115, 149
International Criminal Court, 65

International Crisis Group (ICG), 37
International Monetary Fund, 59
International Network of Engineers and
    Scientists for Global Responsibility
    (INES), 57–58
intervention (humanitarian), 36,
    120–121, 281
    in Darfur, 120–121
    by European states, 40
    in Kosovo, 284
interviewing, 109, 111, 113–114
    See also methods
Iran, 80, 88, 89, 91, 279
    Hezbollah and, 85, 87, 88, 89
    hostage crisis and, 262
    terrorism and, 241
Iraq
    outreach in, 247–249, 253, 260–261
    sources on, 151
    withdrawal from, 229–230, 239–240
Iraqi Islamic Party, 259
Islam
    factionalism within, 88, 92, 94
    ideology, 92, 254, 255
    in Lebanon, 88
    Shi'ite (Shi'a), 89, 91, 93
    Sunni, 89, 93
    See also clerics (Muslim); Hezbollah;
        mosques; Sunni Endowment
Islamic Development Bank, 73–74
Israel, 82–86, 88, 93
Italy, 87

Joint Special Operations Command, 262
Joint Task Force (JTF), 286
Jordan, 86, 228
justice, 31
"just war" (concept), 66, 279

Kant, Immanuel, 33, 34, 79, 80
    neo-Kantian approach, 79–80, 301
Kedia, Satish, 62
Kennedy, John F., 263
key informants, 111, 113
kidnapping, 20, 90, 104, 162
Kindleberger, Charles, 49

Knop, Ed, *111*
Kosovo, 41, 80, 99, 199
Kothari, Kajni, 59
Kristof, Nicholas, 50, 64
Kurds, 58, 118
Kysis (Egypt), 192

language (study), 235
law, 35, 59, 65, 66, 152
leadership (in Iraq), 251–255, 258–261
League of Nations, 41
Lebanon, 82–86, 301
    factionalism in, 88
    See also Hezbollah
lessons learned. *See* best practices
Locally Engaged Staff (LES), 235, 236
Logistics Civil Augmentation Program
    (LOGCAP), 98
London Missionary Society, 39, 42
Lord's Resistance Army (LRA; Uganda),
    95, 297
Lucas, George, Jr., 32–33
Lutz, Catherine, 292

M-19 (NSA), 265
Ma'moun (governor), 259, 261
Manumission Society, 30
map (interpretation), 154
marijuana, 264
Marshall Plan, 49
martial arts training, 143–145
Martin, Jim, 57
Masaki, Katsuhiko, 34
McChrystal, Stanley, 177
McNeill, William, 81
media, 174, 188–190
medical care
    civilian, 212–213, 244, *245*, 245–246,
        248
    emergency, 158–159
    See also public health
Merton, Robert, 63–64
Mertus, Julie, 291
methods, 107–109, 110–111, 112–114
    See also rapid ethnographic
        assessment (REA)

Metzler, Barbara, 38
Mexico City, 173–174, *174*, 179–180
migration, 63, 125
Mihai I (king), 198
militarism, 293
militarization, 293
military, 290–291, 292–293
    anthropology and, 287–289
    bases, 191–193
    humanitarian role of, 23
    Romanian, 196–199, 204
    See also civilian-military cooperation;
        technology; warfare
Military Professional Resources, Inc.,
    98–99
Millennium Challenge Accounts, 51
Millennium Development Goals (UN),
    53–54, 61, 63, 130, 190
Milošević, Slobodan, 76
Minear, Larry, 21, 35, 39
mines (land), 165
    See also explosives; IEDs (improvised
        explosive devices)
missionization, 65
modeling, 108, 109, 287
Moldavia, 197
Monterrey Consensus, 50
morality, 67
    See also ethics
mosques, 251–252, 254–255
MPRI (company), 97, 99
Myanmar (Burma), 45, 53

Nansen, Fridtjof, 41
Nasrallah, Hassan, 83, 88
National Telecommunications and
    Information Administration (NTIA),
    183
National Union for the Total Independence
    of Angola (UNITA), 199
NATO, 198, 199–200
    in Afghanistan, 240
    Romania and, 204
natural disasters, 62, 120, 122, 175
    training and, 209, 212, 214, 216, 222
nature versus nurture, 30

Naval Special Warfare Development Group
    (DEVGRU), 262
navigation, 153–155
needs, 105–106
neutrality, 114–115
NGHOs (nongovernmental humanitarian
    organizations), 285–286
NGOs, 41–42, 53, 118, 190, 256
    See also civilian-military cooperation;
       and specific organizations
9/11 (terrorist attack), 21, 36, 122, 128–129
Nobel Peace Prize, 39, 279
nonmalevolence, 31
non-state actors (NSAs), 43, 78, 93–96
    See also NGOs
Nordstrom, Carolyn, 34
North Korea, 279
Northrup Grumman, 97, 149
Noriega, Manuel, 263

Obama, Barack, 266, 278–279
observation (participant), 111, 112–113
Office for the Coordination of
    Humanitarian Affairs (UN), 22, 42
Office of Naval Research, 108, 115, 271, 274
officers (desk), 236–237
    See also Foreign Service Officers
       (FSOs)
Oil-for-Food Program (Iraq), 42
Olmert, Ehud, 84
operational security (OPSEC), 175
Operation Eagle Claw, 262
Operation Jaque, 149
ordnance (unexploded; UXO), 90–91, 165
Ottoman Empire, 40, 76–77, 197
outreach, 188, 190
    in Afghanistan, 241–247
    in Iraq, 238, 247–249, 253, 260–261
    medical, 245–246, 248–249
    presence posts, 224–225, 239
    tribal, 238, 240–241, 260–261
Oxfam International, 41, 47, 73, 103, 228

Pakistan, 21, 36, 49, 189
    opium poppies and, 243, 244
Palestinians, 92–93

parking (convoy), 168–169, 169
participant observation, 111, 112–113
    See also methods
peacekeeping, 87, 198–199
perimeters, 213–214, 222, 258
Petraeus, David (general), 268, 300
Philippines, 41, 96, 195
political science, 48, 59, 65, 152
poppies (opium), 241, 243–244, 246
Posen, Barry, 78
postmodernism, 47, 288
postpositivism, 43, 44
poverty, 59, 68
Powell, John Wesley, 61
power (electrical), 216, 221
power (sociopolitical). See authority;
    leadership (in Iraq)
praxis, 23, 44, 208
Prendergast, John, 42, 43, 174, 267
preparedness, 135–136, 171–172, 205
presence posts, 224–225, 239
Price, David, 33
Prince, Erik, 99
prisoners of war, 56
    camps, 195–196
    exchange of, 83, 90
    of FARC, 149
    Palestinian, 92–93
    treatment of, 65
prisons, 195–196
privacy, 115
    See also informed consent
private military companies (PMCs),
    97–99
    See also Blackwater Worldwide
      (Xe Services)
privatization (of warfare), 97–99
    See also Blackwater Worldwide
proactive engagement teams (PETs), 100
Provincial Reconstruction Teams (PRTs),
    73, 115–117, 239–240
    in Afghanistan, 242
    in Anbar Province, 256, 296
    embedded, 269
    sites, 191–192
    training and, 299–300

Psychological Operations (PsyOps), 188, 244, 269–270
PsyOps. *See* Psychological Operations (PsyOps)
public diplomacy, 188
public health, 40, 59, 64
    See also medical care
public relations, 188–190

Quick Reaction Forces (QRFs), 241, 273

radicalism, 254–255, 256
radio, 180–182, 183–184
Ramadi, 247–248, 255, 261
Ramos-Horta, José, 37, 74
rapid ethnographic assessment (REA), 108, 109–110, 117
rationality (economic), 60
Red Cross (ICRC), 41, 83, 96–97, 115, 149
Redlener, Irwin, 122, 123, 129
Red Zone, 72
refugees, 41, 84, 85, 90
    See also IDPs (internally displaced persons)
Refugees International, 84
religion, 37–38
    See also clerics (Muslim); Islam; mosques
residences, 218–219, 222–224
responsibility to protect, 78–79
Revolutionary Armed Forces of Colombia (FARC), 265
Rice, Condoleezza, 85, 234
Risha, Ahmad abu, 259, 260, 295
Risha, Sattar abu (d. 2007), 254
risk analysis, 124–125, 172–174
Roberts, Bill, 294
Roman Empire, 197
Romania, 196–199
rules of engagement, 32, *33*, 162–164
Rule of Law Complex. *See* Green Zone
Rumsfeld, Donald, 99, 284
Russia, 40
    See also Soviet Union
Rwanda, 80, 299

Sachs, Jeffrey, 50, 59
Sadr, Muqtada al-, 94, 96
Salween River, 53
sampling, 113
satellites. *See* communications
Saudi Arabia, 84, 85, 86, 89
Save the Children, 19, 73
Schneller, Rachel, 237
Schultz, Jack, *111*
SEALS (Navy), 262, 263
security, 21, 130
    in Anbar Province, 259–260
    best practices and, 209, 250
    communications, 187
    operational, 175
    in rural locations, 221, 222–223
    in urban locations, 216–218, 219
    See also risk analysis; vulnerability analysis
Security Assistance Services, 97
self-defense, 145
Sen, Amartya, 59, 68
September 11th (terrorist attack), 21, 36, 122, 128–129
service learning, 203–204
Shi'ite (Shi'a) Islam, 89, 91, 93
    See also Hezbollah
Shin, Dennis, 51
Sierra Leone, 19, 36, 94, 289
Silbert, Mimi, 63
simulations, 297–298
    See also field schools
Singer, Peter, 99
Siniora, Fouad, 83–84, 88
Sison, Michele, 90
sites (fixed) 191–195
    establishing, 206, 212–214
    remote, 225–227
    rural, 220–222
    securing, 213
    temporary, 227–228, 229
    in urban locations, 215–218
Small, Meredith, 30
Smillie, Ian, 35, 39
Smith, Derrin, 23, 36, 141
    analyses by, 91

career of, 220, 235, 279
crash-landing of, 249–250
experiences of, 95, 138, 159, 165,
    186, 218
expertise of, 50, 59, 145, 205, 282
in Iraq, 75, 165, 179, 256, 259
outreach and, 238, 241, *242*
physical fitness and, 143, *144*
risk and, 166, 170, 173
Romania and, 200, 204
society (civil), 58, 281
social scientists, 266–267, 279, 287
    See also anthropology
social work, 59, 63
    See also Addams, Jane
soft measures, *33*, 96–97, 277–278
Somalia, 17, 19, 80, 199
Soviet Union, 198, 263
special forces, 262
special operations, 261–263
Spectrum Policy Initiative (2004),
    182, 183
Spradley, James, 272
Sri Lanka, 289
State Department. *See* U.S. Department of
    State
structural adjustment programs, 59
structural violence, 44–45, 69, 281
Sudan, 19, 159
    See also Darfur
suffering, 68
suicide bombing, 176
Sumatra, 95–96
Sunni Endowment, 251–253, 254–256
Sunni Islam, 89, 93
surveillance, 219, 222
    transit and, 165, 167, *168*
Syria, 84, 85, 88–89, 91
    architecture in, 55

Tactical Human Intelligence Teams
    (THTs), 243
Taiwan, 194
Takasu, Yukio, 286
Taliban, 21, 226, 241, 244
Tax, Sol, 62

teams (humanitarian) and team members,
    42
    clothing for, 148–150
    communication and, 155–156
    driving by, 156
    equipment for, 145–151
    first aid and, 157–159
    fitness and, 142–143
    footwear for, 142–143
    health and hygiene of, 136–141
    martial arts training for, 143–145
    navigation and, 153–155
    training of, 151–153
    weapons and, 156–157
    See also country teams
technology, 77, 81, 182–187, 189–190
telephones, 185
terrain (human), 267, 268
    See also Human Terrain Teams
        (HTTs)
terrorism, 122, 265
    See also al-Qaeda; extremism;
        September 11th (terrorist attack)
theft, 221–222
Thomas-Slayter, Barbara, 52, 125
threat, 121–123, 171–174, 175, 258
Tigray Province. *See* Ethiopia
Tigray Development Association, 107
Timor-Leste, 74, 119
    civil war in, 36, 80
    country teams and, 93
    human rights and, 289
    relief operations in, 41, 119
trade, 192–193
training
    in country operations, 200–207
    of foreign service officers, 235
    results of, 207–212
    of team members, 151–153
transecting, 110–111
transit operations, 161–171
    convoy, 162–164, *164*, 165–167, 170
    planning, 175–177
    training and, 206
Transylvania, 197
triage, 207, 211

Tromp, Maarten, 178
tsunami (Sumatra), 95–96
Turner, Terence, 33

Uganda, 36, 95, 297
United Nations, 41–42, 199
Congo and, 297
Israel-Lebanon conflict and, 84, 85
UN Angola Verification Mission
(UNAVEM III), 199
UN Assistance Mission for Iraq (UNAMI),
73, 74
UN Charter, 35
UN Children's Fund (UNICEF), 41
UN Declaration on the Rights of
Indigenous Peoples, 34
UN Department of Humanitarian Affairs,
42
UN High Commission for Refugees
(UNHCR), 37, 41
country operations and, 74,
118–119
in Darfur, 121
UN Interim Force in Lebanon (UNIFIL),
89, 90, 165
UN Office for the Coordination of
Humanitarian Affairs (OCHA),
42, 286
UN Operation in Somalia II
(UNOSOM II), 199
UN Organization Mission in the DRC
(MONUC), 298
United States
Congo and, 297–299
foreign policy, 278–279, 292
Universal Declaration of Human Rights,
35, 65
University of Denver, 196, 200, 207
field training by, 147, 154, 172, 180,
204, 300
projects of, 112, 140
students of, 25, 112, 202
as subcontractor, 110, 115
Uribe, Álvaro, 149, 266
U.S. Africa Command (AFRICOM), 273,
297, 299

U.S. Agency for International Development
(USAID), 49–50, 266–267, 288
contractors, 98
country assessments and, 73
in El Salvador, 118, 127
U.S. Air Force, 262, 263
U.S. Army, 262, 263, 272
U.S. Central Command (CENTCOM), 268
U.S. Department of Defense, 285,
286–287, 300
U.S. Department of Homeland Security,
122
U.S. Department of State, 234,
237–238, 299
criticisms of, 237, 290, 300
expeditionary diplomacy and,
238–239
Foreign Service and, 234, 300
liaison functions and, 285–286
U.S. Federal Emergency Management
Agency (FEMA), 37, 123
U.S. Foreign Service, 234–237
U.S. Institute of Peace, 285
U.S. Navy, 262, 263
U.S. Special Operations Command
(USSOC), 262
USSR, 198, 263
utilitarianism, 54–55, 66, 115
UXO (unexploded ordnance), 90–91, 165,
282, 285

vaccinations, 137
Van Arsdale, Peter, 200, 297, 299
on benevolence, 31
career of, 50, 108, 267, 287
on Darfur, 228
experiences of, 65, 75, 138, 159, 165
expertise of, 61, 120, 127, 155,
204–205
field work of, 53, 100, 107, 110–111,
220, 283
on humanitarianism, 31, 43, 68, 281
interviews by, 269, 270, 294
on praxis, 62, 204–205
on prison camps, 195
risk and, 173, 176–177

on structural violence, 45
on threat analysis, 122
VASK model and, *111*
van der Cun, Piet (Cunaeus), 31
VASK model, 110, *111*
Vasquez, Jose, 189
VBIEDs (vehicle-borne improvised
    explosive devices). *See* IEDs
    (improvised explosive devices)
Vietnam, 263
violence, 44–45, 121, 281
    See also kidnapping; warfare
Viviano, Frank, 58
voting, 256, 295
vulnerability analysis, 124–125, 172–174
    convoys and, 176–177

Wallachia, 197
warfare, 77–78
    anthropology and, 288–289
    changes in, 80–81, 292
    guerilla in Colombia, 264, 265
    human terrain and, 267
    humanitarianism and, 40–41, 76–77,
        282–284
    interventions and, 54
    as "just," 66, 279
    privatization of, 97–99
Washington, George, 30, 55
Water and Sanitation Consultancy Group,
    107
water systems, 109–110, 112, 127, *128*
Way Seputih/Way Sekampung project, 53
weapons (safety), 156–157
Weiss, Thomas, 36, 39, 40, 80, 115
Welch, Alyson, 20

Wesley, John, 30
Williams, Holly Ann, 105
wills, 160
withdrawal, 194, 297
    from Iraq, 229–230, 239–240
Womeldorff, Javier, 149
women, 245, 247, 295
Woodrow, Peter, 122
World Bank (IBRD; International Bank for
    Reconstruction and Development),
    59, 118
World Food Programme (WFP), 41, 74
World Health Organisation, 74, 84
World Vision, 41, 104, 118, 137
World War I, 76, 292
    chaplains and, 56
    humanitarianism and, 40–41
World War II, 82, 292
    chaplains and, 56
    foreign aid and, 49
    humanitarianism and, 40–41
    military anthropology and, 287–288
    prisoners of war and, 195
    Romania and, 198
    teams and, 42

Xe Services (Blackwater Worldwide), 95,
    97, 99–101

YMCA (Young Men's Christian
    Association), 40
Yugoslavia, 99, 198
Yunus, Mohammad, 59

Zahner, Luke, 237–238
Zeelandia, 194

ABOUT THE AUTHORS

Peter W. Van Arsdale is Senior Lecturer at the Josef Korbel School of International Studies at the University of Denver, where he also serves as Director of African Initiatives. On a consultancy basis, he is Senior Researcher with eCrossCulture Corporation. Through June, 2006, he served as faculty advisor to the university's Center On Rights Development (CORD), a graduate student organization that sponsors human rights activities. Through June, 2008, he served as director of the school's new Program in Humanitarian Assistance. Trained as an applied cultural and medical anthropologist, with an early subspecialty in psychology and a later subspecialty in refugee studies, Van Arsdale has conducted fieldwork in the United States, Romania, Bosnia, Indonesia, Sudan, Ethiopia, Guyana, Peru, and El Salvador, and he recently helped initiate a program in Timor-Leste with Nobel Peace Laureate José Ramos-Horta. He is a former staff member of the Colorado Division of Mental Health and researcher for the Colorado Mental Health Institute. He recently served as a member of two national human rights committees and is author of (among a number of publications) *Forced to Flee: Human Rights and Human Wrongs in Refugee Homelands*. He cofounded The Denver Hospice and the Rocky Mountain Survivors Center. Further humanitarian activities, including a water/sanitation project in Kibera, Kenya, are conducted through his membership in the Rotary Club of Denver Southeast.

Derrin R. Smith is Political Officer at the U.S. Embassy in Beirut, Lebanon. His responsibilities include terrorism finance and sanctions, trafficking in persons, Iraqi refugees and internally displaced persons, and broader issues involving human rights, labor, and democracy. With degrees in technical management, finance, and international economics, from 2007 through 2008 he served as a diplomat and political action officer with PRT Anbar, Iraq, specializing in tribal outreach and development of the provincial governing council. From 2006 through 2007 he served as a diplomat and deputy chief of American Citizen Services in Guadalajara, Mexico, for the U.S. Department of State. His portfolio included narcotics and major crimes, and he also covered Huicholes tribal outreach. Before that, his PRT experience in Afghanistan contributed to studies on disarmament, demobilization, and reintegration programs, while building on still earlier *shura* and village assessments he had conducted in Iraq. As a member of the U.S. Marine Corps years earlier, he worked on intelligence issues. Civilian experience includes serving as a corporate executive for high-technology corporations and investment banking, and teaching on intelligence and international security at the University of Denver. He is a life member of the Association of Former Intelligence Officers and an academic fellow of the Foundation for Defense of Democracies.